CONTENT

ESSAYS ON THE STATE OF BLACK AMERICA

SPECIAL SECTION: BLACK WOMEN'S HEALTH

COMMENTARY

APPENDICES

Awakenings

by Dr. Dorothy I. Height

With all that we have seen in recent years, from Don Imus' vicious name-calling, to the lingering tragedy that was and is Katrina, the one thing that is certain is the need to hear and amplify the voices of black women. Too often, our needs, concerns, struggles, and triumphs are diminished and subordinated to what is believed to be the more pressing concerns of others.

But who better than us understand and empathize with the very real challenges that our brothers, fathers, husbands and sons face as they make their way in a nation that still has far to go to adequately address issues of race? And who better than us can understand the very real boundaries that all women face in navigating a cultural dynamic that still assigns roles and oftentimes limitations based upon gender. Yet, it is also true, that there are special, dual challenges intricately linked to blackness and womanhood that we black women face and navigate alone.

With no apologies, the time is now, to finally focus on us.

It is black women who face most strikingly a double disadvantage in the world of work. Our earnings, for example, are reflective of both a race and gender pay gap. Yet despite this double disadvantage, we clearly understand what it means to work and work hard. Our participation in the labor force eclipses that of all other women and by 2014, is projected to grow by twice the amount expected among white women. Still, in spite of this effort, too many of us continue to live life on the economic fringe; black women's poverty more than doubles that of white women and noticeably outpaces that among Latinas. And even with all of the employment struggles that black men face, it is black women who are, in the final analysis, most likely to be poor.

Yet, despite black women's struggles, we remain key contributors to the economic well-being of our families and communities. About half of the growth in black homeownership in recent years has occurred because of black women. But in the wake of the recent subprime loan crisis, it is black women who have been most distinctly disadvantaged. It was black women who were most likely to have been targeted and ultimately victimized by unscrupulous mortgage lenders. And it was upper-income black women who, in the end, faired the worst, being nearly five times more likely to have received a high-cost loan than upper-income white men—thereby putting their economic futures as well as that of their families in serious peril.

Our challenges, though, don't begin and end with our economic hardships. It is black women who are most likely to endure the work and responsibility of raising children on our own. It is black women who are experiencing exponential growth in the number of those who find themselves ensnarled in our criminal justice system. It is black women who are overrepresented among those afflicted with a wide range of serious illnesses, yet underrepresented among those who have access to health insurance, and as a result, suffer too long without the treatment that is needed for survival.

The National Council of Negro Women echoes the concerns reflected throughout the pages of this book. We understand that these and other issues of importance to black women are rarely addressed. We've done our part to help fill this void through the establishment of our Research, Public Policy and Information Center. We see this Center as a special place meant to both highlight the distinctive concerns of women of African descent while also reaching out to them so as to inform, catalyze and mobilize black women to bring about change. As our efforts move forward, we hope to continue to examine many of the themes highlighted throughout this work for many years to come.

In the meantime, this book represents a long overdue clarion call. Through its pages, we can all now finally hear black women's voices—clearly and distinctly. We can all now finally begin to more fully understand the real, daily struggles, associated with living life as a black woman. With any luck, this effort will bring understanding, and will serve as just the beginning of an awakening that will continue and grow in the days, months and years ahead; ultimately, for the betterment of us all.

by Marc H. Morial

The State of Black America 2008: In the Black Woman's Voice comes out this year in the midst of troubling times. Last year's report concluded that our nation stood at a tipping point. That magic moment has unfortunately led us to a bleak reality.

Over the past year, a recession, precipitated in part by the subprime mortgage debacle, falling house sales and values, and a tighter credit market, has reared its ugly head in a year of what promises to be one of the most competitive and historic presidential elections in decades.

All of this uncertainty grips us with both trepidation and excitement. African Americans stand at a crossroads—we can make a change for the better or lose our chance to resolve our nation's inequalities for once and for all.

Our 2007 *State of Black America: Portrait of the Black Male* report examined the plight of young black males faced with grim prospects. This year's report explores the challenges encountered by the females within our community—the mothers, grandmothers, aunts and sisters who have been the backbone of the black family. Women typically hold the family together, especially in the African-American community, where the marriage rate is lower than in other communities and where a higher percentage of single mothers are the heads of households.

These women are the matriarchs and leaders of our community. They have risen to the challenge of maintaining the black family unit in spite of trying conditions and limited opportunity.

Today there is a great deal of anxiety among African Americans across the nation. There's anxiety about our economic future. There's anxiety about our children, our families and our communities. There's anxiety about America's standing in the global arena. There's anxiety about whether we have become too cynical and prosperous to tackle the challenges of this generation. There's anxiety about the gap between the haves, the have-nots and the have-a-lots that is growing exponentially.

In the past year, the subprime mortgage meltdown has done irreparable harm to African-American homeowners, who are more likely than other groups to receive high-cost and high-interest home loans. As Andrea Harris points out in her essay, *Unsustainable Loans Wipe Out Gains Made by African-American Women*, it is black women who bear an unfair burden. According to 2006 Home Mortgage Disclose Act data, African-American women received 51.4 percent of subprime loans. Worse yet, upper-income black women were five times as likely as white men to receive such loans.

Additionally, because home equity accounts for a larger percentage of personal wealth for African Americans than it does for whites, increasing foreclosures of subprime borrowers translate into a major financial hit for the black community, targeting African-American women of all income brackets.

That is why our women must have the opportunity to obtain low-cost financing to become homeowners—not these deceptive mortgage products with jack-in-the-box interest rates that end up tainting the American Dream and wreaking havoc on urban communities. That is why we propose stronger homeownership counseling and the establishment of homeownership development accounts similar to 401-K accounts, among other things.

Intergenerational wealth is also a key component in bridging the economic divide between whites and blacks, in large part because of the empowerment opportunities wealth offers to future generations. A child who grows up in a household that has even nominal wealth is more likely to attend college, have the connections to obtain a good job, the resources to put a down payment on a home and the resources to start a business.

Unfortunately, the relative lack of intergenerational wealth and the lack of monetary connections that come along with wealth make blacks less likely to have the collateral needed to obtain traditional business loans. Micro-financing however, can help. As demonstrated in other countries, micro-financing has given countless women the opportunity to own and grow their own businesses. They got it right—give the seed money to the women and it'll grow.

The same strategy could work in the African-American community, where the average black business is a sole proprietorship. Some just need a little help— seed money to get their business off the ground.

The National Urban League is responding to these challenges facing black women—and all African Americans—through our direct service programs, policy and advocacy. A critical tool in this effort is our *Opportunity Compact: Blueprint for Economic Equality*. Unveiled during our 2007 Annual Conference in St. Louis and endorsed by several 2008 presidential candidates, the *Compact* sets out our top 10 public policy prescriptions needed to nurse urban America back to health. They are: 1) Provide mandatory early childhood education and access to college for all; 2) Ensure universal healthcare for all children; 3) Establish policies that provide tools for working families to become economically self-sufficient; 4) Create an urban infrastructure bank to fund reinvestment in urban communities, e.g. parks, schools, roads; 5) Index the minimum wage to inflation and expand the Earned Income Tax Credit to benefit more working families; 6) Expand "second chance" programs for high school drop outs, ex-offenders and at-risk youth to secure GEDs, job training and employment; 7) Adopt the "Homebuyer's Bill of Rights"; 8) Reform public housing to assure continuing national commitment to low-income families; 9) Strongly enforce federal minority business opportunity goals to ensure greater minority participation in government contracting; and 10) Build capacity of minority business through expansion of micro financing, equity financing and the development of strategic alliances with major corporations.

Although the *Compact* revolves around four core issues – children's wellbeing, jobs, homeownership and entrepreneurship – key components of the American dream, its underlying intent is to strengthen the African-American family. And we know that in order to strengthen the family, we must support our women.

We can help black mothers raise their children in safe and nurturing atmospheres by indexing the minimum wage to inflation and expanding the Earned Income Tax Credit. Ensuring a decent wage for working mothers translates into more time spent between mother and child and reduces the need for mothers to work a multitude of jobs. This will in turn improve the children's future prospects and keep them out of trouble.

Also, as National Urban League Resident Scholar Renee R. Hanson points out in her essay, *A Pathway to School Readiness: The Impact of Family on Early Education*, early childhood education equalizes the playing field when children enter school. Those who enter these programs are more likely to stay in school, go to college, and become successful and independent adults. Healthier and better-prepared children ultimately mean stronger and happier families, especially in cases where parents, particularly single mothers, are already overstressed.

When black women hurt, the American family suffers. When we ignore black women's issues, we ignore an entire community. But by uplifting black women, especially those struggling hardest to keep their families together and their dreams on track, we lift up every American community.

That is why I encourage you to read this year's edition of the *State of Black America: In the Black Woman's Voice* with special attention to the *Opportunity Compact*. Our country urgently needs a new vision to close the gaps between black and white Americans. *The State of Black America* and the *Opportunity Compact* will help guide the way.

The National Urban League 2008 Equality Index™

Index by Sophia Parker and Ana Orozco of Global Insight, Inc. Analysis by Valerie Rawlston Wilson, Ph.D. of the National Urban League Policy Institute

Introduction

Change. It's a word that has been on the lips of virtually every 2008 presidential hopeful this election season and there's no doubt that a change is on the horizon as an African American or a woman stands poised to receive the nomination of the Democratic Party for the first time in history; a nomination that also positions the country to potentially make history when we head to the polls in November. At the same time, we've witnessed the winds of change blowing through the economy as oil prices continue to rise and fallout from the ever-deflating housing bubble is being felt in multiple sectors of the U.S. economy and other markets abroad. Just one month into 2008, the country was forced to confront the very real prospect of a recession, calling for an economic stimulus plan that is expected to take effect by the spring or early summer of 2008.

As the nation's overall barometer for economic growth, trends in the gross domestic product (GDP) along with other economic indicators signal the direction in which the economy is headed, but the smaller components that actually move that number (i.e. consumer spending and business investment) are the targets considered when designing a strategy to steer the economy along the desired path of continued growth. Similarly, the National Urban League Equality Index, now in its fifth year, is an aggregate measure of the relative status between blacks and whites in this country. However, this index is driven by a number of underlying moving parts that can be seen as targets for accomplishing the goal of bringing about greater economic equality.

Interpreting the Equality Index

The Equality Index can be interpreted as the relative status of blacks ver-sus whites in American society, measured according to five areas—eco-nomics, health, education, social justice and civic engagement. For any given measure, the index refers to the ratio between that measure for blacks and whites. To use median household income as an example, an index of 61% = $31,969/$52,423, where $31,969 is the median household income for blacks and $52,423 is the median household income for whites. The interpretation of this index is that the median household income for blacks is only 61 percent of that of whites. Equality would be indicated with an index of 100%. Therefore, an Equality Index less than 100% sug-gests that blacks are doing worse relative to whites, and an Equality Index greater than 100% suggests that blacks are doing better than whites.

The overall Equality Index is a weighted average of indices calculated for each of the five sub-categories—economics, health, education, social justice and civic engagement. In turn, the indices for each of the five sub-categories are themselves weighted averages[1] of indices calculated from individual variables (like the example of median household income used above) available from nationally representative data sources. The appro-priate data sources and data years are indicated in the accompanying tables at the end of this chapter.

What's New in the Equality Index this Year?

This year, the 2007 Equality Index (last year) was revised from its previously published value of 73.3% to 72%. This revision reflects data points that were removed (for greater comparability across years), corrected or updated. The 2008 Equality Index is 73%, up 0.41 percentage point from the revised 2007 Index. While the overall index has remained relatively stable for the past four years (large swings in the demographics of a population usually aren't observed over the short-run, nor are new data available every year for all vari-ables in the index), there were significant changes in areas such as the digital divide, school enrollment, and sentencing.

This year's index reflects an improvement in the digital divide, a compo-nent of the economics sub-index. The ratio for the percentage of adult users with broadband access increased from 61% the year before to 82% this year.

More than half of that increase was the result of increased access among African Americans.

Within the education sub-index, there was an especially large jump (49 percentage points) in the school enrollment index for the 30 to 34 year-old age cohort. Within this age group, African-American enrollment increased from 7.2% to 10%[2] and much of this increase in overall school enrollment occurred at the college level. At the same time, there was a 15 percentage point drop in the index for college enrollment of recent high school graduates with recent African American high school graduates remaining less likely to enroll than their white counterparts (index of 76%). The index for high school dropouts also improved (88% compared to 79%) as the percentage of black dropouts decreased from 15% to 13%. Whites also saw a one percentage point decline from 12% to 11%. In the course quality category, the greatest improvement in index values was for enrollment in Algebra 2 courses. However, while there was an increase in the value for Precalculus enrollment, the index value for Calculus enrollment declined.

Under the health sub-index, equality in elderly care showed the most significant deterioration (from 83% to 72%) due to a rapid increase in the Medicare expenditures of blacks. On the other hand, there were improvements in children's health. While the percent of white children without a health care visit in past 12 months showed an increase, the percentage of black children without a visit continued to decline, resulting in a 28 percentage points increase in the index for this variable (from 91% to 119%).

Finally, the social justice sub-index saw the most improvement. The gap in average jail sentencing narrowed by 15 percentage points (from 77% to 93%) as the average sentence for blacks decreased from 44 months to 40 months and the average sentence for whites increased from 34 months to 37 months. The index for average sentence for drug trafficking by males increased 23 percentage points (from 84% to 108%) as the average sentence for white males actually surpassed the average sentence for black males.[3] The average sentence for drug trafficking among white males increased from 38 months to 41 months while the average sentence for black males decreased from 45 months to 38 months. Also, there was a significant improvement in high school students carrying weapons (both on school property or elsewhere).

Given the relatively small changes in the overall Equality Index from one year to the next, the true substance of this measure can be found in the analy-

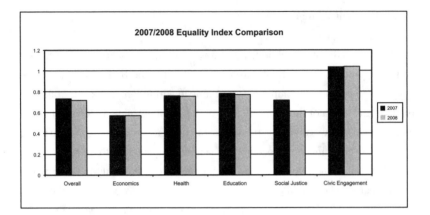

2007/2008 Equality Index Comparison

sis of inequality in economic outcomes—income, employment, poverty and housing and wealth—that have been persistent over time and the underlying inequalities in areas like education, health, social justice and civic engagement that under gird these economic disparities.

Inequality in Economic Outcomes (30% of total Equality Index)

This year, the economic sub-index is 56.8%, unchanged from the year before. New to the calculation of the economics sub-index was the addition of high-priced mortgage data. In terms of overall economic well-being, African Americans in this country are doing over half as well as whites. This overall gap is born out in a number of factors including median household income and earnings, poverty and housing and wealth.

Income and Earnings

The index for real median household income remains at 61% again this year. So, while real median household income has decreased for all Americans since the inception of the Equality Index in 2005, the black-white gap persists. When broken out according to gender, the gap in median earnings between black men and white men is 72%, 14 points larger than the gap between black and white females (86%). Were equality achieved in median household income, and median earnings for both males and females, the economic sub-index would be increased to 64%, raising the overall Equality Index to 75%.[4]

Poverty

Though the poverty index has changed little between 2007 and 2008[5], since 2005, the poverty gap has actually widened as the percentage of whites living below the poverty line has decreased 2 percentage points since 2005 while blacks in poverty has remained essentially stable. According to the 2008 index, nearly three times as many African Americans as whites (31% compared to 11%) are living below 125% of the poverty line. Were poverty eliminated in this country, the economic sub-index would rise to 63% and the overall Equality Index would increase to 75%.[6] Additionally, empowering all families to live above 125% of the poverty level would raise the economic index another 4 percentage points to 67% and raise the overall Equality Index to 76%.[7]

Unemployment

While still hovering just below 50%, the black-white unemployment gap decreased between 2007 (45%) and 2008 (49%).[8] This improvement was in large part attributable to the decline in black unemployment (from 9% to 8.3%), particularly among black females (from 8.5% to 7.5%). As is the case with earnings, the black-white female unemployment gap (ratio of 53%) was less than the black-white male unemployment gap (ratio of 46%). For people over age 25, black labor force participation exceeded that of whites at every level of education beyond high school, suggesting that although a larger proportion of African Americans are seeking employment, they continue to be less likely to be employed than their white counterparts. Teens continue to have the largest rate of unemployment—29% for African Americans and 14% for whites—as well as the lowest labor force participation rate. Equality in unemployment for men, women and teens would raise the economic sub-index to 62% and the Equality Index to 75%.

Housing & Wealth

There were no new data available on homeownership rates this year, but each of the indices for mortgage application and home improvement loan denials decreased 3–4 percentage points from the year before, indicating less equality in these outcomes. Mortgage application denial rates for blacks, already twice that of whites, increased by 3.4 percentage points (from 24.5% to 27.9%) while the corresponding rate for whites increased by less than one percentage point (from 13% to 13.7%). African Americans also remained more than three times as likely to receive a high-priced loan (having an interest rate more than 3% above the Treasury rate). The importance of equality in being able to obtain a mortgage loan and purchase a home is reflected in the fact that by eliminating gaps in denial rates, the economic sub-index would increase to 60%, resulting in an Equality Index of 74%.[9]

Inequality in Causes of Economic Disparities

The elimination of many of the economic disparities discussed above is dependent upon the elimination of inequalities in other areas that create and sustain these gaps. In order for the nation to be successful at eliminating the economic gaps, we must also consider ways to close the gaps in these underlying areas, some of which are discussed below.

Education (25% of total Equality Index)

The 2008 education sub-index of 78.2% represents a less than one percentage point drop (0.6) from the previous year (78.6%).[10] The enrollment category was the only category to show a decrease from last year's index values, mainly due to declines in preprimary enrollment and college enrollment of recent high school graduates. The gap in school enrollment for 3–4 year olds increased as the index went from 113% in 2007 to 96% in 2008, due primarily to a decline in the percentage of black children enrolled (from 59.6% to 52.2%) and a slight increase in enrollment for whites (from 52.8% to 54.2%). At the college level, the enrollment gap between black and white recent high school graduates also widened significantly (from 91% to 76%) as the African American enrollment rate fell from 63% to 56% and the corresponding rate for whites increased from 69% to 73%. On the other hand, there were improvements in the high school dropout rate with the ratio between blacks and whites going from 79% in 2007 to 88% in 2008.

Though school enrollment for African Americans generally exceeded that of whites for all age cohorts (58% compared to 56%), attainment or completion rates are lower. For example, 19% of African Americans over age 25 have a college degree, compared to 28% of whites. These disparities in educational attainment typically translate into differences in rates of employment and earnings, which are not directly estimated in this index.[11] Equality in college enrollment of recent high school graduates as well as high school and college attainment translates into an education sub-index of 80%.[12]

Health (25% of total Equality Index)

Last year's (2007) health sub-index was revised to 75.3% from 77.8%. As a result, this year's health sub-index increased 0.4 percentage point to 75.7%.[13] Most notable was the negative shift in health insurance. For example, the gap in total uninsured increased this year as the index fell from 56% in 2007 to 53% in 2008. Though there was little change in the gap in children's health insurance, black children remain more than twice as likely as whites to be uninsured (52%).

Health status is an important factor in economic outcomes because it affects an individual physically (i.e. one's ability to work) as well as financially. Poor health creates added healthcare expenditures, particularly for the uninsured or those without adequate healthcare coverage. Diabetes, HIV/AIDS and violence resulting in homicide continue to plague the African American community at alarming rates.[14] For example, the age-adjusted death rate from diabetes was more than four times higher for African Americans (48 per 100,000) than for whites (21.5 per 100,000). The African American death rate from HIV/AIDS was ten times the rate for whites (20.4 versus 1.9 per 100,000). For young black men (ages 15–24) the death rate from homicide (77.6 per 100,000) are over 16 times higher than they are for young white men (4.7 per 100,000).

Though the direct effects on economic outcomes are not discernable using this model, gaps in insurance coverage coupled with higher incidences of certain diseases that result in shorter life expectancy among African Americans can conceivably be linked to observed gaps in labor force participation, employment and wealth accumulation. Eliminating gaps in health insurance coverage as well as death rates from all causes would increase the health sub-index to 84% and the overall Equality Index to 75%.[15]

Social Justice (10% of total Equality Index)

The Social Justice sub-index saw the most improvement, increasing 6 percentage points from a revised 65.4% in 2007 to 71.7% in 2008. The social justice index improved overall, mostly due to narrowing of sentencing gaps (from 77% to 93%) and a significant turn-around in students carrying weapons to school (from an index of 80% to 120%). Also, there was a 3 percentage point improvement in the index of prisoners as a percentage of arrests (from 34% to 37%). Despite this improvement, African Americans were 3 times more likely than whites to be incarcerated following an arrest.

There was also some improvement in the "stopped while driving" category, going from 96% in the 2007 index to 110% this year. This suggests that whites were more likely than blacks to be stopped while driving, according to the latest Bureau of Justice Statistics data. Equality in sentencing and incarceration resulting from arrests would raise the social justice sub-index to 80% and the overall Equality Index to 74%.[16]

Civic Engagement (10% of total Equality Index)

The 2008 civic engagement sub-index was 103.6%, down 1.3 percentage points from 105% in 2007. Civic engagement remains the only major area where African Americans exceed whites. The 2008 index reflects slightly lower relative rates of volunteerism in the military reserves, as well as other volunteer activities, including religious activities. Decreased participation in the military reserves has been a long-term trend over the last five years, likely due to the Iraq war.

Conclusion

While there seems to be no doubt that the country is on the precipice of change politically and economically, the critical questions that must be answered are what kind of change and how do we begin to make it? As Congress debates the ideal stimulus package for generating optimal economic growth, it is important to remember that regardless of whether GDP is up or down, the full potential of this nation can only be met when all citizens have equal opportunities to thrive, earn, own and prosper. While the Equality Index would suggest that there is still a ways to go in achieving this end, The Opportunity Compact: Blueprint for Economic Equality—released last year by the National Urban League (also published in this volume)—presents a set of ten policy prescriptions for the kind of change needed

NOTES

[1] Weights for individual data points are available from the National Urban League Policy Institute upon request.

[2] Data on school enrollment by age are not weighted and therefore do not affect the final Equality Index.

[3] Data on sentencing by type of crime are not weighted and therefore do not affect the final Equality Index.

[4] These estimates are based upon the author's calculations under the current weighting structure used by Global Insights, Inc. (GII). The calculations were performed by replacing the actual index for median household income, median male earnings and median female earnings with 100% (equality) and reading the resulting sub-index and total index from the GII table.

[5] The poverty index for 2008 and 2007 are based on Census poverty data from 2006 and 2005, respectively.

[6] See note #4. In this case, instead of changing the index for median income and earnings, the actual index for the percentage of people below poverty was set to equality.

[7] Ibid. Additionally, the actual indices for the percentage of people below 50% and 125% of poverty were set to equality.

[8] The total unemployment rate index is not weighted and therefore not included in the Equality Index. Instead the individual unemployment rates for men, women and teens are used.

[9] See footnote #4. In this case, the mortgage application denial rate was set to equality.

[10] This difference is not statistically significant.

[11] Since this index does not account for the effect of educational attainment on employment and earnings, the true impact on overall equality may be understated.

[12] See note #4. In this case, college enrollment of recent high school graduates, high school dropouts, high school educational attainment (25 and over) and college educational attainment (25 and over) were set to equality.

[13] This difference is not statistically significant.

[14] Death rates from individual causes of death are not weighted and therefore not included in the Equality Index. However, the total death rate from all causes is included.

[15] See note #4. In this case, age-adjusted death rates from all causes and the percentage of all uninsured, including the percentage of uninsured children, were set to equality.

[16] See note #4. In this case, the mean incarceration sentence and prisoners as a percentage of arrests were set to equality.

The Equality Index of Black America

	Updated Series	New Series	(Index = 0.73)

ECONOMICS (30%)	Source	Year	Black	White	Index	DIFF ('08-'07)
Median Income (0.25)						
Median Household Income (Real)	Census	2006	31,969	52,423	61%	0.00
Median Male Earnings	ACS	2006	34,480	47,814	72%	(0.01)
Median Female Earnings	ACS	2006	30,398	35,151	86%	(0.00)
Poverty (0.15)						
Poverty Line (% Below)	Census	2006	24.3	8.2	34%	0.00
Poverty Line (% Below 50% of Poverty Line)	Census	2006	10.9	3.5	32%	0.02
Population Living Below 125% of Poverty Line	Census	2006	30.7	11.4	37%	0.01
Population Living Below Poverty Line (Under 18)	Census	2006	33.4	10	30%	0.01
Population Living Below Poverty Line (18-64)	Census	2006	19.9	7.8	39%	0.01
Population Living Below Poverty Line (65 and Older)	Census	2006	22.7	7	31%	(0.03)
Employment Issues (0.20)						
Unemployment Rate	BLS	2007	8.3	4.1	49%	0.04
Unemployment Rate-Male	BLS	2007	9.1	4.2	46%	0.04
Unemployment Rate-Female	BLS	2007	7.5	4.0	53%	0.06
Unemployment Rate-Persons 16-19	BLS	2007	29.4	13.9	47%	0.02
Percent Not in Workforce-Ages 16 to 19	BLS	2007	69.7	55.6	80%	(0.01)
Percent Not in Workforce-Ages 16 and Older	BLS	2007	36.3	33.6	93%	(0.01)
Labor Force Participantion Rate	BLS	2007	63.7	66.4	96%	(0.00)
LFPR 16 to 19	BLS	2007	30.3	44.4	68%	(0.05)
LFPR 20 to 24	BLS	2007	68.3	76.4	89%	(0.01)
LFPR over 25-Less than High School Grad	BLS	2007	39.1	47.9	82%	(0.03)
LFPR over 25-High School Graduate, No College	BLS	2007	65.4	62.3	105%	(0.02)
LFPR over 25-Some College, No Degree	BLS	2007	74.4	69.0	108%	0.01
LFPR over 25-Associate's Degree	BLS	2007	77.6	76.1	102%	(0.01)

The Equality Index of Black America

Legend: ■ Updated Series ■ New Series

	Source	Year	Black	White	Index	DIFF ('08–'07)
					(Index = 0.73)	
LPR Over 25–Less than Bachelor's	BLS	2007	75.3	71.4	105%	0.01
LPR Over 25–College Graduate	BLS	2007	83.0	77.4	106%	0.01
Employment to Pop. Ratio, %	BLS	2007	58.4	63.6	92%	0.00
Housing & Wealth (0.34)						
Home Ownership	Census	2006	47.9	75.8	63%	
Mortgage Application Rate (Total), %	HMDA	2006	27.9	13.7	49%	(0.04)
Mortgage Application Denial Rate (Male), %	HMDA	2006	29.7	16.4	55%	(0.04)
Mortgage Application DenialRate (Female), %	HMDA	2006	28.2	15.6	55%	(0.04)
Mortgage Application Denial Rate (Joint), %	HMDA	2006	22.8	10.1	44%	(0.04)
Home Improvement Loans Denials (Total), %	HMDA	2006	51.6	30.9	60%	(0.04)
Home Improvement Loans Denials (Male), %	HMDA	2006	52.9	35.6	67%	(0.04)
Home Improvement Loans Denials (Female), %	HMDA	2006	53.4	35.4	66%	(0.04)
Home Improvement Loans Denials (Joint), %	HMDA	2006	46.6	25.9	56%	(0.04)
Percent of High-Priced Loans (More than 3% above Treasury)	HMDA	2006	53.4	17.5	33%	0.02
Home Values (Median)	Census	2000	80,600	123,400	65%	
Median Net Worth	SWA	2004	11.8	118.3	10%	
Equity in Home	Census	2000	35,000	64,200	55%	
Percent Investing in 401k	Census	2000	19.6	32.9	60%	
Percent Investing in IRA	Census	2000	6.5	27.5	24%	
U.S. Firms by Race (% Compared to Employment Share)	Census	2002	0.509	0.951	54%	
Digital Divide (0.05)						
Households with Computer at Home, %	Census	2003	44.6	66.6	67%	
Households Using the Internet, %	Census	2003	36.0	59.9	60%	
Adult Useres with Broadband Access, %	Stat. Ab.	2006	37.0	45.0	82%	0.22
Transportation (0.01)						
Car Ownership, %	Census	2000	70.2	89.2	79%	

The Equality Index of Black America

Updated Series | New Series | (Index = 0.73)

	Source	Year	Black	White	Index	DIFF ('08-'07)
Drive Alone	ACS	2006	70.7	79.6	89%	(0.00)
Reliance on Public Transportation	ACS	2006	11.6	2.8	24%	0.01
Economic Weighted Index					**56.8%**	(0.00)
HEALTH INDEX (25%)						
Death Rates & Life Expectancy (0.45)						
Life Expectancy at Birth	CDC-H	2004	73.1	78.3	93%	
Male	CDC-H	2004	69.5	75.7	92%	
Female	CDC-H	2004	76.3	80.8	94%	
Life Expectancy at 65 (Additional Expected Years)	CDC-H	2004	17.1	18.7	91%	
Male at 65	CDC-H	2004	15.2	17.2	88%	
Female at 65	CDC-H	2004	18.6	20.0	93%	
Death Rates						
Age-Adjusted Death Rates (per 100,000)–all causes	CDC-D	2004	1,027.3	797.1	78%	0.00
Age-Adjusted Death Rates (per 100,000)–Male	CDC-D	2004	1,269.4	949.0	75%	0.00
Age-Adjusted Death Rates (per 100,000)–Female	CDC-D	2004	855.3	677.5	79%	(0.00)
Age-Adjusted Death Rates (per 100,000)–Heart Disease	CDC-D	2004	280.6	216.3	77%	0.00
Ischemic Heart Disease	CDC-D	2004	179.8	150.9	84%	0.00
Age-Adjusted Death Rates (per 100,000)–Stroke (Cerebrovascular)	CDC-D	2004	69.9	48.3	69%	(0.00)
Age-Adjusted Death Rates (per 100,000)–Cancer	CDC-D	2004	227.2	188.6	83%	0.01
Trachea, Bronchus, and Lung	CDC-D	2004	59.8	56.0	94%	0.00
Colon, Rectum, and Anus	CDC-D	2004	24.7	17.9	72%	0.01
Prostate (Male)	CDC-D	2004	55.5	23.6	43%	(0.00)
Breast	CDC-D	2004	32.2	24.5	76%	0.02
Age-Adjusted Death Rates (per 100,000)–Chronic Lower Respiratory	CDC-D	2004	28.2	44.9	159%	0.09
Age-Adjusted Death Rates (per 100,000)–Influenza and Pneumonia	CDC-D	2004	22.3	19.6	88%	(0.07)
Age-Adjusted Death Rates (per 100,000)–Chronic Liver Disease and Cirrhosis	CDC-D	2004	7.9	8.7	110%	0.03

The Equality Index of Black America

Legend: Updated Series | New Series | (Index = 0.73)

	Source	Year	Black	White	Index	DIFF ('08-'07)
Age-Adjusted Death Rates (per 100,000)–Diabetes	CDC-D	2004	48.0	21.5	45%	(0.00)
Age-Adjusted Death Rates (per 100,000)–HIV2003	CDC-D	2004	20.4	1.9	9%	(0.00)
Unintentional Injuries	CDC-D	2004	36.3	39.7	109%	0.02
Motor Vehicle-Related Injuries	CDC-D	2004	14.8	15.6	105%	0.01
Age-Adjusted Death Rates (per 100,000)–Suicide	CDC-D	2004	5.3	12.9	243%	(0.01)
Age-Adjusted Death Rates (per 100,000)–Suicide Males	CDC-D	2004	9.6	21.0	219%	(0.10)
Age-Adjusted Death Rates (per 100,000)–Suicide Males Ages 15-24	CDC-D	2004	12.2	19.0	156%	(0.15)
Age-Adjusted Death Rates (per 100,000)–Suicide Females	CDC-D	2004	1.8	5.4	300%	0.37
Age-Adjusted Death Rates (per 100,000)–Suicide Females Ages 15-24	CDC-D	2004	2.2	4.0	182%	(0.18)
Age-Adjusted Death Rates (per 100,000)–Homicide	CDC-D	2004	20.1	2.7	13%	0.01
Age-Adjusted Death Rates (per 100,000)–Homicide Male	CDC-D	2004	35.1	3.6	10%	0.00
Age-Adjusted Death Rates (per 100,000)–Homicide Males Ages 15-24	CDC-D	2004	77.6	4.7	6%	0.00
Age-Adjusted Death Rates (per 100,000)–Homicide Female	CDC-D	2004	6.3	1.8	29%	0.00
Age-Adjusted Death Rates (per 100,000)–Homicide Females Ages 15-24	CDC-D	2004	8.8	2.3	26%	0.07
Age-Adjusted Death Rates (per 100,000) by Age Cohort: >1 Male	CDC-D	2004	1,414.2	625.2	44%	(0.02)
Age-Adjusted Death Rates (per 100,000) by Age Cohort: 1-4 Male	CDC-D	2004	48.6	29.0	60%	0.03
Age-Adjusted Death Rates (per 100,000) by Age Cohort: 5-14 Male	CDC-D	2004	26.0	17.9	69%	0.01
Age-Adjusted Death Rates (per 100,000) by Age Cohort: 15-24 Male	CDC-D	2004	164.3	104.8	64%	0.02
Age-Adjusted Death Rates (per 100,000) by Age Cohort: 25-34 Male	CDC-D	2004	252.3	130.9	52%	0.01
Age-Adjusted Death Rates (per 100,000) by Age Cohort: 35-44 Male	CDC-D	2004	397.0	235.7	59%	0.02
Age-Adjusted Death Rates (per 100,000) by Age Cohort: 45-54 Male	CDC-D	2004	954.9	510.5	53%	0.02
Age-Adjusted Death Rates (per 100,000) by Age Cohort: 55-64 Male	CDC-D	2004	1,960.8	1,076.4	55%	(0.00)
Age-Adjusted Death Rates (per 100,000) by Age Cohort: 65-74 Male	CDC-D	2003	3,818.3	2,617.9	69%	(0.00)
Age-Adjusted Death Rates (per 100,000) by Age Cohort: 75-84 Male	CDC-D	2004	7710.3	6,461.5	84%	0.01
Age-Adjusted Death Rates (per 100,000) by Age Cohort: 85+ Male	CDC-D	2004	14,452.5	15,489.2	107%	(0.02)
Age-Adjusted Death Rates (per 100,000) by Age Cohort: >1 Female	CDC-D	2004	1,149.9	500.7	44%	(0.01)

The Equality Index of Black America

Updated Series   New Series   (Index = 0.73)

	Source	Year	Black	White	Index	DIFF ('08-'07)
Age-Adjusted Death Rates (per 100,000) by age cohort: 1-4 Female	CDC-D	2004	40.9	24.4	60%	(0.03)
Age-Adjusted Death Rates (per 100,000) by Age Cohort: 5-14 Female	CDC-D	2004	21.1	13.0	62%	(0.07)
Age-Adjusted Death Rates (per 100,000) by Age Cohort: 15-24 Female	CDC-D	2004	53.7	44.3	82%	0.00
Age-Adjusted Death Rates (per 100,000) by Age Cohort: 25-34 Female	CDC-D	2004	112.3	60.3	54%	(0.00)
Age-Adjusted Death Rates (per 100,000) by Age Cohort: 35-44 Female	CDC-D	2004	256.0	136.0	53%	0.02
Age-Adjusted Death Rates (per 100,000) by Age Cohort: 45-54 Female	CDC-D	2004	564.1	292.9	52%	0.02
Age-Adjusted Death Rates (per 100,000) by Age Cohort: 55-64 Female	CDC-D	2004	1,128.6	683.8	61%	0.01
Age-Adjusted Death Rates (per 100,000) by Age Cohort: 65-74 Female	CDC-D	2004	2,386.1	1,752.0	73%	0.01
Age-Adjusted Death Rates (per 100,000) by Age Cohort: 75-84 Female	CDC-D	2004	5,300.0	4,571.1	86%	(0.01)
Age-Adjusted Death Rates (per 100,000) by Age Cohort: 85+ Female	CDC-D	2004	12,896.9	13,609.6	106%	(0.00)
Physical Condition (0.10)						
Overweight and Obese: 18+ years (% of Population)	CDC	2006	71.8	61.0	85%	0.02
Overweight-Men 20 Years and Over (% of Population)	CDC-H	2004	67.0	71.0	106%	
Overweight-Women 20 Years and Over (% of Population)	CDC-H	2004	79.6	57.6	72%	
Obese (% of population)	CDC	2006	36.7	24.2	66%	0.04
Obese-Men 20 Years and Over (% of Population)	CDC-H	2004	30.8	30.2	98%	
Obese-Women 20 Years and Over (% of Population)	CDC-H	2004	51.1	30.7	60%	
Diabetes: Physician Diagnosed in Ages 18+ (% of Population)	CDC-H	2005	11.6	6.1	53%	
AIDS Cases per 100,000 Males Ages 13+	CDC-H	2005	95.1	12.1	13%	
AIDS Cases per 100,000 Females Ages 13+	CDC-H	2005	45.5	2.0	4%	
Substance Abuse (0.10)						
Binge Alcohol (5 drinks in 1 day, 1x a year) Ages 18+ (% of Population)	CDC-ER	2005	24.0	32.9	137%	
Use of Illicit drugs in the past month ages 12 + (% of population)	CDC-ER	2005	9.7	8.1	84%	
Tobacco: Both Cigarette & Cigar Ages 18+ (% of Population)	CDC-ER	2005	17.3	21.4	124%	
Mental Health (0.02)						
Students Who Consider Suicide: Male	CDC-H	2005	7.0	12.4	177%	

The Equality Index of Black America

Updated Series ▮ New Series ▮ (Index = 0.73)

	Source	Year	Black	White	Index	DIFF ('08-'07)
Students Who Carry Out Intent and Require Medical Attention: Male	CDC-H	2005	1.4	1.5	107%	0.86
Percent of Students that Act on Suicidal Feeling: Male	CDC-H	2005	5.2	5.2	100%	
Students Who Consider Suicide: Female	CDC-H	2005	17.1	21.5	126%	
Students Who Carry Out Intent and Require Medical Attention: Female	CDC-H	2002	2.6	2.7	104%	(0.05)
Percent of Students that Act on Suicidal Feeling: Female	CDC-H	2005	9.8	9.3	95%	
Access to Care (0.05)						
Private Insurance Payment for Health Care: Under 65 Years Old (% of Population)	CDC-H	2004	39.5	59.4	66%	
People Without Health Insurance (% of population)	Census	2006	20.5	10.8	53%	(0.04)
People 18 to 64 Without A Usual Source of Health Insurance (% of Adults)	CDC-H	2005	19.0	14.6	77%	
People in Poverty Without a Usual Source of Health Insurance (% of Adults)	CDC-H	2005	28.3	26.8	95%	
Population Under 65 Covered by Medicaid (% of population)	CDC-H	2005	24.8	8.5	34%	0.02
Elderly Health Care (0.03)						
Population Over 65 Covered by Medicaid	CDC-H	2005	23.6	6.1	26%	0.06
Medicare Expenditures per Beneficiary	CDC-H	2004	18,111.0	13,064.0	72%	(0.11)
Pregnancy Issues (0.04)						
Prenatal Care Begins in 1st Trimester	CDC-B	2004	76.5	88.9	86%	
Prenatal Care Begins in 3rd Trimester	CDC-B	2004	5.7	2.2	39%	
Percent of Births to Mothers 18 and Under	CDC-H	2004	6.5	2.0	31%	
Percent of Live Births to Unmarried Mothers	CDC-B	2004	69.3	24.5	35%	
Mothers With Less than 12 Years of Education (% of Live Births)	CDC-H	2004	23.4	11.0	47%	
Mothers Who Smoked Cigarettes During Pregnancy (%)	CDC-B	2004	8.4	13.8	164%	
Low Birth Weight (% of Live Births)	CDC-B	2004	13.7	7.2	52%	
Very Low Birth Weight (% of Live Births)	CDC-B	2004	3.2	1.2	38%	
Reproduction Issues (0.01)						
Abortions (Per 100 Live Births)	CDC-H	2003	49.1	16.5	34%	
Women Using Contraception (% in Population)	CDC-H	2002	57.6	64.6	89%	

The Equality Index of Black America

Updated Series ■ New Series (Index = 0.73)

	Source	Year	Black	White	Index	DIFF ('08-'07)
Delivery Issues (0.10)						
All Infant Deaths: Neonatal and Post (per 1000 Live Births)	CDC-D	2004	13.6	5.7	42%	0.00
Neonatal Deaths (per 1000 Live Births)	CDC-D	2004	9.1	3.7	41%	(0.00)
PostNeonatal Deaths (per 1000 Live Births)	CDC-D	2004	4.5	2.0	44%	0.00
Maternal Mortality (per 100,000 Live Births)	CDC-H	2004	32.3	7.8	24%	
Children's Health (0.1)						
Babies Breastfed (%)	CDC-H	2001	45.3	68.7	66%	
Percent of children without a health care visit in past 12 months (children up to 6 years old)	CDC-H	2005	4.3	5.1	119%	0.28
Vaccinations of Children Below Poverty: Combined Vacc. Series 4:3:1:3 (% of Children 19-35 Months)	CDC-H	2006	72.0	70.0	103%	(0.03)
Uninsured Children	CDC-H	2005	6.1	3.2	52%	0.01
Overweight Boys 6-11 Years Old (% of Population)	CDC-H	2004	17.2	16.9	98%	
Overweight Girls 6-11 Years Old (% of Population)	CDC-H	2004	24.8	15.6	63%	
AIDS Cases per 100,000 All Children Under 13	CDC	2005	0.6	0.0	4%	
Health Weighted Index					**75.7%**	0.45
EDUCATION (25%)						
Middle Grades—Teacher Lacking at Least a College Minor in Subject Taught	ET	2000	49%	40%	85%	
HS—Teacher Lacking at Least a College Minor in Subject Taught	ET	2000	28%	21%	91%	
Per Student Funding in Low and High Poverty Districts (Dollars)	ET	2004	5,937	7,244	82%	
Teachers with <3 Years Experience (Hi vs. Low Minority Schools)	ET	2000	0.21	0.1	48%	
Distribution of Underprepared Teachers (California Only) Small vs. High Minority	SRI	2005-06	0.08	0.03	38%	
*had not completed a preparation program and obtained a full credential before beginning to teach						
Course Quality (0.15)						
All College Entrants	ET	1999	0.45	0.73	62%	
Of All College Entrants What Percent Had a Strong HS Curriculum (Algebra II Plus Other Courses)	ET	1999	0.75	0.86	87%	
HS Students: Enrolled in Chemistry	NCES	2005	63.6%	67.1%	95%	(0.00)
HS Students: Enrolled in Algebra II	NCES	2005	69.2%	71.2%	97%	0.03

The Equality Index of Black America

	Updated Series	New Series	(Index = 0.73)

	Source	Year	Black	White	Index	DIFF ('08-'07)
Students Taking: Precalculus	CB	2007	35%	55%	64%	0.01
Students Taking: Calculus	CB	2007	15%	31%	48%	(0.02)
Students Taking: Physics	CB	2007	43%	55%	78%	
Students Taking: English Composition	CB	2006	0.43	0.53	81%	0.01
Students Taking: Grammar	CB	2006	0.51	0.56	91%	
Attainment (0.20)						
Graduation by Enrolled Students for 2-year Institutions	NCES	2002	27.2%	33.8%	80%	0.01
Graduation by Enrolled Students for 4-year Institutions	NCES	1999	40.4%	58.9%	69%	0.00
NCAA Div. I College Freshmen Graduating within 6 Years	NCAA	2000-01	46%	64%	72%	0.02
Degrees Earned (Assoc) (% of population aged 18-24 yrs)	NCES	2005	12.0%	2.6%	76%	0.01
Degrees Earned (Bach) (% of population aged 18-29 yrs)	NCES	2005	1.9%	3.5%	55%	0.00
Degrees Earned (Master) (% of population aged 18-34 yrs)	NCES	2005	0.6%	0.9%	62%	0.02
HS Educational Attainment (25 and Over)	Census	2006	80.7%	86.1%	94%	(0.01)
College Educational Attainment (25 and Over)	Census	2006	18.5%	28.4%	65%	0.02
Degree Holders (% of Persons Over 18)						
Agriculture/Forestry	NCES	2001	0.7	1.2	56%	
Art/Architecture	NCES	2001	3.3	2.9	114%	
Business/Management	NCES	2001	19.5	18.1	108%	
Communications	NCES	2001	3.2	2.4	135%	
Computer and Information Sciences	NCES	2001	3.9	2.2	177%	
Education	NCES	2001	15.3	15.3	100%	
Engineering	NCES	2001	3.6	7.7	47%	
English/Literature	NCES	2001	2.6	3.3	80%	
Foreign Languages	NCES	2001	0.8	0.9	96%	
Health Sciences	NCES	2001	5.4	4.5	120%	
Liberal arts/humanities	NCES	2001	4.6	6.1	75%	

The Equality Index of Black America

Updated Series ■ New Series (Index = 0.73)

	Source	Year	Black	White	Index	DIFF ('08-'07)
Mathematics/Statistics	NCES	2001	2.4	1.4	169%	
Natural Sciences	NCES	2001	6.0	5.6	106%	
Philosophy/Religion/Theology	NCES	2001	0.9	1.3	70%	
Pre-professional	NCES	2001	1.6	1.1	146%	
Psychology	NCES	2001	4.9	3.9	126%	
Social Sciences/History	NCES	2001	8.1	4.9	165%	
Other Fields	NCES	2001	13.1	17.2	76%	
Preschool 10% of Total Scores (0.015)						
Children's School Readiness Skills: Ages 3-5 (% with 3 or 4 skills*)	NCES	2005	44	47	94%	
*Recognizes all Letters, Counts to 20 or higher, Writes Name, Reads or Pretends to Read						
Elementary 40% of Total Scores (0.06)						
Proficiency Test Scores for Selected Subjects (NAEP) Elementary Ages						
Geography Scores for 8th Graders (Public & Private)	NCES	2001	234	273	86%	
History Scores for 8th Graders (Public & Private)	NCES	2001	243	271	90%	
Math 13 Yr Old (8th Grade)	NCES	2004	262	288	91%	
Math 9 Yr Old (4th Grade)	NCES	2004	224	247	91%	
Reading 13 Yr Old (8th Grade)	NCES	2004	244	266	92%	
Reading 9 Yr Old (4th Grade)	NCES	2004	200	226	88%	
Science Scores for 4th Graders (Public Schools)	NCES	2005	129	162	80%	
Science Scores for 8th Graders (Public Schools)	NCES	2005	124	160	78%	0.02
Writing Proficiency at or above Basic 4th Grade	NCES	2002	79	91	87%	
Writing Proficiency at or above Basic 8th Grade	NCES	2002	75	91	82%	
High School 50% of Total Scores (0.075)						
High School Scores						
Writing Proficiency at or above Basic 12th Grade	NCES	2002	59	80	74%	
Science Scores, 12th Graders	NCES	2005	120	156	77%	

The Equality Index of Black America

■ Updated Series ■ New Series (Index = 0.73)

	Source	Year	Black	White	Index	DIFF ('08-'07)
High School GPAs for those taking the SAT	CB	2007	3.00	3.40	88%	(0.00)
SAT Reasoning Test	CB	2007	862	1,061	81%	0.00
Mathematics (Joint)	CB	2007	429	534	80%	
Mathematics (Male)	CB	2007	437	553	79%	
Mathematics (Femal)	CB	2007	423	519	82%	
Verbal (Joint)	CB	2007	433	527	82%	
Verbal (Male)	CB	2007	429	529	81%	
Verbal (Female)	CB	2007	436	526	83%	
Writing (Joint)	CB	2007	425	518	82%	
Writing (Male)	CB	2007	414	511	81%	
Writing (Female)	CB	2007	433	524	83%	
ACT	ACT	2007	17.0	22.1	77%	(0.00)
Enrollment (0.10)						
School Enrollment: Ages 3-34 (% of Population)	Census	2005	58.4%	55.9%	104%	(0.02)
Preprimary School Enrollment	Census	2005	62.0%	65.1%	95%	(0.10)
3 and 4 Years Old	Census	2005	52.2%	54.2%	96%	(0.17)
5 and 6 Years Old	Census	2005	95.9%	95.3%	101%	0.02
7 to 13 Years Old	Census	2005	98.6%	98.6%	100%	(0.00)
14 and 15 Years Old	Census	2005	95.8%	98.3%	97%	(0.03)
16 and 17 Years Old	Census	2005	93.1%	95.4%	98%	(0.04)
18 and 19 Years Old	Census	2005	62.8%	68.0%	92%	0.01
20 and 21 Years Old	Census	2005	37.6%	49.3%	76%	(0.05)
22 to 24 Years Old	Census	2005	28.0%	26.0%	108%	0.08
25 to 29 Years Old	Census	2005	11.7%	11.3%	104%	(0.14)
30 to 34 Years Old	Census	2005	10.0%	6.2%	161%	0.49
35 and Over	Census	2005	3.1%	1.8%	172%	(0.01)

The Equality Index of Black America

Updated Series | New Series | (Index = 0.73)

	Source	Year	Black	White	Index	DIFF ('08-'07)
College Enrollment by Age Cohort (15 Years and Over)	Census	2005	8.0%	7.2%	112%	(0.03)
15 to 17 Years Old	Census	2005	1.5%	1.2%	128%	(0.16)
18 to 19 Years Old	Census	2005	35.9	50.6	71%	(0.00)
20 to 21 Years Old	Census	2005	32.3%	53.6%	60%	(0.04)
22 to 24 Years Old	Census	2005	24.2%	25.9%	94%	0.10
25 to 29 Years Old	Census	2005	10.4%	12.2%	86%	(0.14)
30 to 34 Years Old	Census	2005	8.5%	6.7%	128%	0.31
35 Years Old and Over	Census	2005	2.7%	1.7%	153%	(0.15)
College Enrollment of Recent High School Graduate	Census	2005	55.7%	73.2%	76%	(0.15)
Adult Education Participation	NCES	2004-05	46.0%	46.0%	100%	
Student Status & Risk Factors (0.10)						
High School Dropouts: Status Dropouts--Not Completed HS and Not Enrolled, Regardless of When Dropped	Census	2005	12.9%	11.3%	88%	0.09
Children in Poverty	USDC	1999	0.331	0.093	28%	
Children in all families below poverty level	Census	2005	33.2%	14%	42%	
Children in families below poverty level (female householder, no spouse present)	Census	2005	49.5%	38.7%	78%	
Children with No Parent in the Labor Force	USDC	2000	0.203	0.055	27%	
School Age Children (5-15) with a Disability	USDC	2000	0.07	0.057	81%	
Public School Students (K-12): Repeated Grade	NCES	2003	17.1%	8.2%	48%	(0.05)
Public School Students (K-12): Suspended	NCES	2003	19.6%	8.8%	45%	
Public School Students (K-12): Expelled	NCES	2003	5.0%	1.4%	28%	
Center Based, Child Care of Preschool Children	NCES	2005	66.5%	59.1%	89%	(0.05)
Parental Care Only, Preschool Children	NCES	2005	19.5%	24.1%	81%	0.21
Teacher Stability: Remained in Public School	NCES	2001	84.3	85.0	99%	
Teacher Stability: Remained in Private School	NCES	2001	83.2	79.0	105%	
Zero Days Missed in School Year (%)	NCES	2002	16.5	13.0	127%	
3+ Days Late to School (% of students Reporting)	NCES	2002	46.1	31.5	68%	
Never Cut Classes (% of students)	NCES	2002	64.6	72.9	89%	

The Equality Index of Black America

Updated Series ▪ **New Series** (Index = 0.73)

	Source	Year	Black	White	Index	DIFF ('08-'07)
Home Literacy Activities (Age 3 to 5)						
Read to 3 or More Times a Week	NCES	2005	78	92	85%	
Told a Story at Least Once a Month	NCES	2005	54	53	102%	
Taught Words or Numbers Three or More Times a Week	NCES	2005	81	76	107%	
Visited a Library at Least Once in Last Month	NCES	2005	44	45	98%	
Education Weighted Index					**78.2%**	(0.58)
SOCIAL JUSTICE (10%)						
Equality Before the Law (0.80)						
Stopped While Driving	BJS	2005	8.1%	8.9%	110%	0.14
Speeding	BJS	2002	50.0%	57%	114%	
Vehicle Defect	BJS	2002	10.3%	8.7%	84%	
Roadside Check for Drinking Drivers	BJS	2002	1.1%	1.3%	118%	
Record Check	BJS	2002	17.4%	11.3%	65%	
Seatbelt Violation	BJS	2002	3.5%	4.4%	126%	
Illegal Turn/Lane Change	BJS	2002	5.1%	4.5%	88%	
Stop Sign/Light Violation	BJS	2002	5.9%	6.5%	110%	
Other	BJS	2002	3.7%	4.0%	108%	
Mean Incarceration Sentence (In Average Months)	BJS	2004	40.0	37.0	93%	0.15
Average sentence for incarceration (All Offenses) - Male	BJS	2004	43.0	39.0	91%	
Average sentence for incarceration (All Offenses) - Female	BJS	2004	23.0	24.0	104%	
Average Sentence for Murder-Male	BJS	2004	256	232	91%	0.02
Average Sentence for Sexual Assault-Male	BJS	2004	104	110	106%	0.16
Average Sentence for Robbery-Male	BJS	2004	101	88	87%	0.02
Average Sentence for Aggravated Assault-Male	BJS	2004	51	42	82%	0.07
Average Sentence for Other Violent-Male	BJS	2004	47	43	91%	0.01

The Equality Index of Black America

			Updated Series		New Series	(Index = 0.73)
	Source	Year	Black	White	Index	DIFF ('08–'07)
Average Sentence for Burglary–Male	BJS	2004	47	44	94%	0.10
Average Sentence for Larceny–Male	BJS	2004	23	21	91%	(0.04)
Average Sentence for Fraud–Male	BJS	2004	25	27	108%	0.25
Average Sentence for Drug Possession–Male	BJS	2004	23	22	96%	0.09
Average Sentence for Drug Trafficking–Male	BJS	2004	38	41	108%	0.23
Average Sentence for Weapon Offenses–Male	BJS	2004	34	32	94%	0.04
Average Sentence for Other Offenses–Male	BJS	2004	25	25	100%	0.04
Average Sentence for Murder–Female	BJS	2004	231	152	66%	0.17
Average Sentence for Sexual Assault–Female	BJS	2004	55	88	160%	0.34
Average Sentence for Robbery–Female	BJS	2004	80	55	69%	(0.26)
Average Sentence for Aggravated Assault–Female	BJS	2004	31	31	100%	0.14
Average Sentence for Other Violent–Female	BJS	2004	31	41	132%	(0.24)
Average Sentence for Burglary–Female	BJS	2004	22	27	123%	0.05
Average Sentence for Larceny–Female	BJS	2004	17	17	100%	0.00
Average Sentence for Fraud–Female	BJS	2004	21	21	100%	0.13
Average Sentence for Drug Possession–Female	BJS	2004	15	16	107%	0.13
Average Sentence for Drug Trafficking–Female	BJS	2004	25	28	112%	0.21
Average Sentence for Weapon Offenses–Female	BJS	2004	20	26	130%	0.56
Average Sentence for Other Offenses–Female	BJS	2004	17	20	118%	0.44
Probation Granted for Felons (% granted)–Male	BJS	2002	27.0	34.0	79%	
Probation Granted for Murder	BJS	2002	4.0	6.0	67%	
Probation Granted for Robbery	BJS	2002	11.0	14.0	79%	
Probation Granted for Burglary	BJS	2002	23.0	27.0	85%	
Probation Granted for Fraud	BJS	2002	37.0	42.0	88%	
Probation Granted for Drug Offenses	BJS	2002	31.0	42.0	74%	
Probation Granted for Felons (% Granted)–Female	BJS	2002	47.0	45.0	104%	

The Equality Index of Black America

	Updated Series		New Series	(Index = 0.73)

	Source	Year	Black	White	Index	DIFF ('08-'07)
Probation Granted for Murder	BJS	2002	5.0	17.0	29%	
Probation Granted for Robbery	BJS	2002	24.0	31.0	77%	
Probation Granted for Burglary	BJS	2002	24.0	32.0	75%	
Probation Granted for Fraud	BJS	2002	57.0	50.0	114%	
Probation Granted for Drug Offenses	BJS	2002	45.0	49.0	92%	
Incarceration rate: prisoners per 100,000	BJS	2006	2,086	337	16%	0.01
Incarceration Rate: Prisoners per 100,000 People - Male	BJS	2006	3,042	487	16%	0.01
Incarceration Rate: Prisoners per 100,000 People - Female	BJS	2006	148	48	32%	0.04
Prisoners as a % of Arrests	FBI, BJS	2006	23.1%	8.5%	37%	0.03
Victimization & Mental Anguish (0.20)						
Homicide Rate per 100,000	BJS	2004	19.7	3.3	17%	
Homicide Rate per 100,000: Firearm	NACJD	2003	14.1	2.1	15%	
Homicide Rate per 100,000: Stabbings	NACJD	2003	2.0	0.5	25%	
Homicide Rate per 100,000: Personal Weapons	NACJD	2003	0.9	1.7	197%	
Homicide Rate per 100,000 - Male	BJS	2004	37.1	5.3	14%	0.00
Homicide Rate per 100,000 - Female	BJS	2004	6.4	1.9	30%	(0.01)
Murder Victims (Rate per 100,000)	USDJ	2005	18.8	3.6	19%	(0.01)
Hate Crimes Victims (Rate per 100,000)	USDJ	2005	8.5	0.5	6%	0.00
Victims of Violent Crimes (Rate per 100,000)	BJS	2005	32.7	23.2	71%	(0.03)
Delinquency Cases, Year of Disposition (Rate per 100,000)	NCJJ	2004	2,876.7	1,358.8	47%	(0.02)
Prisoners Under Sentence of Death (Rate per 100,000)	BJS	2006	5.0	1.2	23%	0.00
High School Students Carrying Weapons on School Property	CDC	2005	5.1%	6.1%	120%	0.40
High School Students Carrying Weapons Anywhere	CDC	2005	16.4%	18.7%	114%	0.17
Firearm-Related Death (All Ages, Males)	CDC	2004	36.4	15.6	43%	
Ages 1-14	CDC	2004	2.0	0.7	35%	
Ages 15-24	CDC	2004	80.7	14.3	18%	

The Equality Index of Black America

Updated Series | New Series | (Index = 0.73)

	Source	Year	Black	White	Index	DIFF ('08-'07)
Ages 25-44	CDC	2004	59.2	17.4	29%	
Ages 25-34	CDC	2004	83.6	16.9	20%	
Ages 35-44	CDC	2004	35.1	17.8	51%	
Ages 45-64	CDC	2004	18.3	19.2	105%	
Age 65 and Older	CDC	2004	14.6	27.6	189%	
Firearm-Related Death (All Ages, Females)	CDC	2004	3.7	2.9	78%	
Ages 15-24	CDC	2004	6.9	2.5	36%	
Ages 25-44	CDC	2004	5.7	3.9	68%	
Ages 45-64	CDC	2004	3.0	4.1	137%	
Age 65 and Older	CDC	2003	1.8	2.2	122%	
Social Justice Weighted Index					**71.7%**	6.25
CIVIC ENGAGEMENT (10%)						
Democratic Process (0.4)						
Registered Voters	Census	2004	64.4	67.9	95%	
Actually Voted	Census	2004	56.3	60.3	93%	
Community Participation (0.3)						
Percent of Population Volunteering for Military Reserves	USDD	2006	0.9%	0.9%	94%	(0.05)
Volunteerism	BLS	2006	19.2%	28.3%	68%	(0.05)
Civic and Political	BLS	2006	4.6%	6.3%	73%	
Educational or Youth Service	BLS	2006	26.1%	26.4%	99%	
Environmental or Animal Care	BLS	2006	0.4%	1.8%	22%	
Hospital or Other Health	BLS	2006	5.2%	8.4%	62%	
Public Safety	BLS	2006	0.6%	1.4%	43%	
Religious	BLS	2006	43.3%	34.2%	127%	(0.08)
Social or Community Service	BLS	2006	11.9%	12.8%	93%	
Unpaid Volunteering of Young Adults	NCES	2000	40.9	32.2	127%	

The Equality Index of Black America

		Updated Series		New Series	(Index = 0.73)
	Source	Year	Black	White	Index	DIFF ('08–'07)
Collective Bargaining (0.2)						
Unionism (Members)	BLS	2006	14.5	11.7	124%	0.00
Union Rep.	BLS	2006	16.1	12.8	126%	0.03
Governmental Employment (0.1)						
Federal Executive Branch (Nonpostal) Employment	OPM	2006	1.2%	0.8%	146%	0.00
State and Local Government Employment	EEOC	2003	4.3%	2.5%	167%	
Civic Engagement Weighted Index					**103.6%**	(1.33)

The Opportunity Compact
Blueprint for Economic Equality

National Urban League Policy Institute

Valerie Rawlston Wilson, Ph.D.

Renee Hanson

Mark McArdle

INTRODUCTION TO THE OPPORTUNITY COMPACT

> **Opportunity** _ noun
> : a good chance for advancement or progress
> **Compact** _ noun
> : a signed written agreement between two or more parties
> to perform some action

What is the Opportunity Compact?

The Opportunity Compact is a comprehensive set of principles and policy recommendations set forth by the National Urban League (NUL) designed to empower all Americans to be full participants in the economic and social mainstream of this nation. In pursuit of this end, NUL 1) identifies principles that reflect the values inherent in the American dream; 2) examines the conditions that have separated a significant portion of the American population—particularly the poor and disadvantaged residents of urban communities—from accessing that dream; 3) proposes, for honest evaluation and discussion, several policy recommendations intended to bridge the gap between conceptualization and realization of the American dream.

The Opportunity Compact is the culmination of extensive research and policy analysis by the National Urban League Policy Institute (NULPI) and is based upon the input of dozens of policy experts from academia, public policy think tanks, non-profit service and advocacy organizations, the business sector, and the Urban League movement. Among other things, the NULPI hosted a series of five roundtable discussions and obtained feedback and recommendations from numerous experts concerning the development of a coherent and comprehensive plan for empowering the nation's urban communities. As the foundation for such a plan, NUL has clearly identified four cornerstones that reflect the values represented by the American dream: (1) The Opportunity to Thrive (Children), (2) The Opportunity to Earn (Jobs), (3) The Opportunity to Own (Housing) and (4) The Opportunity to Prosper (Entrepreneurship). These cornerstones are supported by a list of ten policy priorities.

Who Are the Entities Involved?

The words *opportunity* and co*mpact,* as defined above, offer a concise and self-explanatory description of what *The Opportunity Compact* represents—an agreement between interested parties to take actions that will improve the chances for advancement and progress of those living in America's cities. The diversity of talents, experiences, ideas and interests represented in the population of the United States is the greatest asset this country possesses. As such, NUL believes that the collaborative efforts of private citizens, national, state and local governments, community-based service providers and the business community will expand opportunities for advancement and progress among the poor, disadvantaged and underserved. The policy recommendations offered in this report are not a laundry list of things for the federal government to perform on behalf of a select group of citizens. Rather, there is a role for all parties—public and private - to play as we together seek to strengthen our nation by maximizing the potential of all our citizens.

What is the Desired Outcome?

The National Urban League embarked upon the task of developing The Opportunity Compact with the goal of drawing upon the strength of NUL's ninety-seven year history as the nation's oldest and largest community-based movement for social and economic empowerment to reassert the organization as a proactive and effective agent in the development of public policy. This document serves as a vehicle through which to assert specific principles and policy recommendations as the foundation for a plan of action to address the challenges faced by those in urban communities throughout the country. As such, this document is also intended to elicit serious responses from the 2008 presidential candidates, legislators, the private sector, the public and other community-based organizations with the ultimate objective of putting in place a comprehensive plan for advancing the promise of America's cities. By generating new ideas, initiating productive partnerships and fostering collaboration, The Opportunity Compact seeks to expand access to the incentives and rewards that act as the driving force behind what makes this country great—personal responsibility, initiative and hard work.

CORNERSTONES & GUIDING PRINCIPLES OF THE OPPORTUNITY COMPACT

There are four cornerstones to The Opportunity Compact:

1 Opportunity to Thrive (Children)

- Every child in America deserves to live a life free of poverty that includes a safe home environment, adequate nutrition, and affordable quality health care.
- Every child in America deserves a quality education that will prepare them to compete in an increasingly global marketplace.

2 Opportunity to Earn (Jobs)

- Every willing adult in America should have a job that allows them to earn a decent wage and provide a reasonable standard of living for themselves and their families.
- Every adult in America should have equal access to the resources that enhance employability and job mobility, including postsecondary education and other investments in human capital.

3 Opportunity to Own (Housing)

- Every adult in America should have access to the financial security that comes from owning a home.

4 Opportunity to Prosper (Entrepreneurship)

- Every individual in America who possesses entrepreneurial vision, ingenuity, drive and desire should have access to the resources needed to establish and grow a viable business enterprise.

45

TOP TEN POLICY PRIORITIES OF THE OPPORTUNITY COMPACT
Opportunity to Thrive (Children)

1. Commit to mandatory early childhood education beginning at age three as well as guarantee access to college for all.

2. Close the gaps in the health insurance system to ensure universal healthcare for all children.

3. Establish policies that provide tools for working families to become economically self-sufficient.

Opportunity to Earn (Jobs)

4. Create an urban infrastructure bank to fund reinvestment in urban communities (e.g. parks, schools, roads).

5. Increase economic self-sufficiency by indexing the minimum wage to the rate of inflation and expanding the Earned Income Tax Credit to benefit more working families.

6. Expand "second chance" programs for high school drop outs, ex-offenders and at-risk youth to secure GEDs, job training and employment.

Opportunity to Own (Housing)

7. Adopt the "Homebuyer's Bill of Rights" as recommended by the National Urban League.

8. Reform public housing to assure continuing national commitment to low-income families.

Opportunity to Prosper (Entrepreneurship)

9. Strongly enforce federal minority business opportunity goals to ensure greater minority participation in government contracting.

10. Build capacity of minority business through expansion of micro-financing, equity financing and the development of strategic alliances with major corporations.

IMPLEMENTATION OF THE TOP TEN POLICY PRIORITIES
Opportunity to Thrive (Children)

1. Commit to mandatory early childhood education beginning at age three as well as guarantee access to college for all.

All children must enter school ready to take advantage of teaching and learning. According "Years of Promise", the report of the Carnegie Task Force on the Primary Grades, these early years are crucial in a young person's life when a firm foundation is laid for healthy development and lifelong learning. The National Urban League recommends that all three- and four-year olds have access to full day, developmentally appropriate, high quality early childhood education. Incentives should be put in place to encourage all service providers to become NAEYC (National Association for the Education of Young Children) accredited.

In addition to a commitment to education in early childhood, The National Urban League also recognizes that although the current system of K-12 education as a free public right may have been sufficient at a time when a high school education qualified people for most jobs in this nation, it is no longer enough. In a competitive global economy, more training, education and skills are needed for the jobs of the future. A program which provides sufficient per student funds to pay for basic tuition at most public universities (at least for two years) is a necessary component of a system that meets the needs of the future.

2. Close the gaps in the health insurance system to ensure universal healthcare for all children.

While Medicaid and the State Children's Health Insurance Program (SCHIP) have made tremendous progress in improving children's health insurance coverage, nine million children in America, almost 90 percent living in working households and a majority in two-parent families, are still uninsured. If enacted, the All Healthy Children Act (H.R. 1688) would close the coverage gap by simplifying and consolidating Medicaid and SCHIP while expanding eligibility for more children as well as pregnant women below 300% of poverty. In addition to the provision of health insurance, The National Urban League also recommends that the policies advancing universal healthcare encompass improvements in access and quality of care in poor communities.

3. Establish policies that provide tools for working families to become economically self-sufficient

Family support policies are a crucial part of moving low-income families into economic self-sufficiency. Since many of the country's low-income families are headed by single mothers, the National Urban League urges the creation and implementation of policies that include, but are not limited to, quality child and infant care, transportation assistance, education and training programs that encourage, rather than penalize, additional skills attainment, and paid leave time for all working parents as proposed by the Healthy Families Act. The National Urban League also urges reconsideration of the 5-year lifetime limit for Temporary Assistance for Needy Families (TANF).

Opportunity to Earn (Jobs)

4. Create an Urban Infrastructure Bank to fund reinvestment in urban communities (i.e. parks, schools, roads).

The Urban Infrastructure Bank would be financed by a stream of federal bond revenue used to create a large pool of funds to rebuild schools, water, wastewater, parks, playgrounds, community centers, recreation centers, as well as streets in economically underserved urban areas. Such a bank would allow a significant infusion of capital expenditures into employment generating activities in urban communities.

5. Increase economic self-sufficiency by indexing the minimum wage to the rate of inflation and expanding the Earned Income Tax Credit (EITC) to benefit more working families.

The National Urban League has consistently supported increases in the federal minimum wage and has called for future increases to be indexed to inflation so that workers never again have to beg politicians to protect their income during the economy's inevitable ups and downs. At least four states currently index their minimum wage to prices; maintaining purchasing power for minimum wage workers without creating adverse effects for the broader state economy.

As accomplished through the EITC, alleviating the tax burden and supplementing the wages of low-income working families have been effective means of encouraging economic self-sufficiency through employment. The National Urban League recommends building upon the success of the EITC through: 1) simplification of the process for claiming the credit; 2) more outreach to eligible families who have not claimed the credit; and 3) increasing the size of benefits for all eligible families, including those without minor children and those with three or more minor children, in such a way that further reduces poverty and hardship among working families.

6. Expand "second chance" programs for high school drop outs, ex-offenders and at-risk youth to secure GEDs, job training and employment.

"Second chance" programs may include anything from blended high schools that provide flexibility for non-traditional students by integrating academic and career education to the development of a comprehensive reentry mechanism for ex-offenders that includes housing, job training, adult basic education, psychological counseling and drug treatment. The evidence suggests that local agencies could play an important intermediary role with employers in low-wage labor markets by providing job placement, transportation, basic skill enhancements, and assistance in developing career advancement strategies for low-wage adults. In addition to these "second chance" efforts it is also important to have in place a well-defined pipeline that facilitates the transition of socially and economically disadvantaged youth into the labor force through college, apprenticeships or internships.

Opportunity to Own (Housing)

7. Adopt the "Homebuyer's Bill of Rights" as recommended by the National Urban League.

The National Urban League Homebuyer's Bill Of Rights asserts that every homebuyer in America should have: 1) The right to save for home-ownership tax free; 2) The right to high quality homeownership education; 3) The right to truth and transparency in credit reporting; 4) The right to production of affordable housing for working families; 5) The right to be free from predatory lending; and 6) The right to aggressive enforcement of fair housing laws. The full list of recommendations for accomplishing these goals can be found at p.135.

8. Reform public housing to assure continuing national commitment to low-income families

In the judgment of the National Urban League, the HOPE VI program, while well-intentioned, is broken and in need of overhaul. Therefore, the National Urban League proposes a return to the core stated tenets of the program: to transform public housing communities from islands of despair and poverty into a vital and integral part of larger neighborhoods; and, to create an environment that encourages and supports individual and family movement toward self-sufficiency. The following actions are important in accomplishing this end: 1) HUD should be required to publish an updated list of public housing developments eligible for HOPE VI funds according to a new definition of 'severe distress' created in collaboration with public housing residents, housing advocates, housing experts, and others; 2) All public housing units subject to demolition or redevelopment under HOPE VI should be replaced with new public housing units on a one-for-one basis; 3) HUD should be required to issue regulations governing the administration of HOPE VI redevelopment activities, which should provide enforceable, on-going rights of resident participation; 4) Public housing residents should be guaranteed the right to occupy units redeveloped under HOPE VI, and the relocation rights of displaced residents should be strengthened and clarified.

Opportunity to Prosper (Entrepreneurship)

9. Strongly enforce federal minority business opportunity goals to ensure greater minority participation in government contracting.

In addition to the enforcement of established minority contracting goals, it is also imperative that these goals are updated and revised as the marketplace changes and grows. Compliance with established goals should be supplemented by appropriate matching between government agencies and potential minority contractors as well as maintenance of an appropriate mix of contracts attainable to businesses of various sizes. The National Urban League also calls for greater transparency in the government contracting process by making RFPs easier to access, conducting ongoing disparity studies, and providing truth in procurement spending through disclosure of the competitive and non-competitive bidding processes.

10. Build capacity of minority business through expansion of micro-financing, equity financing and the development of strategic alliances with major corporations.

Capacity building is an important part of sustaining a profitable business enterprise of any scale. The National Urban League proposes three distinct methods for providing access to the capital necessary to sustain and grow a business at any stage of development. These methods include: 1) micro-financing, which provides small business loans (typically under $100,000) to microentrepreneurs (those with five or fewer employees); 2) equity financing (money acquired from investors or the small-business owner) for businesses seeking to expand beyond the scale of a small-business; and 3) strategic alliances between major corporations and larger-scaled minority-owned businesses in search of the kind of synergistic relationships necessary for major industry presence and scale.

MAKING THE CASE
The Opportunity to Thrive (Children)

America's performance, relative to other global leaders, in the provision of services to children offers a sobering picture of our national priorities. According to UNICEF, among developed countries, the United States ranks 20 out of 24 in children's material well-being, 14 out of 24 in children's educational well-being, and last in children's health and safety.[1] These international comparisons only tell part of the story about the unforgiving injustices that minority children face daily due to disproportionate rates of poverty, inadequate education and a lack of accessibility to healthcare.

U.S. Childhood Poverty

On a daily basis we see the harsh and brutal toll that poverty has on the children of third-world countries. As a world leader, America along with the United Nations has made eradicating poverty a priority in less-developed countries. However, given the resources available in the United States, the statistics on childhood poverty in this country are alarming and inexcusable. Despite moderate economic growth, about 1.3 million more children were living in poverty in 2005 than in 2000.

Figure 1

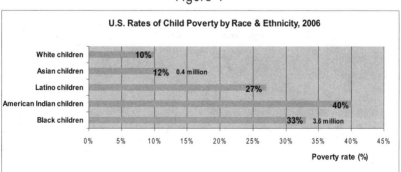

Source: National Center for Children in Poverty, 2007

The fact that nearly 13 million American children live in families with incomes below the federal poverty level doesn't tell the entire story of disparities based on locale and race. Children in urban areas are more likely to live in low-income families than are rural or suburban children and the rate of poverty for African-American children (33%) is second only to that of American Indian children (Figure 1). The poverty disproportionately experienced by minority children and families have led to experiences in poor education and school facilities, a lack of quality health care, isolation in poor, segregated urban neighborhoods, and high unemployment and underemployment of family members.

Education and the Achievement Gap

Despite the goals of the No Child Left Behind (NCLB) Act, African-American and Latino students continue to lag behind their white and Asian American peers on national standardized achievement tests. However, the achievement gap is not the result of innate differences in ability. Rather, the disadvantages many minority students face on a daily basis can have a serious impact on their educational experiences. For example, minority students often attend high-poverty, poorly resourced schools with less rigorous curricula[2] (Figure 2). They also experience the injustices of overrepresentation in special education classes and under-representation in gifted and advanced placement classes.[3] In addition to inadequate resources, minority students are more likely to be taught by poorly qualified or inexperienced teachers.[4] Research also suggests students of color may experience bias, such as lower teacher expectations and less challenging academic standards than their white counterparts.[5]

Figure 2

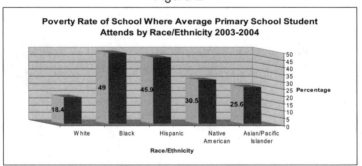

Source: National Center for Education Statistics, Common Core of Data. Public Elementary/Secondary School Universe Survey

The gaps that exist in grade school often have their roots in the early stages of child development. Before entering kindergarten, the average cognitive scores of pre-school age children in the highest socioeconomic group are 60% above the average scores of children in the lowest socioeconomic group.[6] At age 4, children who live below the poverty line are 18 months behind what is normal for their group; by age 10 that gap is still present.[7] Third graders are supposed to know about 12,000 words; however, third grade children from low-income families with uneducated parents have vocabularies around 4,000 words, one-third as many as their middle-income peers.[8] These statistics eventually translate into achievement gaps in high school as well. Statistics show that 12th grade African-American and Latino students have reading and math skills that are almost equivalent to eighth-grade white students.[9]

Health Disparities and Healthcare for Poor Families

Poor and minority children, especially African-American and Latino children, continue to lag behind whites and affluent children in almost every health indicator. Poor children and children of color are at a disproportionate risk for exposure to environmental hazards like lead paints, dampness and mold, and inadequate ventilation. As a result, African Americans and Latinos are two to six times more likely than whites to die from asthma[10] and African-American children are 5 times more likely than white children to suffer from lead poisoning.[11] The pandemic of childhood obesity is also more common among African-American children. In 2003-2004, a quarter of non-Hispanic black females ages 12 to 19 were overweight, compared to 15 percent of non-Hispanic whites and 14 percent of Mexican American youth.[12] Children who are overweight run the risk of developing type-2 diabetes, cardiovascular problems and arthritis.

Children from communities of color are less likely to have employer-based coverage and are more dependent upon government programs such as Medicaid and the State Children's Health Insurance Program (SCHIP) which provide a safety net for the growing number of families without private health insurance. Slightly more than half of insured African-American (51.3%) and Latino children (50.3%) are covered by these programs.[13] However, even since the inception of SCHIP, African Americans remain twice as likely than whites to go uninsured, while Latinos remain three times as likely to go uninsured than whites (Figure 3). The sad reality is that 74% of the 8 million Americans who went uninsured in 2004 were eligible for coverage.

Figure 3

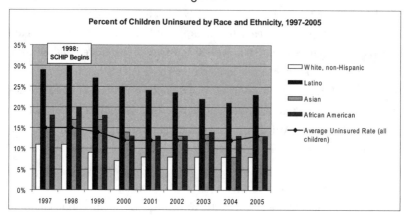

Source: Families USA analysis of U.S. Census Bureau Current Population Survey

Uninsured African-American children are also at higher risk for reduced access to health care. For example, they are 26 percent more likely to have delayed medical care due to cost and have an 81 percent higher likelihood of having no usual place of health care.[14]

The Opportunity to Earn (Jobs)

The Economic Plight of Working Families

The existence of a relatively large middle class makes the United States unique among nations and represents a real opportunity for social and economic mobility as a bridge between the extremes of poverty and wealth. For many Americans, attainment of middle class status has become synonymous with achieving the "American dream;" a dream rooted in a shared work ethic and sense of independence which says that there is value in work that empowers people to be responsible for their own well-being. By their own hard work people are able to provide certain necessities and comforts for themselves and their families including economic security, a safe home, a quality education for their children, reliable health care, and a comfortable retirement. This strong sense of independence, however, is balanced by a sense of fairness and social connectedness, as demonstrated by the public provision of certain types of safety nets.

Maintaining the economic security of middle class families, as well as access into the middle class for lower income families, is a vital part of preserving the very principles that make this country unique. It is also a vital part of eliminating gaps in income, wealth and educational attainment within this country that are too often defined along racial lines. Unfortunately, for a growing segment of the population, particularly working and middle-class families, economic security has grown increasingly difficult to maintain. In fact, according to a 2006 report from the Center for American Progress, the increase in downward short-term mobility from 1997-98 to 2003-04 was driven by the experiences of middle-class households (those earning between $34,510 and $89,300 in 2004 dollars).[15] On the other hand, households in the top quintile saw no increase in downward short-term mobility, and households in the top decile ($122,880 and up) saw a reduction in the frequency of large negative income shocks.[16] Some of the factors affecting the economic well-being of working families include low wage growth, rising costs of food, housing, medical care, child care, higher education and gasoline, and the disappearance of employer-provided pensions and health care benefits.

The following tables and graphs offer some insight into the economic plight of America's working families,[17] with special attention directed toward differences between white and non-white working families.

Income Growth and Changes in the Cost of Living
Working families have experienced a dramatic increase in the cost of living, while wage growth has failed to keep pace with these increases. For example, between 2000 and 2006, overall inflation increased by 17%.[18] This was accompanied by a less than 17% increase in the median family earnings of many low- and moderate-income working families (Figure 4). Between 2001 and 2006, there were especially dramatic increases in the price of goods such as gasoline (79%), college tuition and fees (45%), child care (26%), and medical care (23%).

Figure 4

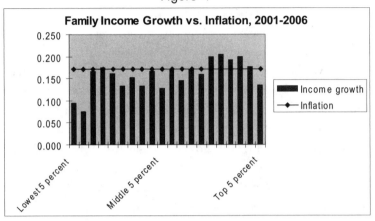

Source: NULPI analysis of U.S. Census Bureau Current Population Survey, March 2001 and 2007

In addition to the wages earned through employment that enable families to pay for basic necessities like housing, food and clothing, health insurance coverage and pensions have also historically been closely linked to employment. The likelihood of receiving either of these benefits increases with a family's income which is representative of the fact that workers in better paying jobs are more likely to have access to employer-provided health insurance and pensions However, between 2000 and 2006 the percentage of working families with access to these benefits decreased across the board (Figures 5 & 6). At all levels of income, Hispanic workers are least likely to work for an employer that provides these benefits.[19]

Figure 5

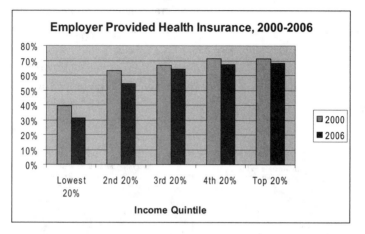

Source: NULPI analysis of U.S. Census Bureau Current Population Survey, March 2001 and 2007

Figure 6

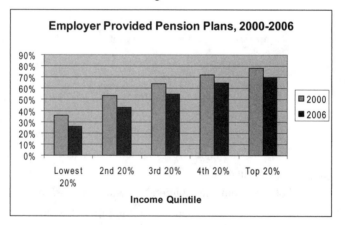

Source: NULPI analysis of U.S. Census Bureau Current Population Survey, March 2007

Poverty

Based on data from the 2007 March Supplement of the Current Population Survey (CPS), in 2006, 7% of working families were living below the poverty threshold, while more than one-fourth (26%) of working families lived below 200 percent of poverty (Figure 7). Working families with a minority parent were three to four times as likely to be in poverty as families with a white parent (Figure 8). This statistic has intergenerational implications. Research suggests that African-American children born in the bottom quartile are almost twice as likely to remain there as adults as white children born to parents with identical incomes.[20] These differences persist even after controlling for parental background factors, such as whether the household was female-headed or receiving public assistance.

Figure 7   Figure 8

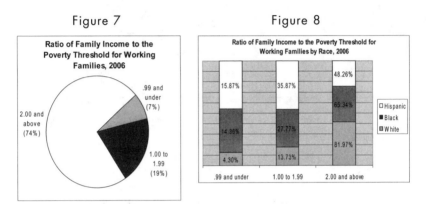

Source: NULPI analysis of U.S. Census Bureau Current Population Survey, March 2007

Family Composition and Educational Attainment

Two of the underlying factors in the existence of economic disparities along racial lines are differences in family composition and educational attainment. Family composition has a major effect on the number of wage earners in a home and thus the family's total income. Less than one-fourth of families in the lowest 20% of the income distribution have more than one member in the labor force, compared to 77% of families in the top 20 percent. In terms of family composition, more than half (54%) of African-American working families are headed by a married couple compared to 82% of white and 78% of Hispanic families. Over three-fourths (78%) of all single parent working families are headed by a female.[21]

Educational attainment is also closely related to earnings. For example, according to 2006 estimates from the Bureau of Labor Statistics, individuals with a bachelor's degree earn more than one and a half times as much as high school graduates and more than twice as much as those without a high school diploma. Also, the black-white earnings gap narrows considerably when you compare median earnings of blacks and whites with a bachelor's degree or higher.[22] In 2006, 39% of adults in white working families had a bachelor's degree or higher, compared to 22% of African-American working families and 13% of Hispanic working families. (Figure 9).

Figure 9

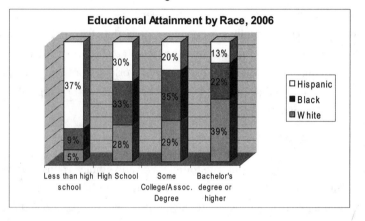

Source: NULPI analysis of U.S. Census Bureau Current Population Survey, March 2007

Occupations of Adults in Working Families

Finally, the majority of non-white adults in working families are employed in service occupations (23% of African-American and 22% of Hispanic workers) while the majority of whites (24%) are employed in professional occupations .[23] This too reflects differences in average educational attainment and much of the resulting differences in family income by race. However, based upon research in The State of Black America 2006, there is a general pattern of exclusion in the most desired management and professional occupations even for black males with the requisite educational qualifications. This pattern, known as "crowding out", also holds for the sales and office occupations.[24] As a matter of fact, only 14% (67 out of 475) of occupations in the U.S. exhibit no "crowding out" and the average wage across "crowded" occupations is 74% lower than the average wage across "crowded out" occupations.[25]

Invisible Men: The Urgent Problems of Low-Income African-American Males

The State of Black America 2007 was dedicated to various aspects of the plight of African-American males. In many ways, two different worlds exist for African-American males. In one world, the number of black men graduating from college has quadrupled since the passage of the 1964 Civil Rights Act; in the other, more black men are earning high school equivalency diplomas in prison each year than are graduating from college. In one world, black families consisting of a father and a mother have a median family income nearly equal to white families; in the other, more than half of the nation's 5.6 million black boys live in fatherless households, 40 percent of which are impoverished.[26] The existence of these two worlds is both an example of what is possible, and a warning about the consequences of marginalization, racism and inequality.

Unemployment

Although the unemployment rate for all racial and ethnic groups follows the economic cycle (higher during recessions, lower during recoveries), black male unemployment is consistently higher than any other group and usually twice that of whites (Figure 10). If broken down by age group, one-third of black teens were unemployed in 2007, compared with only 16% of white teens (Figure 11). Although unemployment declines as men age, black unemployment is still double that of whites for each age group. These high rates of unemployment among black males have been attributed to a lack of skills necessary for participation in today's mainstream labor force, a shortage of relatively well-paying jobs for those with less than a college education, and disproportionately high rates of incarceration, accompanied by discrimination by employers against former prisoners.

Figure 10

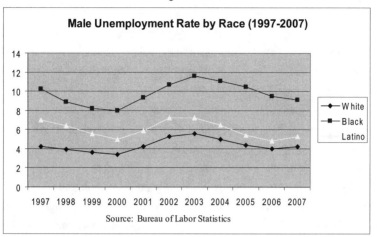

Source: Bureau of Labor Statistics

Figure 11

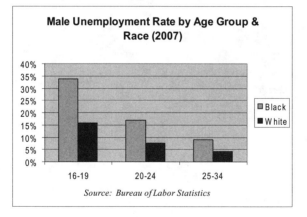

Education

One explanation for why black men experience higher rates of unemployment is the fact that the average level of educational attainment is lower for this group. In many inner cities, more than half of all black men do not finish high school,[27] and in 2004, 72 percent of black male high school dropouts in their twenties were jobless.[28] In 2007, nearly 13 percent of all black men over age 25 had no high school diploma compared with only 7 percent of white men (Figure 12). At the upper end of the educational spectrum, black men attain master's degrees, PhD's and professional degrees at half the rate of white men. It has been well-documented that education is a major determinant of earning power and employability. In 2006 college graduates (bachelor's degree) earned over twice as much as high school dropouts and the unemployment rate of those without a high school diploma was nearly three times the unemployment rate of those with a bachelor's degree (Figure 13).

Figure 12

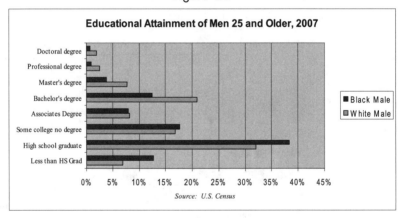

Figure 13

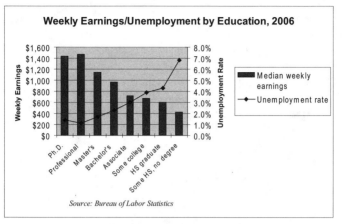

Weekly Earnings/Unemployment by Education, 2006

Source: Bureau of Labor Statistics

Incarceration

Another contributing factor to higher unemployment for black men is their much higher incarceration rates. Although comprising only 12 percent of the U.S. population, 37 percent of all prison inmates were black in 2006 (Figure 14), and the black incarceration rate was over 6 times the incarceration rate for whites (Figure 15). The rate of incarceration is highest for men between the ages of 25 and 29, when over 7% of black men are in prison, compared with only 1% of white men (Figure 16). The rate of incarceration among black males has been increasing since the 1990s due in large part to harsher punishments for repeat offenders (e.g. "three strikes law") and drug laws that impose harsher sentences on those found in possession of crack cocaine. In 2005, drug offenders comprised 20 percent of state prisoners and almost 55 percent of federal prisoners.[29] The U.S. now has the highest reported incarceration rate in the world, at 737 inmates per 100,000 persons in the population (followed by Russia at 611 per 100,000). A history of incarceration not only interferes with educational attainment, but also becomes a significant employment barrier; therefore, the effect of even a short imprisonment lasts a lifetime.

Figure 14

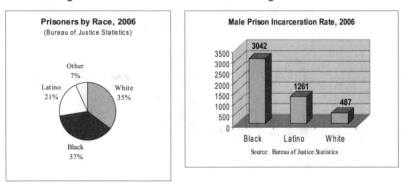

Prisoners by Race, 2006
(Bureau of Justice Statistics)

White 35%
Other 7%
Latino 21%
Black 37%

Figure 15

Male Prison Incarceration Rate, 2006

Black 3042
Latino 1261
White 487

Source: Bureau of Justice Statistics

Figure 16

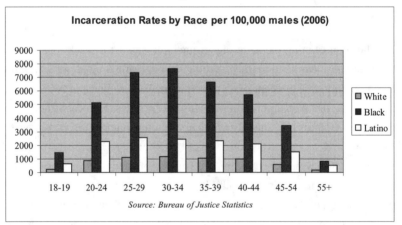

Incarceration Rates by Race per 100,000 males (2006)

White
Black
Latino

18-19 20-24 25-29 30-34 35-39 40-44 45-54 55+

Source: Bureau of Justice Statistics

The Opportunity to Own (Housing)

For most Americans, the largest single asset they will ever own will be their home. Homeownership means greater personal wealth; therefore, empowering more Americans to become responsible homeowners takes us a step closer to closing the wealth gap that exists between blacks and whites in the United States. In addition to the economic benefits, homeownership has also been linked to educational gains for children, increased civic participation and even health benefits.[30]

Unfortunately, race has proven to be a prevailing factor in securing the neccesary capital for home ownership. Many minority buyers face the problems of discrimatory lending practices, decreased housing affordability, high rates of home foreclosures, and increased incidence of high-cost loans.

Homeownership Rates

According to the U.S. Census, nearly 70 percent of Americans owned their homes in 2006—down slightly from the all time high in 2004. Yet there are troubling disparities in homeownership rates when segmented by race (Figure 17). After increasing for the previous ten years, homeownership declined for blacks between 2004 and 2006 (from 49.1% in 2004 to 47.9% in 2006; nearly 28 points below non-Hispanic whites).

Figure 17

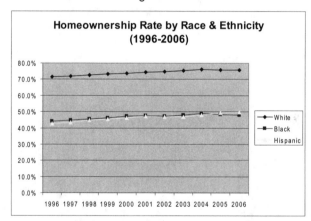

Source: U.S. Census

The National Urban League Homebuyer's Bill Of Rights, released in March 2007, identifies four major obstacles standing in the way of more Americans owning their own homes: 1) lack of net savings for down payments and closing costs; 2) lack of information on how to shop for homes and apply for loans; 3) lack of quality affordable units in livable locations; and 4) lack of consumer protection. Other studies have found that lower homeownership rates for African Americans are related to lower application rates, which in turn were caused by differences in the role that families play in helping to generate mortgage down payments, as well as differences in wealth, income and marital status.[31]

Lending Practices

The now deflating housing bubble was preceded by a lending industry that could be characterized by three main trends: (1) an increase in lending products, (2) more places to get a loan, and (3) a distinct need for housing counseling. Compared with only a handful of products available ten years ago, there are now a myriad of lending products including interest-only loans, reverse mortgages, and 15-year loans with balloon payments. Whereas commercial banks were once the primary providers of home loans, mortgage brokers now account for half of all originations and 70% of originations in the subprime market.[32] With the loosening of lending standards, minimal oversight of brokers and far more options, there is a greater chance that a borrower can be placed in an inappropriate loan. For example, between 35 percent and 50 percent of those with subprime loans could have qualified for a prime loan.[33]

Figure 18

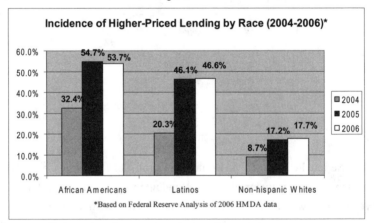

According to Home Mortgage Disclosure Act (HMDA) data, in 2006 there was a 36 percentage point gap between African Americans and whites in the incidence of high-priced loans, compared to a gap of 23.7 percentage points in 2004 (Figure 18). A Federal Reserve study found that almost 17.4 points of the difference is due to choice of bank resulting from aggressive marketing, lack of consumer education or fewer local lending choices. Six points of the difference was due to borrower characteristics in the data such as loan size and income, while the remaining 12.6 points of the difference could not be explained by available lender or borrower characteristics.

Housing Segregation and Discrimination

While racial segregation has decreased over the last three decades, in part due to fair housing enforcement, segregation still persists in many areas and neighborhoods that are predominately minority are much more likely to be poor. On average, homes in predominantly minority neighborhoods are often worth less (according to one study, 18% less value), even accounting for differences in income.[34] The Census Bureau's Racial and Ethnic Segregation in the United States identifies only 8 of 220 metropolitan areas which had an increase in black-white segregation, while 203 experienced a decrease.

NFHA believes that there are at least 3.7 million violations of the fair housing act against minorities in rental and sales alone, but less than one percent is reported or even detected. Support for fair housing enforcement has remained essentially level over the last few years, despite continued evidence of discrimination in rental, sales and lending markets.

The Opportunity to Prosper (Entrepreneurship)

Minority business enterprises (MBE) are defined as business entities in which minorities own 51 percent or more of the stock or equity. In 2002, MBEs represented 18 percent (4.1 million) of classifiable firms, grossed 8 percent of all annual gross receipts ($668 billion), and employed 9 percent of all paid employees (4.7 million).[35] In that same year, there were 1.2 million African-American-owned firms in the U.S. employing 754,000 persons and generating $89 billion in revenue.[36] The importance of minority-owned businesses to urban economic development is well documented. Minority-owned firms are more likely to locate in urban communities, making them more likely to hire minority workers, lowering local unemployment rates. They are also more likely to purchase from minority-owned suppliers, contributing to the growth of other minority-owned businesses. Despite these benefits, MBEs continue to face a number of barriers to firm formation and growth including lack of financial capital, lack of social capital, lower human capital endowments, and limited access of minorities to broader consumer markets[37].

Government Contracting of Minority Business Enterprises
Procurement provides governments with a powerful way of promoting opportunities for MBEs and counteracting the effects of discrimination. Although set-aside programs exist at all levels of government including federal, state, city, county and special district,[38] the established contracting goals often go unmet. A widely cited 1996 disparity study[39] by the Urban Institute reported that at the state and local government levels, minority-owned firms received only $0.57 for every dollar they would be expected to receive based on their availability.[40] The House Small Business Committee reports that since the beginning of the Scorecard report in 1999, failure of the federal government to meet its 5 percent small disadvantaged business goal has cost minority entrepreneurs $21.2 billion in contracting opportunities (Figure 19).

Figure 19

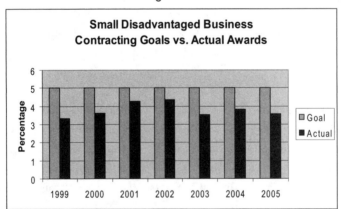

Source: House Small Business Committee, Scorecard VII

The three main barriers to minority participation in government contracting are contract bundling, subcontracting and coding errors. Bundling contracts is the act of combining 2 or more contracts into a large single agreement. This has most often pushed smaller minority-owned firms out of the competition while subcontracting has most often benefited prime contractors over (typically minority) subcontractors. Procurement data can also be distorted by coding errors in that companies coded as "small" are sometimes misidentified as such or in fact no longer qualify as small as a result of having been acquired by larger businesses during the course of the contract.

Small Business Financing

Loan markets have become more competitive over the past decade due to an expanding nationwide market for credit lines & credit cards along with the entry of large regional banks in local markets. Although banks are the most often used credit source for small firms in general,minority firm owners are less likely to have bank loans of any kind.[41] Research has also found that African-American and Latino firm owners face significantly greater loan denial probabilities than white male firm owners and are often charged higher interest rates.[42]

In recent years, microfinancing has grown in popularity as source of capital for microenterprises (a business with five or fewer employees), which account for 94 percent of all firms and are overwhelmingly owned by minorities and women. Patterned after the successful Grameen Bank in Bangladesh, microfinancing promises great benefits. The Aspen Institute has estimated that it can be implemented at one-tenth of the cost of creating opportunities through tax breaks and other public subsidies. However, there are some challenges to microfinancing, including the fact that competition limits interest rates U.S. microlenders can charge, making it less profitable than in developing nations, and U.S. businesses typically have greater capital requirements and need larger-sized loans faster.

CONCLUSION

The Opportunity to Thrive. The Opportunity to Earn. The Opportunity to Own. The Opportunity to Prosper. Each of these opportunities for upward economic and social mobility are available in few other countries outside the United States. Therefore, maintaining equal access to these opportunities is a vital part of preserving the very principles that make this country unique and will prove to be an effective way to eliminate gaps in income, wealth and educational attainment within this country that are too often defined along the lines of race or socioeconomic status.

Although this document serves as a vehicle through which to develop a serious plan of action to address the persistent inequalities faced by those in urban communities; all Americans, regardless of place of residence or racial identity, can benefit from the policy recommendations presented in The Opportunity Compact. Furthermore, there is a role for all parties to play – private citizens, national, state and local governments, community-based service providers and the business community – as we together seek to strengthen our nation by maximizing the potential of all its citizens. By generating new ideas, initiating productive partnerships and fostering collaboration, The Opportunity Compact seeks to expand access to the incentives and rewards that act as the driving force behind what makes this country great—personal responsibility, initiative and hard work.

The National Urban League thanks the following individuals whose participation in the Opportunity Compact Roundtable Discussions provided an invaluable source of information and insight.

Jobs I: Working Families

Dr. Bernard Anderson (University of Pennsylvania); Dr. Jared Bernstein (Economic Policy Institute); Ms. Cecelie Counts (AFL-CIO); James Reid (NUL, Vice-President of Workforce Development)

Jobs II: African-American Males

Dr. Darrick Hamilton (The New School for Management and Urban Policy); Dr. Harry Holzer (Georgetown Public Policy Institute); Dr. James Lanier (Re-entry & Sanctions Center); Dr. Silas Lee (Dr. Silas Lee & Associates)

Children

Dr. Avis Jones-DeWeever (Institute for Women's Policy Research); Ms. Julia Isaacs (Brookings Institution); Dr. Valerie Polakow (Eastern Michigan University)

Housing

Alan Fishbein (Consumer Federation of America); Dr. Lance Freeman (Columbia University); Dr. Roberto Quercia (University of North Carolina at Chapel Hill); Cy Richardson (NUL, Vice-President of Housing & Community Development)

Entrepreneurship

Dr. Quintus Jett (Dartmouth College); Dr. Jeffrey Robinson (New York University); Dr. Mark Turner (Optimal Solutions); Donald Bowen (NUL, Sr. Vice President of Programs); Donald McMichael (NUL, Vice-President of Entrepreneurship); Terry Clark (NUL, Vice-President of Economic Empowerment)

Special thanks to the staff of the National Urban League Policy Institute for their hard work and commitment to this project.

NOTES

[1] See UNICEF. "Child Poverty in Perspective: An Overview of child well-being in rich countries," Innocenti Report Card 7, 2007.

[2] See Christopher B. Knaus. "Still Segregated, Still Unequal: Analyzing the Impact of No Child Left Behind on African-American Students." *In The State of Black America 2007.* National Urban League. 2007.

[3] See Caroline Rothert. "Achievement Gaps and No Child Left Behind." *Youth Law News.* April–June 2005.

[4] Ibid.

[5] Ibid.

[6] See Lisa G. Klein and Jane Knitzer. "Promoting Effective Early Learning: What Every Policymaker and Educator Should Know." National Center for Children in Poverty. January 2007.

[7] Ibid.

[8] Ibid.

[9] See Caroline Rothert. "Achievement Gaps and No Child Left Behind." *Youth Law News.* April–June 2005.

[10] National Institute of Allergy and Infectious Diseases. 2002.

[11] See "Update: Blood Lead Levels in the United States, 1991–1994." *Morbidity and Mortality Weekly Report,* 46(7). Centers for Disease Control. 1997.

[12] See Cynthia Ogden et al. "Prevalence of Overweight and Obesity in the United States, 1999-2004." *Journal of the American Medical Association.* April 2006.

[13] See Kaiser Family Foundation. "SCHIP and Children's Health Coverage: Leveling the Playing Field for Minority Children." December 2006. (www.kff.org)

[14] See Children's Defense Fund. *The State of America's Children: Yearbook 2004.* July 2004.

[15] See Tom Hertz. "Understanding Mobility in America." Center for American Progress publication. April 2006.

[16] Ibid

[17] For the purpose of this analysis, a family is defined as a married couple or single parent primary family with at least one child under the age of 18. A family is considered working if in the last 12 months, family members age 15 and older have a combined work effort of at least 39 weeks or a combined work effort of at least 26 weeks plus one unemployed parent actively looking for work in the past four weeks.

[18] All inflation estimates in this paragraph are based upon the Consumer Price Index for All Urban Consumers (CPI-U).

[19] Based on NULPI analysis of U.S. Census Bureau Current Population Survey, March 2007.

[20] See Tom Hertz. "Understanding Mobility in America." Center for American Progress publication. April 2006.

[21] Based on NULPI analysis of U.S. Census Bureau Current Population Survey, March Supplement, 2007.

[22] See http://nces.ed.gov/programs/coe/2006/section2/table.asp?tableID=475

[23] Based on NULPI analysis of U.S. Census Bureau Current Population Survey, March 2007.
[24] See Darrick Hamilton. "The Racial Composition of American Jobs." In *The State of Black America 2006* report. National Urban League. 2006.

[25] Ibid.

[26] See Michael A. Fletcher. "At the Corner of Progress and Peril." *The Washington Post.* June 2, 2006.

[27] See Gary Orfield, ed. *Dropouts in America: Confronting the Graduation Rate Crisis.* Harvard Education Press. 2004.

[28] See Bruce Western. *Punishment and Inequality in America.* Russell Sage Foundation. 2006

29 Bureau of Justice Statistics

30 National Association of Realtors. 2006.

31 See Kerwin Kofi Charles and Erik Hurst. "The Transition to Home Ownership and the Black-White Wealth Gap". *The Review of Economics and Statistics*. March, 2000; Donald Haurin, et al. "Homeownership Gaps Among Low-Income and Minority Households". *Ohio State University Working Papers*, 07-02. January, 2007.

32 See "Residential Mortgage Origination Channels." *MBA Research Data Notes*. September 2006.

33 Fannie Mae, 2001.

34 See David Rusk. "The Segregation Tax: The Cost of Racial Segregation to Black Homeowners". Brookings Institution. 2001.

35 See *The State of Minority Business Enterprises*. Minority Business Development Agency. August 2006.

36 Ibid.

37 See Maria Enchautegui, et. al. "Do Minority-Owned Businesses Get a Fair Share of Government Contracts?" Urban Institute. 1996.

38 Special district includes airports, water, sanitation, parks and schools.

39 Disparity is measured by comparing the percentage of all government contract dollars received by minority-owned (women-owned) businesses to the percentage of all businesses "ready, willing and able" to carry out government contracts that are minority-owned (women-owned).

40 See Maria Enchautegui, et. al. "Do Minority-Owned Businesses Get a Fair Share of Government Contracts?" Urban Institute. 1996.

41 See Karlyn Mitchell and Douglas Pearce. "Availability of Financing to Small Firms Using the Survey of Small Business Finances." For SBA Office of Advocacy. May 2005.

42 Ibid.

Shouldering The Third Burden: The Status of African-American Women

by Julianne Malveaux, Ph.D.

B ennett College for Women is a special place, an oasis where women are educated, celebrated, and developed into twenty-first century leaders and contributors. It is one of only two educational institutions in our nation where women of color are at the center, not the periphery, of the universe. Indeed, one might argue that it is one of just a handful of places where African-American women are systematically celebrated, not cursorily ignored and vilified. Bennett College for women also offers a special lens through which to view the status of African-American women, as many of the choices, challenges, and triumphs that women face are reflected in the hurdles that our students clear, and those over which they sometimes stumble.

In an election year when women of color are being asked if they are voting their race or voting their gender—as if we could divide them—it is important to note that race and gender are intertwined for African-American women, and that both are determinants in our economic, social, political, and educational status. The intersection of race and gender, additionally create a third burden for African-American women in that part of our status is a function of the way that the majority society marginalizes and demonizes African-American men.

A most stunning example of this third burden is evident in the labor market, where both African-American men and women experience unemployment rates that are higher than those for the overall population. While the unemployment rate in January 2008 was 4.9 percent, it was 7.3 percent for adult African-American women, and 8.3 percent for African-American men. Moreover, a full million more African-American women held jobs than African-American men, with 8.3 million black women and 7.3 million African-American men working.[1] The underemployment of African-American men represents a burden to the African-American women who, then, often shoulder disproportionate responsibility in supporting households and children without sufficient contribution from spouses, partners, or fathers. A full understanding of the third burden explains, at least partly, why African-American women cannot separate interests of race and issues of gender in analysis of political candidates, economic realities, or social and cultural realities.

There are other important critical economic realities that shape the status of African-American women. While more likely to be employed than African-American men, African-American women earn lower wages than African-American men and white women do, with white women earning a median $663 per week in 2007, compared to $629 for African-American men and $566 for African-American women. All three groups earn less than white men, whose 2007 weekly median earnings were $850.[2] And, while African-American women represent two-thirds of all African-American undergraduates, and the majority of graduate students,[3] African-American women are less likely than African-American men to reach the pinnacle of their occupations, especially in corporate America. Indeed, while a handful of African-American men lead Fortune 500 corporations, as do a dozen or so white women, not a single African-American woman has ever led such a corporation.

If a pie chart illustrates distribution of economic benefits within a race, then African-American women have a larger slice of pie than white women within their race group. Thus, historical, institutional, and sociological forces slice the pie differently for African-American women than for white women, with gender playing a different role in the African-American community because of the way society has dealt with African-American men. At the same time, the pie that African Americans have to slice is smaller than it should be. African Americans are 13 percent of the population, but we have 8 percent of the income and less than 2 percent of the nation's wealth. For some, the focus has been on increasing the size of the pie that African Americans have to divide, looking at issues of race instead of gender. At the same time, when we view gender status in the African-American community, it is clear that the pie analogy is imperfect unless the size of the pie African-American women have is viewed as both benefit and burden. Further, the pie analogy is imperfect because it does not capture issues that are not strictly economic—family and family formation, the role of African-American women in popular culture, and the challenges that African-American girls face in a society that routinely ignores the third burden of African-American women.

A focus of women at the top should not preclude attention to the material struggles for African-American women at the bottom of the economic spectrum. One in four African-American people, and more than forty percent of African-American children live in poverty. Many of these poor are working poor—women who earn little more than the minimum wage in service occupations, especially as home health workers, janitors and cleaners, and in other occupations. These women almost always lack sick leave, health care, and benefits that other workers take for granted. They struggle to make ends meet, often bridging the gap between living expenses and inadequate paychecks with credit cards and other forms of high-interest debt. These economically vulnerable African-American women's stories are often swallowed by more compelling headlines, yet their reality is a common reality for a significant portion of the African-American female population. The third burden is a lens through which we may view African-American women's poverty. Too often, especially when public assistance is involved, the status of African-American women is linked to the economic role that African-American men do not play in poor families. The male and female unemployment that results from the deindustrialization of our nation's cities, and the policy failure to develop jobs policies especially disadvantages African-American men and places the family survival burden on African-American women.

Family Status And Family Formation

Since the 1980s, women head more than 40 percent of African-American families. The majority of African-American children grow up in households headed by women. While there is nothing inherently wrong with female-headed households, there is much sociological data that suggests that children who grow up in healthy, intact families (it is important to emphasize "healthy" as violent or abusive intact families are not preferable to families headed by one parent) are less likely to be involved in violence and more likely to attend college and lead productive lives. Part of the reason why African-American households are so often headed by African-American women are economic and structural—African-American men are more likely to be unemployed or incarcerated, and are often unwilling or unable to make long-term family commitments based on their economic status. African-American women have had no choice but shoulder the burden of family leadership in the African-American community.

The status of African-American men becomes a third burden to young women who would like to marry and raise families. The difference in educational attainment between African-American men and women, and the difference in labor market participation, means that African-American women are less likely to marry than their white counterparts. College-educated African-American women also often marry later than their white sisters do. Many choose single motherhood as their only motherhood option. While these women have the means to raise children, they would often prefer to raise children with contributing partners.

College-educated African-American women are by no means the only women who want marriage, family, and stability. Their realities are often shaped by gaps in labor market opportunities between men and women, and gaps in the training possibilities that men and women face. While clerical and service work provide some opportunities for African-American women without college educations, the decline in manufacturing work has eliminated many opportunities for African-American men.

Thus, the educational and economic status of African-American men becomes a policy and community concern for African-American women, and part of the third burden that African-American women shoulder. The extent to which African-American men are not allowed to fully participate in our nation's economic life, means that African-American women have the opportunity, responsibility, and burden to more fully participate.

Images In Popular Culture

Through the lens of the third burden, aspects of African-American women's depiction in popular culture become partly understandable, though wholly unacceptable. The rap music artists who insist on portraying African-

American women as sexual objects, as "-itches" and "hos" seem to have a seething resentment for African-American women that is partly rooted in the economic realities described in the paragraphs above. References to "gold diggers" and images of credit cards swiped through a woman's buttocks demean women to a beat so enticing that other women dance to the sounds of their debasement. When the talk jock Don Imus broadcast hateful words to describe a graceful group of Rutgers women basketball players, African-American people around the nation exploded in rage. The conversation was quickly hijacked in both productive and destructive ways. On one hand, the conversation about Imus quickly became a productive conversation about images of African-American women in media. On the other hand, the conversation about Imus also attempted to equate rap music artists, some with very limited distribution, with the power that an Imus, with tens of millions of viewers and listeners, had. In some ways, the conversation became one in which segments of the African-American community seemed to turn on each other, with younger hip hop artists pitted against older, more established leaders and scholars. It became a conversation much like the prevailing political conversation—are you supporting your race or supporting your gender, as if the two can be separated.

Interestingly, the attention focused on the depiction of African-American women in popular culture has barely touched on indelible images of African-American women on public assistance and in public housing, and the demeaning images invoked by members of Congress in the 1996 welfare deform debate. While changes in the way that public assistance is delivered and our society's shift away from the poverty debate have blunted sharp images of African-American women as lazy and dependent, those women who still receive public assistance, and those who attempt to use education as their escape from poverty while on public assistance find that demeaning images often shape their ability to find jobs and opportunities. White women are more likely to be allowed to attend college while on public assistance than African-American women are, partly because caseworkers have some discretion in making exceptions to rules governing college attendance and images of African-American women too often influence willingness to make exceptions.

Nearly a year after the Imus flap, the image of African-American women in popular culture has only barely improved. The bastion of Sunday morning pale, male talking heads shows little more diversity than it did a decade ago. The gyrating, undulating images of African-American women in rap music videos and, by extension, on cable television is as prevalent as ever. And though African-American women have organized in response and in resistance to these images, conducting conversations and negotiations with entertainment industry executives and also elected officials who might regulate decency in the absence of its natural occurrence, the progress toward depicting African-American women positively in media has been slow.

Media imagery invades the mind and spirit and is at least partly responsible for the unequal, and often dismissive, treatment that African-American women face in the labor market and in society. There is bountiful anecdotal evidence that while African-American women have been climbing the corporate ladder, images of black women in popular culture are an ankle-weight that slows the climb. Thus, while economic issues such as workplace discrimination and equal pay must interest those who are concerned with the status of African-American women, issues of image may well have an impact on economic status.

In this context, it is important to note the many powerful images of African-American women that exist at the other end of the spectrum. Dr. Dorothy Height, Dr. Maya Angelou, Oprah Winfrey, Susan Taylor, and Michele Obama are among the many African-American women whose names and images invoke strength, dignity, and grace, and are an antidote to the demeaning images that so often prevail.

Young Women, Girls, And The Third Burden

While demeaning images may well lightly touch adult African-American women, young women and girls often feel the burden of these images acutely, and act out their reaction to these images unwittingly. There is an obesity challenge among African-American women that has trickled down to young women and girls, many who face debilitating disease if they cannot get their weight under control. Some girls are also embracing the violence that has shattered so many young black male lives and acting out their pain in ways that is ultimately self-destructive. The incarceration of African-American women has increased exponentially in the past two decades, with some women being incarcerated because of their involvement in the drug culture (translation—their relationship with a man who was involved in drugs), and others because of alarming acts of violence.

Terri Williams has written brilliantly of the pain that many in the African-American community deny, the depression that has both debilitating personal and societal effects. Those black women who attempt to manage and respond to images of Sapphire and Superwoman, oversexed video vixen and over-worked beast of burden may also be managing a pain they cannot address. The extent to which young women and girls are constantly exposed to conflicting, and often demeaning, images, may play some role in the future status of these women and, indeed, of the African-American community at large.[4]

Conclusion

Dr. Dorothy Height has often said that "African-American women do not do what we want to do, we do what we have to do". That daunting adage of service and community, of shouldering the third burden, remains applicable. Those who ask African-American women to choose between race and gender ignore the fact that race and gender only partly explain African-American women's reality. The third burden, the intertwining of African-American male and female lives in the context of patriarchy and economic oppression, is an important way of viewing the complexities of the African-American woman's existence in these United States. In the context of this patriarchy, we are consumers, not producers, of our images in popular culture, the target of a drive-by public policy analysis that asks us to choose between race and gender as we navigate our reality. To invoke the South African proverb, "black women hold up half of the sky" in the African-American community. Whether operating from a strong economic base, or from the poverty status that affects more than one in four of us, we shoulder a third burden as we hold up half the sky. Race, gender, and society's treatment of African-American men shape and define our reality and determine our status.

NOTES

[1] Bureau of Labor Statistics, The Employment Situation: January 2008.

[2] Bureau of Labor Statistics, Employment and Earnings, January 2008.

[3] National Center for Educational Statistics, Digest of Educational Statistics, 2006.

[4] Terrie Williams, *Black Pain: It Just Looks Like We're Not Hurting*, New York: Scribner, 2008.

The "Invisibility Blues" of Black Women in America

by Maudine R. Cooper

anita Jacks disappeared behind the doors of her rowhouse in Southeast Washington, D.C. with her four daughters—invisible to the world. She remained invisible until the fateful day—January 9, 2008— when marshals came to evict her from that home. What they found finally made Banita visible. Her four daughters, who had vanished from their classrooms at two different schools, were invisible unto death. Brittany, 17, Tatiana, 11, N'Kia, 6 and Aja, 5, dying at the hands of their mother who told authorities "they had demons."

Banita Jacks represents the nearly 60 percent of black families headed by black women, and her children could be counted among the 3.7 million black children who lived in poverty, more than half of them with their mothers. Even in their invisibility, "black women are expected to be workers, to hold the broom or care for the children or type the memo or cook the meal...these daily experiences of oppression take a tremendous toll," according to Stephanie Y. Mitchem, Professor at the University of Detroit Mercy in Michigan. Poor black women live and die in the U.S. and hardly anyone notices, so giving voice to black women's realities is a necessity.

It takes a tremendous amount of energy for poor black women to deal with the dynamics of race, gender and class. There is no social safety net for the invisible black woman who often struggles alone with children abandoned by the males who fathered them. These women are left with little or no income and bureaucratic red tape that wraps around them until they smother. When they seek help, they are ignored; seen as lazy, worthless or crazy. The system that was put in place to help poor, single mothers, does its best to humiliate them, despising their situation and pinching off only a portion of what they need to survive in a decent fashion. Working class and poor black women only become highly visible when they encounter domestic violence, sexual promiscuity, strained family relations and other personal difficulties in part because of their race and economic class.

The continuous struggle of black women against misrepresentation in a society that still undervalues them is an experience black feminist Michele Wallace calls "invisibility blues."

Dropping the Ball

The path to visibility was a long and difficult one for Banita Jacks. She applied for housing assistance on Dec. 6, 2005, and for Temporary Assistance to Needy Families, Medicaid and Food stamps on Dec. 21, 2005; moved to the D.C. General Hypothermia Shelter on Dec. 14, 2005, and left on April 9, 2006; Banita had a behavioral health Medicaid visit June 16, 2006; food stamp benefits were terminated on Nov. 20, 2006; her male partner died of leukemia in a Maryland hospice on Feb. 19, 2007; Temporary Assistance for Needy Families ("TANF") benefits were terminated Oct. 31, 2007; lights were cut off in her home sometime in September 2007.

Since 2005, Banita sought help in getting housing, food stamps, medical care, and educational placements for her children, from five D.C. government agencies—including Child and Family Services Agency, D.C. Public Schools, Metropolitan Police Department, the Department of Human Services and the Department of Health. Each agency failed in carrying out its mandate to provide services to those in need and gave up without thoroughly assessing Banita Jacks' situation. Every one of those agencies dropped the ball.

Banita and her daughters went without food because she had failed to be recertified for food stamps.

The staff at D.C. Superior Court failed to intervene after being notified by a school attendance counselor that 16-year-old Brittany Jacks had extensive absences from school. The court's social services division referred the matter to D.C. public schools, never received further information and didn't follow up on the case.

And she didn't get the mental health care she needed. According to health experts, women who are poor, on welfare, less educated, unemployed and from certain racial and ethnic populations are more likely to experience depression.

Medications and psychological treatments are available that can help prevent 80 percent of those with depression and enable people like Banita to function satisfactorily in their lives. But the stigma attached to mental illness prevents African Americans from seeking professional help and their depression goes untreated keeping them incapacitated for weeks or months. Banita presents textbook evidence that ignoring mental health problems can have long lasting and devastating effects on black families including homelessness, incarceration, suicide, and exposure to violence. Children deserve a life free of poverty that includes a safe home environment, adequate nutrition and affordable quality health care.

Lifting the Veil of Invisibility

Steps taken by D.C. Mayor Adrian Fenty in response to Banita Jacks' tragedy are a good start to preventing a repeat of this tragedy. He mandated that the Child and Family Services Agency review every closed case to assure that everything possible had been done for each client. In addition, he revamped policies regarding case work completion, and plans to implement a better tracking and monitoring system for home school families and for transient school children who move from school to school within the D.C. Public Schools and Public Charter schools.

Social service strategies need to be put in place that will lift poor black women out of invisibility. Successful implementation of these policies will take the collaborative efforts of private citizens, national, state and local governments, community-based service providers and the business community to secure a social safety net for the least of these.

Toward that end, the National Urban League, through the *Opportunity Compact*, has laid the foundation for a strategy that reflects the values represented in the American dream: providing the opportunity for children to thrive, for adults to hold jobs and earn, to own housing and to prosper through entrepreneurship.

Housing, a basic necessity for rich and poor alike, is the foundation that props up the other components of this social service strategy. The national commitment to housing for low-income families must continue and public housing policy must be reformed. The strategy is to transform public housing from islands of despair and poverty into vital and integral parts of larger neighborhoods and to create an environment that encourages and supports individual family movement toward self-sufficiency.

Such a policy could have saved Banita Jacks as can family support policies including reconsideration of the five-year-lifetime limit for TANF, quality child and infant care, transportation assistance, education and training programs that encourage rather than penalize participants trying to attain additional skills.

Poor black women who possess entrepreneurial vision, ingenuity, drive and desire should have access to the resources needed to establish and grow a viable business enterprise. And they should have access to the financial security that comes from home ownership. In order to accomplish the latter, the National Urban League's "Homebuyer's Bill of Rights" must be adopted and public housing must be reformed to assure the continuing national commitment to low- income families.

Every poor black woman who is willing should have a job that allows her to earn a decent wage and provide a reasonable standard of living for herself and her family. These women also must have equal access to resources that enhance employability and job mobility and allows the family to move to economic self-sufficiency. But having a job is not enough. In order for poor black women to benefit from employment, the minimum wage must be indexed to the rate of inflation to protect income during economic downturns, and the Earned Income Tax Credit (EITC) must be expanded in such a way that it further reduces poverty. We must put a policy in place that simplifies the process for claiming EITC; that increases the size of benefits for all eligible families; and that reaches out to eligible families who have not claimed the credit.

Policies also must be implemented that help the children of black women thrive, including mandatory early childhood education beginning at age three and universal healthcare for children. Medicaid and the State Children's

Health Insurance Program have gone a long way in improving health insurance, but almost nine million children are still uninsured. NUL urges passage of the All Healthy Children Act, which would close the coverage gap by simplifying and consolidating Medicaid and SCHIP while expanding eligibility to more children as well as pregnant women who are poor. In addition, poor children and youth also need education beyond high school to compete in the global economy. Toward that end a policy should be initiated that would provide funds per student to pay tuition for two years of study at public universities.

Conclusion

The struggle of living as black women in American society is "anomaly of sorts," says theologian Diana Hayes. "It is, on the one hand to be treated as someone who has performed miracles simply by continuing to persist in living life as she and she alone sees fit. On the other hand, it is to be narrowly watched, critiqued and judged for every action, every step, almost every breath taken…"

Invisible black women are legion. Banita Jacks is just one of them. She now languishes in a jail cell where she has the right to remain silent. Before, she lived in silence without certain rights, like the right to a decent home for herself and her children, the right to economic self-sufficiency, the right to mental and general health care, and the right to lift herself and her children out of poverty through education, training and a job with decent wages.

Banita Jacks has the right to remain silent. But we do not. We must speak up for, reach out to and lift up every black woman who struggles to be seen, heard, and helped.

REFERENCES

Metchem, Stephanie Y., "Introducing Womanist Theology," Maryknoll, New York: Orbis Books, 2002, p. 19.

Wallace, Michele, "Variations on Negation and the Heresy of Black Feminist Creativity, p.55 as cited in Mitchem.

Hayes, Diana L., Hagar's Daughters: Womanist Ways of Being in the World (New York: Paulist Press, 1955) p. 54.

A Pathway to School Readiness: The Impact of Family on Early Childhood Education

by Renée R. Hanson

Early childhood education is an important aspect of any child's life. Birth to three years old represent critical years when children begin to communicate and build other positive developments that are shaped through the preschool experience. Early childhood education can also produce long-term effects on academic achievement and social adjustment. According to a recent report by the National Center for Children in Poverty (NCCP), low-income young children attending high-quality programs are more likely to stay in school, go to college, and become successful, independent adults. They are also less likely to need remediation, be arrested, or commit violent crimes.[1]

The primary goal of early childhood education programs is to create a solid start to school readiness. "School readiness is described as a combination of experiences and care that a child has received from birth to school entry. There are five dimensions included in a child's school readiness. They are 1) physical health and well-being and motor development; 2) social and emotional development; 3) approaches to learning; 4) language and literacy development; and 5) cognition and general knowledge".[2] According to the National Education Goals Panel, school readiness can also mean, "children's readiness to enter school; schools' readiness for children; and family and community supports that contribute to the readiness of children".[3]

As a child's first teachers, parents also play a critical role in children's early learning and school readiness by transmitting basic knowledge and skills, as well as through nurturance and cultivation of other socio-emotional developments. For example, research has shown that parent participation in child-centered activities, specifically play, is important for children's social and emotional development.[4] It has also been reported that "parent participation with their children in activities such as arts and crafts is associated with children's literacy development".[5]

This study uses data from the Early Childhood Longitudinal Study: Kindergarten Class of 1998–1999 (ECLS-K) to examine the role of family background and parental involvement in determining early learning outcomes of children in kindergarten. Based on a sample of 5,528 African-American, white and Hispanic kindergarten students enrolled in public schools throughout the United States during the fall of 1998, I address several questions:

How does early academic achievement vary by race and socioeconomic status?

To what extent do differences in family background alone account for differences in early academic achievement?

Does a child's preschool setting have a significant effect on early learning?

To what extent does parental involvement, specifically parents reading to their children, improve early academic achievement?

Preschool Attendance and Kindergarten Math & Reading Scores

The two most basic academic skills acquired by school-aged children are the ability to read and perform mathematical operations. For the ECLS sample, reading and math skills were assessed during one-on-one testing sessions during the fall of the kindergarten year.[6] The reading test assessed knowledge of letters and word recognition, beginning and ending sounds, vocabulary and passage comprehension. The math test assessed understanding of numbers, geometry and spatial relations.

Table 1 displays average reading and math scores of children from four types of preschool programs—relative care, non-relative care (nanny or babysitter), Head Start, and other center-based care. The average math score for children who came from Head Start or some other type of center-based care was slightly higher than the average for all students in the sample. There was also less variation between the different types of preschool care when it came to math scores than there was in the reading scores. The lowest average reading scores were for those children coming from relative care and non-relative care and again students from Head Start were more likely to score slightly above the average.[7]

The effectiveness of Head Start programs at preparing children for school has been well-documented. According to a 2003 study by Abbott-Shim, et al., Head Start children performed better in cognitive, language, and health measures than their comparison group counterparts.[8] Also, recent Head Start Family and Children Experience Survey (FACES) data show that Head Start graduates, by spring of their kindergarten year, were essentially at national norms in early reading and writing and were close to meeting national norms in early math and vocabulary knowledge.[9]

Table 1. Average Reading and Math Test Scores by Type of Preschool Program

Types of Preschool	Math Scores	Reading Scores
All Types	50.78 (10.57)	48.37 (14.27)
Relative Care	50.53 (10.24)	47.86 (15.04)
Non-Relative Care	50.65 (10.56)	47.87 (14.11)
Head Start	50.92 (10.91)	49.16 (13.64)
Center-based	50.83 (10.73)	48.43 (14.34)

The Effect of Family Background, Parental Involvement and Preschool Attendance on Early Academic Achievement

Regression analysis was used to further explore the extent to which family background contributes to differences in scores on reading and math tests that were administered during the fall of the kindergarten year. The family background variables included were race, gender, number of siblings in the household, mother's education, father's education, and family type (one parent, two parents or other). A measurement of early parental involvement based upon the number of days per week the parent spends reading to the child was included as well.[10] Complete tables of regression estimates are presented in the appendix to this chapter.

The results indicate that differences in family background explained a larger portion of the variance in reading scores (32–44 percent depending upon the type of preschool program attended) than the math scores (15–24 percent). This suggests that to a large extent, a child's language and literacy development tends to be cultivated within the home as opposed to in a formal school setting. Aside from whether the child was from an English-speaking household, the most significant family background determinants of test performance were family size and parental education. Children from larger families tended to score lower as did those whose parents had lower levels of education.

Parental reading was found to be especially important among Head Start participants. For example, children in Head Start whose parents did not read to them at all scored significantly lower on reading (17 points) tests than other Head Start children whose parents did read to them. Overall, the frequency of reading tended not to be as important as the fact that parents read to their children at all. Less than one percent of all families reported that they did not read to their children at all, indicating that the majority of parents are aware of the benefits of reading to their children and have chosen to take this simple step toward preparing their child for school. Children who were in non-relative care (i.e. a nanny or babysitter) prior to entering kindergarten were the least likely to be read to by a parent.

A few racial and gender differences in test performance were also identified. On average, black children scored lower than their white counterparts on math tests, and Hispanic students scored lower on reading tests. The performance gap between boys and girls was identified among those students who attended Head Start or other center-based programs. Boys in Head Start scored lower on reading tests than their female counterparts while boys in other types of center-based programs scored lower than girls on both reading and math tests.

Policy Implications
The results of this study provide support for a number of the National Urban League's policy recommendations for improving education. In The Opportunity Compact: Blueprint for Economic Equality, NUL's 2007 compre-

hensive policy document, the League advocates for "mandatory early child-hood education beginning at age 3" as a means of providing children with an opportunity to thrive. According to the League's recommendations for reau-thorization of No Child Left Behind (NCLB), "it is critical that ALL children enter school ready to take advantage of teaching and learning in order to be successful in their schooling."

Two early learning programs in particular that have demonstrated success in this area are Chicago Child-Parent Centers (1967-present) and the Abecedarian Project (1972–1985). Data on participants in the Chicago Child-Parent Centers provides evidence that children's participation in early school-based intervention coupled with intensive parental involvement was associ-ated with a wide range of long-term positive effects including less frequent grade retention, higher rates of high school and college completion, and high-er rates of full-time employment as adults.[11] Similarly, participants of the Abecedarian Project had higher cognitive test scores from the toddler years through age 21, higher scores on achievement tests in mathematics and read-ing during their elementary and secondary school years, higher rates of high school graduation and college attendance, as well as lower levels of grade retention and placement in special education classes.

In addition to early childhood education, this report also shows the signif-icance of improving opportunities for educational attainment among parents since so much of a child's literacy development is determined by the parent's level of education. Along these lines, NUL urges the creation and implemen-tation of policies that include quality child care and transportation assistance along with education and training programs that encourage, rather than penalize, additional education and skills attainment.

The League has also promoted increased support for family engagement and support for greater student learning at home and in school. Family engage-ment initiatives have already been implemented in Head Start programs, sev-eral of which are operated by Urban League affiliates, where family literacy services were mandated by the Head Start Act of 1998. "Head Start and Early Head Start programs are committed to helping parents, including fathers, con-tribute to their children's learning....By focusing on the literacy of moms, dads, and their children at the same time, family literacy services are an effective way to help parents get involved in their children's development".[12]

Conclusion

This report helps to shed light on existing racial and socioeconomic differences in academic proficiency and school readiness in kindergarten among white, black and Hispanic children. Although the focus of this study was how the family affects early academic achievement, there are undoubtedly a number of other factors also influencing performance including variation in the quality and curriculum of early education programs and teacher effectiveness.

A high quality early learning environment[13] is an essential part of maximizing every child's school readiness. While some early childhood education programs have been successful in implementing an intensive curriculum that prepares young children with a solid start to school readiness before they enter elementary school, not all of our nation's children are receiving the same kind of high quality early learning. In many cases, there is a direct relationship between socioeconomic status and access to high quality early learning programs. In fact, the achievement gap that exists between economically disadvantaged children of color and their white peers is believed to begin as early as pre-kindergarten (pre-K) and continue throughout their academic development. In The Black-White Test Score Gap, researchers estimate that about half of the black –white test score gap at twelfth grade may be attributable to gaps that existed in first grade[xiv].

Effective policies must take account of how variations in the quality of early learning programs interact with the influence of the family to produce positive academic outcomes for all children. Through combined efforts of teachers and parents, perhaps greater equity in academic development can be fostered, contributing to the closing of the 'achievement gap' for low-income children.

Appendix Table A1.
OLS Regression Estimates of Kindergarten Reading Test Scores
(Standard Error in Parentheses)

	Relative	Non-relative	Head Start	Center-based
Black	-1.226	-1.851	-0.510	-1.601
	(1.177)	(1.235)	(1.692)	(0.617)
Hispanic	-12.031	-8.329	-4.044	-6.163
	(1.469)	(1.573)	(1.491)	(0.761)
Male	-0.056	-1.437	-2.268	-2.333
	(0.745)	(0.846)	(0.862)	(0.400)
English speaking	15.758	20.549	22.138	21.432
	(1.735)	(2.102)	(2.382)	(0.983)
Mother has no HS diploma	-6.235	-5.876	-8.048	-5.982
	(1.408)	(1.642)	(1.875)	(0.775)
Mother has a HS diploma	-1.925	-1.920	-1.572	-1.402
	(0.975)	(1.060)	(1.091)	(0.520)
Mother has a bachelor's degree	1.449	3.295	4.758	1.490
	(1.206)	(1.478)	(1.401)	(0.658)
Mother has post baccalaureate degree	1.470	5.286	3.489	3.195
	(1.654)	(1.985)	(1.946)	(0.866)
Father has no HS diploma	-5.325	-5.229	-2.259	-5.525
	(1.404)	(1.581)	(1.822)	(0.759)
Father has a HS diploma	-0.523	-1.854	-2.139	-2.267
	(1.019)	(1.095)	(1.116)	(0.531)
Father has a bachelor's degree	2.537	1.340	1.195	3.057
	(1.204)	(1.464)	(1.417)	(0.671)
Father has a post baccalaureate degree	4.299	2.149	2.871	2.961
	(1.518)	(1.813)	(1.818)	(0.828)
Two parent household	-0.398	-1.071	1.723	2.229
	(2.046)	(2.303)	(3.376)	(1.135)
Other household	0.647	-1.438	-0.414	2.199
	(3.768)	(4.279)	(5.403)	(2.023)
Number of siblings	-1.354	-0.785	-0.700	-0.909
	(0.357)	(0.386)	(0.413)	(0.184)
First Quintile	3.119	-0.677	0.564	1.687
	(1.285)	(1.697)	(1.747)	(0.790)
Second Quintile	3.301	-0.245	2.073	1.463
	(1.149)	(1.313)	(1.324)	(0.619)
Third Quintile	2.431	-1.230	1.360	1.212
	(1.113)	(1.164)	(1.241)	(0.586)
Fourth Quintile	3.016	0.298	1.262	0.843
	(1.155)	(1.149)	(1.149)	(0.544)
Parent does not read to child	-2.129	1.790	-17.976	-0.096
	(3.508)	(4.450)	(8.048)	(2.655)
Parent reads once and twice a week	1.426	2.269	1.502	0.724
	(1.119)	(1.403)	(1.513)	(0.655)
Parent reads everyday	0.272	1.368	0.297	0.205
	(0.813)	(0.911)	(0.935)	(0.435)
R-squared	0.44	0.43	0.32	0.43
N	947	663	705	2934

Appendix Table A2.
OLS Regression Estimates of Kindergarten Math Test Scores
(Standard Error in Parentheses)

	Relative	Non-relative	Head Start	Center-based
Black	-2.227	-5.015	-2.157	-3.693
	(0.958)	(1.070)	(1.510)	(0.547)
Hispanic	-1.829	-2.876	-1.066	-1.426
	(1.195)	(1.362)	(1.331)	(0.675)
Male	0.664	-0.356	-0.943	-0.788
	(0.606)	(0.733)	(0.769)	(0.355)
English speaking	3.433	3.866	7.729	5.630
	(1.412)	(1.821)	(2.126)	(0.871)
Mother has no HS diploma	-4.097	-7.197	-7.067	-4.421
	(1.146)	(1.422)	(1.673)	(0.687)
Mother has a HS diploma	-0.691	-2.075	-1.904	-1.517
	(0.793)	(0.918)	(0.973)	(0.461)
Mother has a bachelor's degree	2.289	1.170	3.658	1.992
	(0.981)	(1.280)	(1.251)	(0.584)
Mother has post baccalaureate degree	1.598	3.261	4.251	3.509
	(1.346)	(1.719)	(1.736)	(0.767)
Father has no HS diploma	-4.108	-4.186	-0.675	-2.851
	(1.142)	(1.369)	(1.626)	(0.673)
Father has a HS diploma	-1.465	-3.321	-1.367	-2.135
	(0.829)	(0.948)	(0.996)	(0.471)
Father has a bachelor's degree	1.775	2.067	0.815	2.098
	(0.980)	(1.268)	(1.264)	(0.595)
Father has a post baccalaureate degree	4.311	0.548	1.508	3.009
	(1.235)	(1.570)	(1.622)	(0.734)
Two parent household	0.023	-1.264	2.698	3.477
	(1.665)	(1.994)	(3.012)	(1.006)
Other household	-0.397	1.543	-0.885	1.943
	(3.065)	(3.705)	(4.822)	(1.794)
Number of siblings	-0.769	-0.420	-0.183	-0.650
	(0.290)	(0.334)	(0.369)	(0.163)
First Quintile	0.956	-0.145	-0.170	1.875
	(1.046)	(1.470)	(1.559)	(0.701)
Second Quintile	1.406	2.129	0.955	1.351
	(0.935)	(1.137)	(1.182)	(0.548)
Third Quintile	1.633	0.827	0.079	0.849
	(0.906)	(1.008)	(1.107)	(0.520)
Fourth Quintile	1.562	0.614	0.002	0.745
	(0.939)	(0.995)	(1.025)	(0.482)
Parent does not read to child	-1.371	5.360	-17.550	-0.327
	(2.854)	(3.854)	(7.182)	(2.354)
Parent reads once and twice a week	1.986	-0.865	0.965	0.785
	(0.910)	(1.215)	(1.351)	(0.581)
Parent reads everyday	-0.476	0.559	0.742	0.627
	(0.661)	(0.789)	(0.834)	(0.386)
R-squared	0.20	0.24	0.15	0.20
N	947	663	705	2934

REFERENCES

Abbott-Shim, M., Lambert, R., and McCarty, F. (2003) "A Comparison of School Readiness Outcomes for Children Randomly Assigned to a Head Start Program and the Program's Wait List" *Journal of Education for Students Placed at Risk* 8(2), pp.210–211.

Bredekamp, S., & Copple, C. (1997) *Developmentally appropriate practice in early childhood programs.* NAEYC: Washington, DC.

"Father Involvement: Building Strong Programs for Strong Families". (2004) *Head Start,* Head Start Bulletin #77

Jencks, C. and Phillips, M. (1998) *The Black-White Test Score Gap,* Brookings Institution Press.

Kagan, S. Lynn; Moore, Evelyn; & Bredekamp, S. (Eds.). (1995) "Reconsidering children's early learning and development: Toward common views and vocabulary." Washington, DC: National Education Goals Panel. http://eric.ed.gov/ERICDocs/data/ericdocs2/content_storage_01/0000000b/80/24/e8/8d.pdf

Klein, L.G. and Knitzer, J. (2007) "Promoting Effective Early Learning: What Every Policymaker and Educator Should Know", *National Center for Children in Poverty.*

National Urban League. (2007) *The Opportunity Compact: Blueprint for Economic Equality.*

Nord, C.W., Lennon, J., Liu, B., and Chandler, K. (1999) "Home Literacy Activities and Signs of Children's Emerging Literacy: 1993 and 1999", *Education Statistics Quarterly,* Vol. 2, Issue 1, Topic: Early Childhood Education, http://nces.ed.gov/programs/quarterly/vol_2/2_1/q3-1.asp

Paley, V.G. (2004) *A Child's Work: The Importance of Fantasy Play,* Chicago, IL: University of Chicago Press.

Reynolds, A.J., Temple, J. and et al., (2007) "Effects of a Preschool and School-Age Intervention on Adult Health and Well Being: Evidence from the Chicago Longitudinal Study", *Foundation for Child Development.*

"School Readiness: Helping Communities Get Children Ready for School and Schools Ready for Children", (2001) *Child Trends: Research Brief,* Washington, DC

NOTES

[1] See Klein & Knitzer (2007). These statistics in this report are based on more than 20 years of data on small and large-scale early intervention programs.

[2] See Bredekamp and Copple (1997); Kagan, Moore and Bredekamp (1995).

[3] See Child Trends (2001); Kagan, Moore and Bredekamp (1995).

[4] See Paley (2004),

[5] See Nord, et al. (1999).

[6] The scores on these tests have been transformed into standardized t-scores with a mean of 50 and standard deviation of 10 (based on the full sample distribution). T-scores provide estimates of achievement level relative to the population as a whole and not mastery of a particular set of skills. Therefore, those with scores above 50 are above the average relative to their peers and vice versa for those with scores below 50.

[7] The differences in average scores between types of preschool were all less than the standard deviation of 10.

[8] See Abbott-Shim, et al. (2003).

[9] See Zill and Sorongon (2004).

[10] Parent-child reading is also likely related to the parents' level of education and /or time spent working or caring for other children. Caution should be taken in interpreting coefficient estimates.

[11] See Reynolds (2007).

[12] See Head Start Bulletin (2004).

[13] High quality early childhood learning is described as an environment with small classes taught by teachers with a bachelors degree and training in early childhood education who implement an intensive, cognitively stimulating curriculum.

The Triumphs and Challenges of Historically Black Colleges And Universities

Johnnetta Betsch Cole, Ph.D.

istorically Black Colleges and Universities (HBCUs), a designation established by the federal government in 1965, are the 100-plus public and private institutions that were founded just before and in the decades following the Civil War, a time when African Americans could not attend American institutions of higher education. Today, when predominately white colleges and universities (PWI's) have a stated goal of increasing the diversity of their student bodies, HBCUs must compete for black students, and they must do so with far fewer resources

Thirty-nine of the private HBCUs form the United Negro College Fund (UNCF) and the National Association for Equal Opportunity in Higher Education (NAFEO), as an umbrella organization for private and public HBCUs. There is considerable diversity among these institutions, because some are small liberal arts colleges and others are large research universities. Some schools are church-related colleges and universities, while others are land grant institutions. There are co-ed institutions and three single-sex colleges—Bennett and Spelman colleges for women and Morehouse College for men.

In the HBCU family, it is often said that if HBCUs did not exist, it would be necessary to invent them. Certainly in terms of the number of students that HBCUs graduate, their value cannot be doubted. Although public and private HBCUs only comprise 3 percent of American colleges and universities, they account for a quarter of all black college graduates. Three quarters of all

African Americans with a Ph.D. did their undergraduate studies in an HBCU.[1] A study by the National Center for Education Statistics documents the economic worth of these institutions to their communities and the nation.[2] For example:

- The total economic impact of the nation's HBCUs in 2001 was $10.2 billion.
- In 2001, the combined initial spending of the 101 HBCUs in their host communities totaled $6.6 billion.
- Collectively, HBCUs generated a labor impact of $4 billion in 2001, including all forms of employment income such as wages, salaries and proprietors' incomes.

When asked what they like about their HBCUs, students respond by saying that they appreciate being in an environment that is relatively free of racism and applaud being able to attend a college that is half the cost of many predominately white institutions. They speak about faculty who set high academic goals and then provide support to help students reach those goals, and staff who help to create a nurturing environment. Students say they appreciate the chance to make friends they will have for the rest of their lives, and they applaud the value placed on developing students intellectually, spiritually, physically and culturally. Many students also acknowledge the importance of being exposed to both the African and African-American history and culture that was missing in their earlier education, and they appreciate HBCUs emphasis on public and community service.

While there are many positive features at HBCUs, there are also a number of serious challenges that must be addressed if these institutions are to remain a viable choice in the world of American higher education.

Financial Challenges

Unlike public HBCUs, private ones do not receive annual funding from the state in which they are located. Therefore, it is especially important for private black colleges to have endowments from which, based on a spending rule, they can draw funds. Although all private HBCUs have some endowments funds, with the exception of a few institutions, the funding is very small.[3] The combined endowments of all HBCUs are less than 2 billion dollars, while the endowment at Harvard University is approximately $35 billion. Only four HBCUs, Hampton, Howard, Morehouse and Spelman, have endowments exceeding $100 million. Spelman College's endowment is worth over $100,000 per student, making it the highest endowment per student of all HBCUs. However, the financial status of this HBCU, the richest of all the HBCU institutions, takes on a different light when Spelman's total endowment and endowment per student is compared to institutions of similar size, such as Williams College and Grinnell College, where financial endowments are over $1 billion.

On many HBCU campuses, the buildings are old and in need of repairs and regular maintenance. But when operating funds are in short supply, which is usually the case, administrators far too often make the decision to defer needed maintenance on campus buildings.

Fundraising

The presidents of private HBCUs must devote a great deal of their time to fundraising, and the presidents and chancellors of public HBCUs are increasingly involved in seeking funds to supplement what they receive from state allocations.

For HBCUs, just as for PWI's, there are four sources of funds: the government, corporations, foundations and individuals. In terms of individuals, alumni at our black colleges and universities must be encouraged to increase their financial support of their alma maters substantially. When a president or chancellor is making a fundraising call, they are frequently asked how many of their graduates donate to the alma mater, and the amount graduates give to the annual fund. Contributions from alumni are especially important because they are a source of unrestricted monies.

Accreditation

In recent years, more than 10 HBCUs have experienced accreditation problems, stemming from reprimands, and in some cases revocations, by accrediting boards. Althougth accreditation challenges can be linked to a range of issues, such as campus infrastructure, student enrollment and faculty quality, fiscal instability is the most common problem.

There are six regional accrediting associations in the United States. However, most HBCUs are located in the South and must be accredited by the Southern Association of Colleges and Schools (SACS). Although HBCUs comprise only 13 percent of the institutional membership, between 1966 and 2005, 25 percent of SACS' actions were against HBCUs, according to findings from Donahoo and Lee.[4] Dr. Belle Wheelan, the current president of SACS, has aggressively moved to provide proactive support for all colleges and universities in the southern region, including our HBCUs.

Recruitment and Enrollment

Because HBCUs are tuition driven, a dip in enrollment can create financial problems for these institutions. With more and more PWIs recruiting African Americans, HBCUs must compete more aggressively for their students, and they must do so with fewer resources.

African-American women are entering college at twice the rate of African-American men. Therefore, a serious recruitment and retention challenge for HBCUs is how to increase the number of black male students in enrolling to and graduating from a college or university.

Student Debt Level

Black students are among the group who graduate with the highest debt level. Some schools, particularly Ivy League institutions such as Brown, Harvard and Yale, have moved to reduce the amount of debt for students they admit. Bowdoin College has boldly announced plans to eliminate loans for all students receiving financial aid, replacing those loans with grants beginning in the fall of 2008. It is almost impossible for HBCUs to compete with these new initiatives.

Reducing student-debt level must be on the agendas of HBCUs', because on average, these institutions admit the most economically challenged students who are least able to assume debt. As Khumosetsile-Taylor once stated, "High risk students who have been unconsciously underserved by our public schools are expected to bear the cost associated with closing educational gaps so they may have a chance to succeed in college."[5]

According to the Journal of Blacks in Higher Education, citing a study by Nellie Mae, the largest nonprofit provider of federal and private education loans in the country, "69 percent of African Americans who enrolled in college but did not finish said that they left college because of high student loan debt, as opposed to 43 percent of white students who cited the same reason."[6]

Retention and Graduation Rates

HBCUs continue their historical commitment to accept students who have different levels of preparation. This means that among the students at these institutions are women and men whose academic preparation would gain them entrance to the most competitive PWI's, and students, who through no fault of their own, have received poor academic training in their K-12 schooling. Consequently, we can continue to expect that graduation rates at HBCUs will be lower than at PWI's. However, HBCUs must continue to develop strategies to address retention and graduation rates.

All HBCUs need to provide their students with the kind of academic programs that will prepare them to be successful in the highly technological, information laden workplaces of the 21st century. Students in our black colleges and universities must also be prepared to work in international settings, as well as in domestic settings among people of diverse backgrounds.

Bennett and Spelman: Historically Black Colleges for Women

The majority of black women who have attended HBCUs have done so at co-educational institutions. Those women who have matriculated at a historically black college for women have had a unique educational experience. Barber-Scotia, and Huston-Tillotson began as women's colleges and became co-ed. Conversely, Bennett college began as a co-educational institution and became a women's college in 1926. Only Spelman college was founded as and has remained a women's college.

Today, Bennett and Spelman are the nation's only historically black colleges for women. In the wider community, the argument is sometimes made that there is no longer a need for such institutions. This argument rests on the false assumption that not only racism but sexism is no longer present in American life and a part of the educational journey of black girls and women. Also, there is a view expressed by some African Americans that while race still matters, and racism is alive and well, gender inequality is not a major issue in black communities. The experiences of the women who attend Bennett and Spelman speak to the contrary, and the opportunity to attend a college where women are not assumed to always be secondary to men is highly valued. At Bennett and Spelman, the experiences of students as African Americans and as women is acknowledged; students are challenged to excel in fields that are traditionally said to be too difficult for women; and the curriculum and extracurricular activities are designed to prepare women for leadership roles that were once reserved for men.

Throughout the United States and the world, alumnae of these two colleges are engaged in the range of professional careers, and they are active participants in their communities. In addition to having a long list of distinguished alumnae, Bennett and Spelman have a great deal in common. The founding of the two colleges followed a similar pattern, a pattern that echoes how all-private HBCUs began. Bennett was founded in 1873, in the basement of a Methodist church in Warnersville, N.C.; Spelman began in 1881, in the basement of a Baptist church in Atlanta, GA. Each of the schools began as a seminary, and their founding was the result of cooperative efforts by white philanthropists and feed slaves who were determined to have a formal education.

There are some striking differences between the two historically Black colleges for women. Spelman has a substantially larger endowment, a larger enrollment, a larger physical plant and more academic programs than Bennett. In recent years, Bennett has faced serious challenges in terms of its fiscal stability, size of the enrollment and deferred maintenance of the physical plant. However, in the last five years, the college has addressed these issues, and today, Bennett College for Women is in a far more stable financial condition.

In the early days of the two institutions, teacher education was a focus in the curriculum. Each college continues to have an education program; however, they are now known for consistently graduating large numbers of students in STEM fields (science, technology, engineering and mathematics). Bennett and Spelman are also known for consistently graduating large numbers of students who go on for post-baccalaureate studies.

In addition to the value of attending any HBCU, students at Bennett and Spelman speak of additional advantages in attending a women's college. "Here at Spelman," one student said, "no one uses words or silent messaging to say to me, ' Honey, are you sure you can do physics?'" Another student comments, "At Bennett College for Women, when you are elected to be the president of a student organization or an academic club, you know you haven't been elected as the token woman."

At each of the nation's only two HBCUs for women, there is a great deal of discussion about "The Sisterhood," with most students concluding that it is not always in full force, but when it is, it is a very special bonding among women. Today, at Bennett and Spelman, like at most HBCUs, there is an openness to exploring how the student body might become more diverse without moving away from the fundamental mission of the institution. The discussions center on the assumption that the educational experience of black women at Bennett and Spelman would be enhanced by the presence of some women students who are Latinas, Native Americans, Asian Americans and white Americans.

A special report by the Thurgood Marshall Scholarship Fund entitled, Understanding Gender at Public Historically Black Colleges and Universities,[7] looked at gender issues on 48 campuses. Drawing on issues raised in this report, a number of questions should be discussed, and where appropriate, acted on at the two historically black colleges for women.

- Does the gender of a faculty member matter to the students?
- Do male and female faculty members experience differences in their performance ratings that impact tenure?
- Are there any differences in how salaries are set for women and men?
- What is the role of Women's Studies on a women's college campus?
- What distinctions do students and faculty make between female and male staff members?
- Does the institution have an effective sexual harassment policy?
- What is the climate on the campus for lesbian, gay bisexual and transgender (LGBT) students, faculty and staff.?
- What preventive measures are in place to guard the safety of women students and all individuals in the college community?
- Bennett College for Women and Spelman College have a unique place within the HBCU family that must be preserved. For, as a saying goes: "When you educate a man, you educate a man. When you educate a woman, you educate a nation."

Conclusion

What conclusions can be drawn about the state of historically black colleges and universities? As the former president of two of these institutions is fond of saying, "there is nothing HBCUs need that money can't buy." The 100-plus public and private HBCUs continue a 200-year tradition of enrolling, educating and graduating students who, because of their economically or educationally challenged background, would otherwise not have the capacity to earn a college degree.

Although some HBCUs can "hold their own" with highly competitive majority institutions, other HBCUs face serious challenges in terms of their fiscal stability. We must be courageous and innovative enough to determine what needs to be done to make sure that students who want an HBCU education will be able to matriculate at financially sound and academically excellent institutions. Does this mean merging some of our HBCUs? Perhaps. Does this mean launching more revenue generating programs such as distant learning? Perhaps. Does this mean exploring ways that several HBCUs could do joint purchasing or pool their endowments for better returns on investments? Perhaps. Whatever it takes must be done so that historically black colleges and universities do not simply survive, but thrive.

Note: Dr. Kassie Freeman, System Vice President for Academic and Student Affairs, Southern University and A&M College System, assisted with locating information for this essay.

NOTES

[1] U.S. Department of Commerce, Bureau of the Census, *Current Population Survey*, March 2005.

[2] U.S. Department of Education, National Center for Education Statistics (NCES). *"Economic Impact of the Nation's Historically Black Colleges and Universities,"* http://nces.ed.gov/pubs2007.

[3] Ronald Taylor, *Diverse Issues in Higher Education*, "Endoements: Investing in Education's Future—Historically African American Colleges." www.diverseeducation.com.

[4] Saran Donahoo and Wynetta Lee, "The Adversity of Diversity: Regional Associations and the Accreditation of Minority Serving Institutions," in *Understanding Minority Institutions*, edited by Marybeth Gasman, Benjamin Baez, and Caroline Sotello Turner. New York State University Press, Forthcoming.

[5] Pelonomi K. Khumoetsile-Taylor, "Access to Higher Education for African Americans," www.bhcc.mass.edu

[6] "Black Student College Graduation Remains Low, But Modest Progress Begins to Show," *Journal of Blacks in Higher Education*, 2006.

[7] Thurgood Marshall Scholarship Fund, Inc., *Understanding Gender: At Public Historically Black Colleges and Universities*, 2007, New York, New York

African-American Women and Work: Still a Tale of Two Cities

by Alexis Herman

For more than 60 years, we have lived through and been part of one of the most remarkable social revolutions in history. That revolution has fundamentally changed the relationship between women and work. In 1940, 28 percent of women were in the labor force, compared to 38 percent in 1970, and 60.6 percent in 2007.[1] In 1940, one in four workers was a woman, today almost one in two are women.[2] However, we must remember that this revolution was mostly about non-African Americans, because African-American women have always worked—in their own homes, in the homes of others, and in the limited areas of the workplace that were open to them. Today, African-American women continue to have the highest labor force participation rate among women at 63.4 percent.

The days of Ozzie and Harriet, a television sitcom family of the 50's and 60's, where Harriet stayed at home with two kids, are long gone, as two-thirds of married couples have two earners. Further, over 70 percent of women with children are in the workforce and even two out of three women with preschool aged kids work. Harriet has joined the 64.9 million employed women as of 2007, and she not only works, but also she is increasingly likely to make more than Ozzie, as one in four wives today make more than their husbands.

While trends in labor force outcomes are similar for black and white women, important differences exist. Another sitcom of the 60's gave us a brief look at some of these differences. Diahann Carroll—like Oprah Winfrey today—made TV history. As "Julia" on her weekly show of the same name, Carroll depicted a widowed African-American woman raising her child alone, while employed as a registered nurse—an occupation few African-American women were held at the time. The experience of African-American women raising children alone has always been a reality, but today it is simply more dramatic. However, even though African-American women have always been heavily invested in the workforce, we are more likely to be found working in education and healthcare where the pay is generally lower.

The plight of African-American women and their overall status in the workplace reminds me still of a tale of two cities. One city sits on the hill—bright and shimmering, reflecting the progress and the promise of tomorrow for women in our economy. The other city sits in the valley, little changed from the reality of our youth, characterized by low pay and limited opportunities.

Some of the shimmer is a reflection of our successes and progress. Women have served as Secretary of State and today a young woman is flying her F-14 into combat over Afghanistan helping to protect us from terrorism. Women's tennis outdraws male tennis, and our daughters can dream of playing professional sports. African-American women, in particular, have dominated the world of professional tennis with the advent of Serena and Venus Williams. And, while African-American women have not broken the ranks of governorship, we have held four presidential cabinet appointments; one of us has served in the United States Senate and we hold the mantle of mayor increasingly in cities across the nation. African-American women hold 14 of 435 Congressional seats; and 215 seats in state legislatures, serving 37 states.[3] We are gaining ground slowly in leadership positions at institutions of higher education and have ascended to the presidency of major educational institutions—at both historically black colleges and universities, as well as mainstream institutions.

All women, including African-American women, make up the majority of those getting associates, bachelor, and masters degrees. African-American women in particular are acquiring higher degrees in record numbers. For instance, most recently, African-American women were awarded 90,312 bachelors, 38,749 masters and 2,007 doctorates.[4] In America, there is an estimated 250,000 women lawyers, 16,000 black; and about 189,000 women physicians and surgeons, of which 13,000 are black.[5] Women have also joined the ranks of sciences and engineering doctorate holders employed in America where 256,900 are women, and 14,800 are African-American women.[6]

Still, progress and lack thereof is reflected in the earnings picture of women today. Women overall make up just 7 percent of those making $250,000 or more a year and 18 percent of those making $100,000 a year or more. African-American women make up less than one percent of those making over $100,000 or more a year. While we are six percent of the overall workforce, we make up 14 percent of those making between $15,000 and $30,000.[7] Between 1979 and 2006, inflation adjusted earnings for white women rose by 29 percent, while earnings growth among black women was only 19 percent.[8] It is particularly interesting to note that even discounting time on the job, and the fact that women have more career interruptions than men do, the pay gap still exists for all women.

The future suggests that, when it comes to women and work, our two cities will still persist. The Bureau of Labor Staristics projects that the fastest growing occupations over the next decade will be found in the computer and health fields, but at the lower end are jobs like home health aides, medical and dental assistants, bill collectors, and medical records technicians, where women in general and African-American women in particular, collectively make up 90 percent of those occupations.[9] At the top end of the earnings distribution are occupations like computer engineers, computer support specialists, systems analysts, financial services sales agents, occupational therapists, and biological scientists.

Perhaps the brightest lights and greatest opportunities in the city on the hill come from women starting their own businesses and for women in corporate America. Today, where one of every eleven adult women is an entrepreneur, women-owned businesses grew 20% between 1997 and 2006.[10] The overall growth rate for privately-owned businesses was 24%, but businesses owned by African-American women grew at the astronomical pace of 147%.[11]

Formerly, the city on the hill did not exist for women in management in corporate America because their numbers were too few to quantify. In the 1970's, I led an effort to place the first African-American and Hispanic women in managerial, white-collar jobs in FORTUNE 500 companies. While we enjoyed breakthrough successes (the first African-American woman in management in the airline industry, the automotive industry, the telecommunications industry, etc.), these efforts were largely tokenistic. Today, much has changed for the better as African-American women continue to make inroads, but gaps and differences still persist. African-American women are twice as likely as all women to hold staff versus line positions, making it harder to get the kind of experience needed to reach the top levels in most organizations. They represent 1.1% of corporate officers at FORTUNE 500 companies and the most recent data indicates that their average compensation was $229,000 compared to $250,000 for white women.[12]

Mary McLeod Bethune, founder of the National Council of Negro Women, once reminded us as African-American women that "our ongoing challenge is to spread out as far and as fast as we can, and to always be mindful of the need to help one another along the way." The city on the hill, with its promise and progress, awaits the arrival of more African-American women. As we enter, we can never forget or leave behind those who still toil in the valley, where most of us still live.

REFERENCES

Bureau of Labor Statistics, Civilian Population Employment Status, Dec 2007

Executive Leadership Council 2004 Census of African Americans on Boards of Directors

National Science Foundation, Division of Science Resources Statistics, Scientists and Engineers Statistical Data System (SESTAT)

NOTES

[1] U.S. Census Bureau

[2] Ibid.

[3] Congressional Black Caucus; www.nobelwomen.org.

[4] National Center for Education Statistics, *Digest of Education Statistics 2006.*

[5] Center for Women's Business Research, *2005 WOW!– Women & Diversity*

[6] Comparison of the National Science Foundation's Scientists and Engineers Statistical Data System (SESTAT) with the Bureau of Labor Statistics' Current Survey (CPS)

[7] Current Population Survey Annual Demographic Survey (2005)

[8] Highlights of Women's Earnings in 2006, U.S. Department of Labor, U.S. Bureau of Labor Statistics (Report 1000)

[9] Employment Outlook: 2006–16, *Occupational Employment Projections 2016*

[10] Center for Women's Business Research, 2006, *WOW! Facts 2006—Women & Diversity,* Entrepreneurship, page 52

[11] Center for Women's Business Research Web site, Minority Numbers

[12] Executive Leadership Council 2004 Census of African Americans on Boards of Directors

Make Room for the New "She"EOs: An Analysis of Businesses Owned By Black Females

by Lucy J. Reuben, Ph.D.

The US economy is moving through the first decade of the twenty-first century with significantly increased reliance upon entrepreneurism and business development for job creation and socio-economic well-being. Moreover, women increasingly impact the economic vibrancy of our entire nation through their educational attainment and business leadership.[1] Given the increasing educational attainment of black women, it should not be surprising that businesses owned by black women are making a significant impact in generating economic activity as well as providing large numbers of jobs across our nation. Indeed, black women-owned business enterprises (BWBEs) are increasingly integral to the enhancement of the economic status of Black America. For example, BWBEs not only provide over 176 thousand jobs, but the payrolls of BWBEs are sufficient to support over 110 thousand families at the median black household income.[2] Nevertheless, myriad challenges remain for this very consequential sector of businesses.

Comparative Status of Black Women-Owned Enterprises

The information provided herein is based upon the latest available data from the U.S. Department of Commerce Census Bureau. According to the latest available Economic Census, black females are the primary owners of at least 547,032 businesses.[3] This means that black women hold at least 51% of the ownership in these important businesses, which are sole proprietorships, partnerships and privately held corporations. These black women-owned businesses represent 45.7% of the total 1,197,567 businesses owned by African Americans. This rate compares favorably with the 28.9% of all firms that are identifiably female-owned. This means that the business ownership rate for black females, when compared with all black businesses, is more than 150% greater than the business ownership rate for all females when compared to all comparable or classifiable U.S. firms. (The term classifiable firms includes U.S. firms that may be classified according to race or gender.[4] Unless otherwise indicated, this discussion refers only to all classifiable firms, excluding the large publicly held firms which have very diverse and disparate ownership by both individuals and institutions.) These BWBEs represent 8.4% of all female-owned businesses. In addition, another 79,034 businesses are classified as equally-owned by black males and black females, thus, giving black females primary or equal ownership in more than fifty (53%) percent of all black-owned businesses.

As shown in Table I, businesses owned by black females generated approximately $20.7 billion in revenues, which comprises over twenty percent (23.3%) of the revenues of all black-owned businesses. Clearly, if BWBEs had generated a share of revenues proportionate to their numbers, the receipts would approximate over $40 billion. On the other hand, the $939.5 billion in revenues generated by all female-owned businesses comprised just over ten percent (10.7%) of the revenues of all businesses. Here again, the relative entrepreneurial proclivity of black female business owners compares favorably with their other female peers.

Table I: Overview of U.S. Firms by Type of Ownership

Type of Ownership	Total Number	Total Revenues (000)	Total Number of Employees	Total Payroll (000)
Black Female-owned Firms	547,032	$20,670,616	176,436	$3,911,432
All Black-owned Firms	1,197,567	$88,641,608	753,978	$17,550,064
All Female-owned Firms	6,489,259	$939,538,208	7,141,369	$173,528,707
All Classifiable U.S. Firms	22,480,256	$8,783,541,146	55,368,216	$1,626,785,430
All U.S. Firms	22,974,655	$22,603,658,904	110,766,605	$3,812,427,806

The term *classifiable firms* includes U.S. firms that may be classified according to race or gender.
This term excludes publicly-held firms, foreign firms, and other firms that cannot be classified by race, ethnicity and/or gender.

The term classifiable firms includes U.S. firms that may be classified according to race or gender. This term excludes publicly-held firms, foreign firms, and other firms that cannot be classified by race, ethnicity and/or gender.

The average revenue for a black female-owned business varies considerably depending upon whether or not the business has grown to the point of hiring workers (employer firms). As is true with black businesses overall, the average revenue for all black female-owned businesses (employer and non-employer firms) is very small—less than $40,000. This average revenue amount for BWBEs is only 54% of the $74,000 for all black-owned businesses. These low revenue amounts are often the result of businesses that may represent part-time activity and/or numerous proprietorships held by a single owner. However, as can be seen in Table II, most of the revenues for black female-owned businesses are generated by employer firms. Indeed, across all categories of firms in the Survey of Business Owners (SBO), the great majority of revenues can be associated with employer firms. There were 27,027 black female-owned businesses (fewer than 5% of the total BWBEs) that generated revenues of approximately $13 billion. That is, just five percent of all BWBE firms generated two-thirds of the BWBE revenues. Moreover, as shown in Table III, these employer firms have average revenues just under one-half million dollars, or more than 12 times the revenues of BWBEs overall. Nevertheless, with revenues of $480,000, the average BWBE employer firm is still too small to meet the criteria established by the Minority Business Development Agency for inclusion in the Strategic Growth Initiative.v This Initiative is a targeted effort to accelerate the growth and productivity of minority-owned businesses.

Table II: Overview of U.S. Employers by Type of Ownership

Type of Ownership	Total Number	Total Revenues (000)	Total Number of Employees	Total Payroll (000)
Black Female-owned Businesses	27,027	$12,975,918	176,436	$3,911,432
All Black-owned Businesses	94,518	$65,799,425	753,978	$17,550,064
All Female-owned Businesses	916,657	$802,851,495	7,141,369	$173,528,707
All Classifiable Firms	5,172,064	$8,039,252,709	55,368,216	$1,626,785,430
All U.S. Firms	5,524,784	$21,836,249,354	110,766,605	$3,812,427,806

Employer Firms are those firms which report that they include hired workers.

Table III: Average Revenues, Number of Employees and Payroll by Type of Ownership

Type of Ownership	Total Number	Average Per Firm		
		Revenues	Number of Employees	Payroll
Black Female-owned Businesses	27,027	$480,109	6.5	$144,723
All Black-owned Businesses	94,518	$696,158	8.0	$185,680
All Female-owned Businesses	916,657	$875,847	8.0	$189,306
All Classifiable Firms	5,172,064	$1,554,361	10.7	$314,533
All U.S. Firms	5,524,784	$3,952,417	20.0	$690,059

BWBEs are crucial sources of employment and job creation. Businesses owned by black females employed more than 176 thousand workers, or 23.4% of the 753, 978 workers at black-owned businesses (See Table II). The average BWBE employed the equivalent of 6.5 workers, or one worker for every $74 thousand of revenue (See Table III). This job generating context can be compared favorably with black-owned businesses overall, which on average generate only one job for every $87 thousand in revenue. In even sharper contrast, for the average across all female-owned businesses, it takes $109 thousand to generate one job. Of course, the caveat may be that BWBEs are either operating in relatively labor intensive industries or perhaps in situations with lower productivity. Nonetheless, despite that caveat, it is clearly the case that businesses owned by black females are making notable contributions in terms of workforce preparation and development.

The critical role of minority businesses in initial employment and work skill development must be continually acknowledged as our society is increasingly populated by people who have historically been the victims of job market discrimination. It is recognized that minorities disproportionately enter the workforce through self-employment or employment by minority-owned businesses (MBEs).[6] As people of color more and more rapidly swell the ranks of the labor force, it is essential to level the playing field for those businesses with a track record of hiring them.

BWBEs paid their employees more than $3.9 billion, which is an amount that could provide the median U.S. household income for more than 75 thousand families. At the lower level of median black household income, BWBEs provide payroll dollars that would be adequate to support more than 110 thousand families. As such, businesses owned by black females provide a source of revenue for household stability as well as increases in the tax bases of numerous states and municipalities.

The Impact of Industry Concentrations

One of the more significant challenges to BWBEs is that they are concentrated in lower margin industries within the categories of health and social services as well as retail trade. These two industry sectors accounts for more than 45% of the industry distribution for BWBEs. The health care and social assistance sector alone accounts for more than thirty percent (35.4%) of the numbers of BWBEs, comprising 193,599 of the 547,110 BWBEs participating in that segment of industry. Generally, the participation of these businesses is at the lower margin, low-skilled, labor intensive sub-sectors. Similarly, the retail trade sector, with nearly 10% of the numbers of businesses, (49,626 of the 547,110 black women-owed businesses) is the second largest industrial segment. Although these two segments include nearly 50% of the businesses, they generate much less than half of the revenues. The health care and social assistance sector generates just over twenty-five percent (25.4%) of the revenues for all black women-owned businesses, and the retail trade sector generates under nine percent (8.7%) of the revenues. It can be seen that the relatively greater participation by BWBEs in these two sectors does not yield large revenue streams. Rather, black women-owned businesses would need to participate in the higher skilled, higher technology sub-segments of these industries in order to realize significant revenue streams and profit margins.

A tremendous boost to BWBE revenues and profitability would also result from increased participation in the retail related industry sector of wholesale trade. For example, in terms of the number of BWBEs engaged in that industry segment, wholesale trade participation is less than one percent (0.8%), yet wholesale trade yields more than eight percent (8.8%) of the revenues for all BWBEs. In other words, although the number of BWBE wholesalers is less than the number of BWBE retail trade establishments, the revenues from the wholesale establishments exceed the revenues of the far more numerous retail establishments. The nearly 50 thousand BWBE retail establishments earn $1.81 billion in revenues, while the much smaller number (4,210) of BWBE wholesale establishments earned a slightly higher amount of $1.82 billion in revenues. To illustrate the point more graphically, based upon the earnings track record of these BWBEs, had the mix had been reversed (meaning there were 49,626 wholesale establishments and only 4,210 retail establishments), BWBEs would likely have earned an additional $18 billion simply due to change of industry concentration. Given the close relationships of the two sectors and the history of varied entrepreneurs who have switched from retail to wholesale business activity, encouragement and support for this shift from retail to wholesale should have immense benefits for BWBEs, their employees and the communities that they serve.

As shown in Table IV, the importance of greater participation in growing, profitable and high margin industries can be illustrated by reviewing a number of other areas of industry and the participation of businesses owned by black females. For instance, greater participation by BWBEs in the traditionally male dominated areas of the construction industry and the manufacturing industry as well as the higher skilled industry segments of the management services industry or the professional, scientific and technical services industry offer the prospects of much higher revenues. For example, while the 8,772 BWBEs in the construction industry comprise less than two percent (1.6%) of the total number of BWBEs, these construction businesses provide more than five percent (5.4%) of the total revenues of all BWBEs.

Table IV: Participation & Revenues of BWBEs by Industry Classification

NAICS Industry Classification	Number of Firms	Percent of Firms	Revenues ($000)	Percent of Revenues
Forestry, fishing & hunting, & ag support services	348	0.1%	D	
Mining	77	0.0	D	
Utilities	104	0.0	D	
Construction	8,772	1.6	1,120,189	5.4
Manufacturing	3,492	0.7	533,577	2.6
Wholesale trade	4,210	0.8	1,823,717	8.8
Retail trade	49,626	9.1	1,805,028	8.7
Transportation & warehousing	10,230	1.9	547,336	2.6
Information	5,566	1.0	D	0
Finance & insurance	10,112	1.9	594,714	2.9
Real estate & rental & leasing	20,508	3.7	701,877	3.4
Professional, scientific, & technical services	46,421	8.5	2,371,353	11.5
Management of companies & enterprises	35	0.006	52,751	0.3
Administrative & support & waste management & remediation service	43,058	7.9	1,510,451	7.3
Educational services	15,127	2.8	328,904	1.6
Health care & social assistance	193,599	35.4	5,251,695	25.4
Arts, entertainment, & recreation	18,789	3.4	586,125	2.8
Accommodation & food services	10,544	1.9	804,475	3.9
Other services (except public administration)	106,064	19.4	1,934,798	9.4
Industries not classified	428	0.1	D	0

A 'D' reported in the Revenues column represents information that business owners did not report.

The manufacturing industry also offers the potential for growth in revenues. Even as lower skilled and certain heavy manufacturing activities are shifted off-shore, there are growing opportunities for higher skilled manufacturing in areas such as biotechnology. Within the manufacturing industry, the contributions to overall BWBE revenues are more than four times the numerical participation of the BWBE companies. The 3,492 manufacturing firms owned by black women comprise fewer than one percent (0.6%) of the total number of BWBEs, yet these firms provide nearly three percent (2.6%) of the total revenues.

Similarly, the revenue streams of BWBEs could profit from a business mix with greater inclusion of industry segments that draw upon the higher skills that result from greater educational attainments. This is sharply illustrated by the fact that although the 35 BWBE management companies comprise far less than one percent (0.006%) of all BWBEs, they yield more than forty times that in terms of their percentage contribution to total revenues of all BWBE firms. These BWBE management companies earn revenues which average $1.5 million dollars per year or more than forty times the average annual revenues of all BWBEs in all industries.

Another example of the potential for changes in business mix to enhance the economic potency of BWBEs in terms of revenue generation (and expected job creation) can be seen from the area of professional, scientific & technical services—another area in which participation yields greater proportions of revenue streams. In this category, the 46,421 BWBE firms numerically comprise less than ten percent (8.5%) of the total, yet these higher skill level firms produce decidedly more than ten percent (11.5%) of the total BWBE revenues. Moreover, in these important knowledge-based arenas technology can be easily employed for economies of scale. In many instances, telecommuting, video conferencing and long-distance data communication among highly skilled employees can considerably reduce certain fixed costs, thus, capturing additional revenues to increase the bottom line.

Taking into account the examples of the high potential for increased revenues through the change in business activity and industrial mix, it is more than worthwhile for BWBEs to be awarded the support to grow in markets and sectors that offer profitable opportunities. One of the requirements for greater participation in these more technologically and educationally advanced sectors is, of course, higher degrees of educational attainment. Fortunately, the record for up and coming black businesswomen is encouraging in this regard. However, the business focus of this discussion requires attention to an even more persistent hurdle – the issue of financing, especially in the current environment of retrenchment in conventional credit markets.

In this regard, especially given the low average number of BWBE employees (average of fewer than 7 employees per BWBE firm), the emergent trend towards microfinance support by financial institutions, foundations and wealthy individuals may be a vehicle worthy of more BWBE participation than has been the case in the past. Unfortunately, black-owned businesses have relied disproportionately more on personal and family credit sources than many other groups. Acknowledging that, this reliance often stemmed from discouragement and perhaps outright discrimination by traditional lenders, the emergence of microfinance opportunities may offer new prospects for smaller, growing businesses with credit needs below conventional commercial funding levels. BWBEs may benefit from greater participation in these microfinance structures as such structures become more established in this country and are associated with more traditional business activities. However, this microfinance trend should in no way allow traditional lenders (banks, finance companies, venture capitalists, etc.) to ignore the merits and financial needs of growing businesses that are owned by black women.

Conclusion

This analysis demonstrates that businesses owned by black females make substantial contributions to the socio-economic progress of Black America, especially in providing jobs, typically through smaller businesses. Moreover, as black females continue to enhance their educational attainment, they will be increasingly positioned to pursue business opportunities in growing, higher margin/profitably sectors of business. Finally, as emphasized in this discussion, as black businesswomen attain increasing levels of education, training and business experience, they should be assisted to participate in industry sectors that can provide higher revenue streams. Thus, encouragement and support for black women-owned businesses can pay enormous dividends to the economic progress of the nation.

REFERENCES

"Young Women Outpace Young Men in Degree Attainment, Census Shows," *The Chronicle of Higher Education*, Friday, January 11, 2008.

Cole, John A. and Lucy J. Reuben, The Status of Black-Owned Businesses in South Carolina," *The State of Black South Carolina: An Action Agenda For the Future 2008*, Columbia, SC Urban League.

MBDA Strategic Plan FY 2007 –FY 2010, Minority Business Development Agency, U.S. Department of Commerce.

Survey of Business Owners(SBO): Geographic Area Series: Economy-Wide Estimates of Business Ownership by Gender, Hispanic or Latino Origin, and Race 2002 Economic Census, U.S. Census Bureau, U.S. Department of Commerce.

The State of Minority Business Enterprises: An Overview of the 2002 Survey of Business Owners," Minority

NOTES

[1] Among younger adults, under age 30, more women (33.1%) than men (26.3%) have earned a college degree by 2007, according to U.S. Census Bureau data reported in the *The Chronicle of Higher Education* (January 11, 2008).

[2] Based upon adjusted median household data from the 2000 U.S. Census and BWBE revenue data from the 2002 Survey of Business Owners.

[3] 2002 Survey of Business Owners, Economic Census, U.S. Department of Commerce.

[4] The term classifiable firms excludes publicly-held firms, foreign firms, and other firms that cannot be classified by race, ethnicity and/or gender.

[5] "MBDA defines companies under the Strategic Growth Initiative (SGI) as minority businesses that generate $500,000 or more in annual gross receipts, and have a high potential for future growth," *The State of Minority Business Enterprises: An Overview of the 2002 Survey of Business Owners*, Minority Business Development Agency, U.S. Department of Commerce.

[6] Ibid, According to the MBDA, "Minorities frequently commence their careers by working for a minority or starting their business."

The Subprime Wipeout: Unsustainable Loans Erase Gains Made by African-American Women

by Andrea Harris

Homeownership is an important economic advantage for most families, but for African-American women, owning a home is not just a smart financial move—it is key to the future well-being of their entire community. Among African-American families, half of all households with children are headed by women.[1] Without homeownership, most of these households own very little and have few opportunities to build economic security. In fact, of the wealth possessed by African-American families, nearly two-thirds of it is in the form of home equity.[2]

The potential for prosperity created by homeownership is vitally important, helping families weather financial storms and increasing their capacity to build oher assets. Home equity translates into wealth—wealth that allows families to start businesses, cover medical emergencies, and pay college tuition for their children. To the extent that a large share of African-American women can achieve sustainable homeownership, the benefits will cascade through their families, their neighborhoods and the entire Black community.

On the other hand, to the extent that African-American women lose their homes because of unsustainable home loans, their children and larger communities will suffer a devastating blow. Unfortunately, the subprime lending crisis has single-handedly turned the tide on vulnerable communities that previously had been making modest gains in homeownership.

Impact of Current Foreclosure Crisis on African-American Women

Over the past few years, the African-American community has been subjected to a flood of predatory lending practices, and African-American women have borne more than their fair share of abusive loans. In fact, a recent report by the Consumer Federation of America notes that subprime loans have gone disproportionately to women, and that African-American and Latina women have the highest rates of subprime lending when compared to all other Americans, especially white men who receive the lowest share of subprime loans.[3] Moreover, the disparity increases as income increases. In fact, upper income African-American women are more than five times more likely to receive a subprime mortgage than white men.[4] According to data provided under the Home Mortgage Disclosure Act, in 2006, African-American women received 51.4 percent of subprime loans while white men only received 21.5 percent.[5]

The Center for Responsible Lending estimates that 2.2 million borrowers who got subprime loans between 1998 and 2006 will lose their homes to foreclosures.[6] About one out of every five subprime loans originated in recent years will end up in foreclosure—even more if you consider loans that will refinance and then go into foreclosure.[7] Taking account of the rates at which subprime borrowers typically refinance from one subprime loan into another, and the fact that each subsequent subprime refinancing has its own probability of foreclosure, this translates into projected foreclosures for more than one-third of subprime borrowers. Furthermore, foreclosures will cost consumers $176 billion in home equity.[8]

When one considers that over half of all loans made to African-American borrowers in 2005 and 2006 were subprime, and that African-American women account for 48.8 percent of all African-American subprime borrowers in 2006, it is easy to imagine the devastation that is headed toward African-American women and their communities.[9] In fact, a January 2008 report issued by United for a Fair Economy says that the subprime mortgage crisis will drain $213 billion in wealth from people of color in America, producing for African Americans the greatest loss of wealth in modern U.S. history.[10]

From Redlining to Predatory Lending

Predatory mortgage lending in the African-American community is the direct outgrowth of the elimination of redlining–arbitrary denial of real estate loan applications in certain geographical areas, without considering an individual applicant's qualifications. Prior to 1977, when the Community Reinvestment Act was enacted to abolish redlining, African-American women along with African-American men were discriminated against in the mortgage lending arena and banks refused to provide them with credit. Additionally, African-American women, like white and Latina women, also faced an additional gender burden and needed a co-signor to qualify for a mortgage loan. Thus, African-American women moved from being locked out of the credit system to being aggressively targeted for abusive products.

Predatory mortgage lending emerged in the early 1990s.[11] It started out as a few unscrupulous lenders targeting people to strip their equity from their homes. The most famous predatory lender then was the Associates group, a company acquired by Citigroup in 2000. Today, predatory lending is almost synonymous with subprime lending. Lightly regulated finance companies have been the worst offenders, but most major banks also offered the abusive products that led to the current foreclosure crisis.

In 2004, at the peak of African American homeownership, the overall homeownership rate in the United States was 69.0 percent and the rate for non-Latino, non-Hispanic white Americans was 76.0 percent.[12] The national homeownership rate for African Americans crested at 49.1 percent.[13] By the end of 2006, the homeownership rate for African Americans had dropped by 1.2 percentage points to 47.9 percent.[14] Much of this drop in homeownership for African Americans is attributed to predatory mortgage lending practices.

Predatory Lending Fueled the Foreclosure Epidemic

Predatory lending is a term for a variety of lending practices that strip wealth or income from borrowers. Predatory loans typically are much more expensive than justified by the risk associated with the loan. Characteristics of predatory loans may include, but are not limited to, excessive or hidden fees, charges for unnecessary products, high interest rates, terms designed to trap borrowers in debt, and refinances that do not provide any net benefit to the borrower.

Some of the most common predatory lending practices include:

• Steering—placing borrowers into higher-priced loans than those for which they qualify

- Prepayment penalties—a fee a borrower incurs for paying the loan off early
- Yield-spread premiums—broker kickbacks for placing borrowers into more expensive loans than necessary
- Abusive loan products that are packed with features that significantly increase the risk of foreclosure (described in more detail below)

These practices are usually tactics used by unscrupulous mortgage brokers and lenders who prey on vulnerable citizens, and in some cases, share an affinity with their targets through their race or ethnicity. People of all ages and colors have been subjected to these practices, but because African-American women receive a disproportionate share of bad loans, they have felt the brunt of subprime abuses.

While not all of subprime lending is abusive lending, recently the most aggressive subprime loans where products designed to increased the borrower's likelihood of foreclosure. Since 2005, most subprime loans were hybrid adjustable rate mortgages (ARMs)—2/28s and 3/27s, so much so that they accounted for two-thirds of all subprime loans during this time.[15] Subprime hybrid ARMs typically have a fixed interest rate for two or three years, and then automatically adjust to a higher rate, adjusting again every six months for the duration of the loan. For example, a subprime ARM may have an initial interest rate around 6.5–7 percent, but at the 25th payment, go up another one to three percent, eventually rising as high as 12–16 percent. The adjustments associated with subprime hybrid ARMs result in significant payment shock to borrowers, due to low teaser rates for the early years and then adjustment to a much higher interest rate. The significant usage of this product has led to the rapid increase in home foreclosures with many African-American women losing their homes to foreclosure on court house steps.

Consider the situation of Anjanette Booker, which was featured in a January 2008 article that appeared in the *New York Times*.[16] Ms. Booker, a 33 year-old African-American woman who owns a hair salon in Baltimore, bought a brick row house for $130,000 in 2004. Unfortunately, her lender convinced her to take a 2/28 ARM, with a monthly payment that spiked up from $841 per month to $1,769.

At the time the article was published, Ms. Booker was trying to save her home, and she was not alone. She represents the fastest growing group of homeowners in Baltimore in recent years. These single women accounted for 40 percent of home sales in 2006, and according to the National Community Reinvestment Coalition, nearly half of these mortgages were subprime.[17] Ms. Booker, noting the number of "for sale" signs in her neighborhood, said "It looks like a ghost town."[18]

Spillover Effects: Subprime Losses Extend Beyond Individual Families

The New York Times feature on Baltimore highlights two important points. Not only is the subprime crisis affecting African-American women, but the negative effects are spreading beyond the families who lose their homes to their entire communities. According to recent research by the Center for Responsible Lending, millions of families who pay their mortgages on time every month will suffer losses because of lower property values triggered by subprime foreclosures.[19] Their report makes the following points:

• Subprime foreclosures will cause 44.5 million homes to lose $223 in value. This is because homes located near a foreclosure become harder to sell—an effect that typically lasts two-to-three years after the foreclosure occurs.

• On average, affected properties will lose $5,000 in value.

• The lowering of property values means a lower tax base for the affected communities—which could ultimately affect local schools, hospitals, police protection and other vital services.

These "spillover" effects will be most severe in highly populated areas and in areas where housing costs are high. Inevitably, the effects also will be most severe in communities of color, where residents received more than their share of non-wealth building home loans to the benefit of mortgage brokers and lenders who took immediate profits and passed along the risk.

What Would Make a Difference Now?

It is too late to prevent the damage caused by abusive subprime lending, but sensible policies could save many homes now and prevent another subprime epidemic in the future. While mitigating damage in the African-American community, these policies also would help strengthen the entire economy.

First, we need to do more to keep people in their homes today. Foreclosures continue to rise and the entire economy is suffering, yet lenders and Wall Street are refusing to take responsibility for years of reckless lending. At the time this article was written, a much-needed proposal was making its way through both the U.S. House and Senate that would allow struggling homeowners to get reasonable loan changes approved and supervised by a court of law.

Current law specifically prohibits homeowners from getting court-approved and supervised changes on abusive and unaffordable home loans. This makes no sense when such court-supervised loan modifications are available on other types of debts, including loans on commercial real estate, investment properties, and even yachts. Congress also provided this same type of bankruptcy relief to family farmers during the farm crisis of the 1980s, and this remains part of bankruptcy law today. It is unfair to deny this same relief to ordinary homeowners. By changing this policy, Congress could prevent 600,000 foreclosures—five times as many as the Treasury Department's plan that depends on voluntary action by lenders.[20]

Second, we need to prevent another foreclosure crisis in the future. It is now well established that the subprime crisis was created by predatory and reckless lending practices, and most of these practices were perfectly legal under current federal law. In recent years, many states have taken actions to curb abusive lending practices, but these laws were not able to keep up with constant "innovations" by predatory lenders. Thus, it is now urgent for Congress to dust off severely outdated predatory lending laws and raise standards among lenders.

An effective law to prevent predatory lending would include several key components. One, it would have strong protections against the most common types of abuses, such as banning prepayment penalties and removing incentives to overcharge borrowers. There should also be strong legal remedies for those who violate the law. And it is absolutely essential that federal law does not override existing state laws or prevent states from taking action in the future. If it had not been for state anti-predatory lending laws, there is no doubt that the loss of wealth from abusive lending would have been even worse than it is today.

Conclusion

For many years the community development movement has strived to correct unfair denial of credit to the African-American community. As an advocate for the enactment of the Community Reinvestment Act (a law that requires banks to make loans to people traditionally underserved-people of color, women, and rural residents), I know firsthand what good lending opportunities look like, and I know that in order for them to be successful they must be based on sound underwriting standards—unlike the products that have led to the current foreclosure epidemic. The goal today must not focus narrowly on more access to credit, but on greater access to sustainable loans that build wealth. Today, the wealth of the African-American community significantly lags behind that of white Americans. African Americans have a median net worth that is 1/14th that of white Americans, figures of $5,988 and $88,621 respectively.[21] Moreover, at least a third of all African-Americans have a zero net worth, and homeownership provides the only savings account that many African-Americans have.[22] Therefore, we must act now to limit the devastation of the foreclosure crisis on African-American women and their communities.

NOTES

[1] According to U.S. Census data in the "2006 American Community Survey," 49.6 of African-American households are headed by single women with children under 18 years old.

[2] Rakesh Kochar, *The Wealth of Hispanic Households: 1996 to 2002*, Pew Hispanic Center (October 18, 2004).

[3] Allen Fishbien and Patrick Woodall, Women are Prime Targets for Subprime Lending: Women are Disproprtionately Represented in High-Cost Mortgage Market, Consumer Federation of America, December 2006, p. 1.

[4] See id, at p. 16.

[5] Home Mortgage Disclosure Act Data, 2006.

[6] One out of every four home loans made today will foreclose (19.4%).
Ellen Schloemer, Wei Li, et. al., *Losing Ground: Foreclosures in the Subprime Market and Their Cost to Homeowners*, p. 11 (December 2006) available at http://www.responsible-lending.org/pdfs/CRL-foreclosure-rprt-1-8.pdf.

[7] See Schloemer, p. 15.

[8] See Schloemer, p. 11.

[9] Home Mortgage Disclosure Act Data, 2005 and 2006.

[10] Amaad Rivera et. al., "Foreclosed: State of the Dream 2008," United for a Fair Economy (January 15, 2008), available at http://www.faireconomy.org/files/pdf/StateOfDream_01_16_08_Web.pdf.

[11] In 2000, Delta Funding Corporation, a subprime mortgage lender, agreed to pay remediation of more than $7 million in response to accusations that brokers working for Delta charged higher fees to African American women than to similarly situated white males. The disparate charges were clearly based on the race of the borrowers rather than any difference in risk of repayment. The case was settled with the Department of Justice, U.S. Attorney General for the Eastern District of New York, the Department of Housing and Urban Development, and the Federal Trade Commission.

[12] Homeownership Rates by Race and Ethnicity of Householder: 1994 to 2006", U.S. Census Bureau, Housing and Household Economic Statistics Division, available at http://www.census.gov/hhes/www/housing/hvs/annual06/ann06t20.html.

[13] Ibid. Footnote 1.

[14] Ibid.

[15] Structured Finance: U.S. Subprime RMBS in Structured Finance CDOs, Fitch Ratings Credit Policy (New York, NY), August 21, 2006, at 2.

[16] John Leland, "Baltimore Finds Subprime Crisis Snags Women," *New York Times*, January 15, 2008.

[17] Ibid.

[18] Ibid.

[19] "Subprime Spillover: Foreclosures Cost Neighbors $202 Billion; 40.6 Million Homes Lose $5,000 on Average," Center for Responsible Lending issue paper (January 18,2008).

[20] "Voluntary Loan Modifications Fall Far Short," Center for Responsible Lending issue brief (January 30, 2008).

[21] *2008 National Urban League Equality Index*, supra, p.

[22] Corporation for Enterprise Development, Assets and Opportunity Scorecard (2007–2008)

Putting Homeownership Back Within Our Reach

by Lisa Mensah

T
he subprime lending crisis in the United States has had disastrous implications for families and entire residential communities across the country. Over seven million families now hold subprime mortgages, and one
in five of the subprime mortgages made from 2005 through 2006 are projected to end in foreclosure. As it now stands, 2.2 million families with a subprime
loan made from 1998–2006 have already lost their homes to foreclosure or
will in the next few years.

The severity of this problem is alarming and calls for immediate action.
Many organizations, such as the National Urban League, are working tirelessly to clean up what has become a devastating mess for minority and low-
income communities around the country, and the Initiative on Financial
Security at the Aspen Institute (Aspen IFS) applauds these efforts.
Furthermore, recent legislation introduced by Senator Christopher Dodd to
curb predatory lending practices and protect home owners is an important
step in the right direction. Fighting for better disclosure, an end to predatory
lending and fair treatment for those who have defaulted on their loans are all
extremely important and worthy causes—especially as millions of families
are losing their homes unfairly and struggling to rebuild their lives.

However, as we react to the current crisis and take measures to address it,
the focus cannot just be on fixing the subprime market—that is, on address-
ing the debt side of the ledger; we must build the savings side of the home

ownership ledger, as well. Futhermore, the current mortgage lending crisis should not be used to call into question the fundamental value of home ownership for all Americans, but instead should serve as a wakeup call to address the underlying issues and promote increased savings.

Savings, Not Just Debt

Given the severity of the subprime mortgage crisis, some might be inclined to back away from promoting home ownership for less affluent households. It is just too risky, they may argue, and very difficult for families to bounce back from the potential fallout.

However, such an attitude would be regrettable. Home ownership is a cornerstone of a household's long-term financial security, and it epitomizes the American Dream and the opportunity to build better lives for our children. And home equity, as a financial asset, can become a springboard to the acquisition of other important assets like a college education, a small business and a secure retirement

But while home ownership represents an important milestone that helps establish solid membership in the American middle class, it remains largely out of reach for many families. The numbers are astounding and speak for themselves: according to the Joint Center for Housing Studies at Harvard University, greater than a 25 percent gap exists between the 2006 home ownership rate for whites at 75.8 percent and blacks at 48.4 percent, and the data also reveal a similarly grim picture for Hispanics and other minorities, with 49.7 percent for Hispanics, 60.8 percent for Asians and other minorities, and 51.3 percent for all minorities. In fact, black home ownership actually decreased slightly from 2005 and was exactly the same in 2001, showing no improvement over a five-year period.[1]

One explanation for the gap in home ownership rates has been the difficulty many have in making a large down payment—a high hurdle, indeed, especially for low- and moderate-income families. But those households who are able to bring more to the table for a down payment on a home are far better off over the long-term. A down payment is fundamental to a lower interest rate and a more secure mortgage, and savings is the key to a down payment.

IFS Approach to Home Ownership Challenge

Housing advocates have advanced many different approaches to stimulating homeownership. Aspen IFS initially considered three different approaches to the home ownership challenge: 1) encouraging the use of alternative data to improve creditworthiness of consumers with poor, little or no credit history; 2) using tax credits to encourage lenders to provide soft second mortgages; and 3) using a matched, down payment account to encourage savings by low- and moderate-income households. We worked with a 12-member advisory board comprised primarily of CEOs and senior executives from the financial services industry to determine which of these three approaches would have the maximum impact and be the most feasible.

After close examination of all three proposals, Aspen IFS concluded that a matched down payment savings account—or Home Accounts—would be the best route to promoting home ownership. Going back to basics and focusing on the down payment may seem to oversimplify the issue when so many other options exist. However, although zero- or low-down payment mortgages eliminate the initial down payment hurdle, they require homebuyers to assume more debt and increase the ultimate costs and risk. Working families would be better served by saving more and borrowing less, which Home Accounts would help facilitate.

Saving over time also gives families a greater ownership stake— both figuratively and literally— in the asset they have sacrificed to own, and it instills a savings mindset that may extend to other important asset goals, such as education and retirement.

The Possibility of Savings

The IFS Home Accounts proposal builds on the positive results of years of experiments with Individual Development Accounts (IDAs), which provide matching dollars to reward personal savings toward a home, small business or education. Their success has shown that there is both capacity and interest among working families to save in a more structured way.

The results of the controlled study portion of the American Dream Demonstration, an IDA study funded by the Ford Foundation, the Charles Stewart Mott Foundation and others, show a significant positive impact on home ownership. Among participants—all of whom had an average household income of under $18,000—the home ownership rate increased by 14 percent compared to non-participants, with an even greater impact on African-

American participants.[2] In fact, IDA programs for home ownership have been successful even in high-cost housing markets like San Francisco.

Other research clearly shows that match is a powerful driver of increased savings, even among lower-income families who may find it most difficult to save. H&R Block has tested the impact of matching contributions on saving by low- and moderate-income Americans through its Express IRA. The company found that, when given the right opportunity and incentive, low-income households will save some or all of their tax refunds in an IRA. More customers contributed to the IRA when a higher match was offered, and these customers also tended to have higher savings rates than those offered a lower match (or no match at all).[3]

Basic Features of Home Accounts

Aspen IFS builds on the success of IDAs and other matching programs through its Home Accounts proposal, which would encourage millions of low- and moderate-income Americans to save for a down payment on a home. A Home Account is a simple savings account at a bank or credit union that could be used only for a down payment and closing costs for first-time homebuyers.[4] Low- and moderate-income savers would be eligible for a 50 percent government match of their own savings, up to a lifetime cumulative cap of $5,000.[5] If an individual maximized the government match, account funds would reach at least $15,000. Matching contributions would be delivered through the tax system and deposited directly into accounts. Home Accounts would be FDIC-insured and interest rates paid on these accounts would vary by participating financial institutions.

Down Payment Savings Account Structure

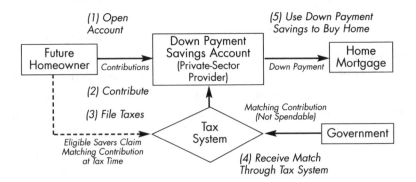

For families struggling to save, Home Accounts are a sensible way to bring the dream of home ownership closer to reality. Making the savings side of the home ownership equation more robust is a smart use of public dollars to help create a pipeline of financially prepared homebuyers. Furthermore, prospective homeowners will have an alternative to zero-down-payment mortgages through a structured and matched savings program.

Account Dynamics—Private Sector Analysis

Home Accounts take the successful IDA experiments one significant step forward by delivering matching contributions directly into a savings account. While these accounts may be modest in size, $15,000 if the full match is gained, they could represent an important new market of savers for the private sector. And because the Community Reinvestment Act provides credit for lending to underserved communities, it is also possible that an additional CRA credit could be offered to institutions that offer the account.

As part of its original research and analysis, Aspen IFS built a financial model projecting savings and home purchases of prospective homebuyers, as well as the market size and government costs for an entire market of down payment savers. Based on conservative assumptions regarding the number of people who would participate, as well as the accumulated savings by prospective homebuyers, the model shows that Home Accounts would create at least four million new homeowners over ten years. These modest savings accounts would leverage $64 billion in mortgages after five years and $457 billion after ten years, at a cumulative government cost of $28 billion over a ten-year period.[6]

Home Accounts in the Real World

For a better understanding of how Home Accounts could facilitate savings for a down payment and result in home ownership, it is useful to consider an individual case:

Mary is single, 29 years old, and lives in Jackson, IA. She earns about $28,000 a year in today's dollars as a receptionist at a doctor's office and would like to buy her own home. She opens up a Home Account and contributes $2,000 each year for five years and earns a $1,000 match from the federal government each year, too.

After five years, Mary has over $16,000 in her account—the result of her savings, her interest and $5,000 of government matching money which she tapped each year at tax time. She uses her entire account to make a down payment and pay closing costs on a house costing $110,000. Mary gets a 30-year fixed-rate mortgage of 6.125 percent, which gives her monthly mortgage payments of $571 – even lower than what she had been paying in rent. She now has home equity valued at $14,000 in her home.

This example illustrates the potential impact of Home Accounts at the individual level. For lower-income, working Americans, these matched savings accounts could make a significant difference in their ability to achieve their home ownership goals with just modest savings over time. And bringing more to the table in the form of a down payment will protect consumers from risky loans and potential default.

Sensible Solutions

Home Accounts embody the Aspen IFS slogan: Smart solutions for a savings society. We believe that a sound national savings policy is essential to achieving the American Dream. And the opportunity to save at every point in the life cycle drives the ability to buy a home, to get an education, to start a business—all springboards to financial security and upward mobility.

Greater personal saving is not a panacea for all problems, of course, either for individuals or for the economy. It certainly won't solve the immediate problems with the subprime lending crisis and rampant predatory lending practices, especially among low-income and minority communities. But it is clear that helping more Americans save, invest and own must be a major element of any serious effort to build greater household and national prosperity.

That is why Aspen IFS spent over two years bringing together policy experts who had new ideas for savings vehicles and the private firms that must ultimately offer and administer these products. Our work together is summarized in our report, Savings for Life: A Pathway to Financial Security for All Americans. Based on several principles that include simplicity, the need for a government match and private sector delivery, we developed a package of four complementary savings vehicles—including Home Accounts— to improve the savings options for all Americans significantly. After careful scrutiny and analysis, we put forth the following proposals in Savings for Life:

• Child Accounts to build savings from the beginning of life. All children born in the United States would receive a beginning endowment provided by the government to open an investment account and matching funds on their own savings until age 18. Based on the United Kingdom's Child Trust Fund, this market-based, retail-sold account product would give every child a financial jump start and help build financial literacy.

• Home Accounts to be used for a down payment on a home, as discussed in detail above.

• America's IRA—standardized, simple Individual Retirement Accounts with a one-time incentive for opening the account as well as government matching funds for low- and moderate-income Americans who do not have access to retirement plans where they work. America's IRA would be similar to existing IRA products and would use existing distribution channels.

• Security "Plus" Annuities—basic life annuities to provide an additional layer of lifetime, guaranteed income as a complement to Social Security. It would partner the familiar and universal Social Security program with the private market. And it would provide many of the 80 million soon-to-retire baby boomers with a simple, low-cost annuity product, provided as part of monthly Social Security benefits that protects them from outliving their savings.

Conclusion

The current subprime lending crisis has put millions of home owners at risk, and it will require a combination of efforts and expertise from private industry, the federal government and community-based organizations to address the problem, protect families and put our economy back on track. At Aspen IFS, we believe these remedies must be immediate and swift in order to protect the millions of families at risk of foreclosure.

While these efforts are underway, however, we must not lose sight of what home ownership symbolizes for so many families. It is possible for all Americans to strive toward this important, potentially wealth-building goal. Although the current crisis underscores the difficult challenge of promoting home ownership for everyone, we cannot ignore the significant racial gap in current home ownership rates or simply accept the status quo. A truly sustainable solution will require significant political will to push new policies forward. And it will build on families' commitments to provide better lives for future generations and on their willingness to sacrifice for long-term financial security. Proposals like Home Accounts will help make the home ownership goal a reality for these families and put the American Dream back within reach.

NOTES

1 Joint Center for Housing, "The State of the Nation's Housing 2007," Harvard University, Joint Center for Housing Studies, 2007.

2 Gregory Mills, Rhiannon Patterson and Donna DeMarco. "Evaluation of the American Dream Demonstration: Final Evaluation Report," Abt Associates Inc., 2004.

3 Esther Duflo, William G. Gale, Jeffrey Liebman, Peter Orszag and Emmanuel Saez, "Savings Incentives for Low- and Moderate-Income Families: Evidence from a Field Experiment with H&R Block," The Retirement Security Project, Policy Brief No. 2005–5, May 2005.

4 Penalties apply for withdrawals used for other purposes, but accounts could be converted into retirement accounts.

5 Households earning under $75,000 per year or single filers earning under $50,000 would be eligible for matching contributions.

6 Lisa Mensah, Pamela Perun, Elena Chávez and Joseph Valenti, "Savings for Life: A Pathway to Financial Security for All Americans," Initiative on Financial Security, The Aspen Institute, 2007.

The National Urban League's Homebuyer's Bill of Rights

1 The Right to Save for Homeownership Tax-Free

Recommendation—Create Individual Development Accounts for Homeownership administered by employers as matched savings plans for the future purchase of a home.

- Similar to 529 plans, the IDA for Homeownership would be a tax-advantaged investment vehicle designed to encourage saving for the future home purchase expenses of a designated beneficiary.

2 The Right to High-Quality Homeownership Education

Recommendation—Redesign of an industry-wide system that integrates pre- and post-purchase homeownership education and counseling; and expansion of HUD's budget for housing counseling from $42 million to $80 million in FY 08.

- HUD funding does not cover all costs of homeownership education and counseling and limits non-profits' ability to collect fees for their services. The private sector contributes only a small share of funding to homeownership education and counseling efforts, and even if the industry's (banks) support matched HUD's, non-profit education and counseling programs would be grossly underfunded if services were expanded to include a larger share of first-time buyers.

3 The Right to Truth and Transparency in Credit Reporting

Recommendation—Demystify the credit reporting system through creation of a public education and awareness campaign about credit scoring and its impact on wealth creation, and establishment of a penalty structure for credit reporting bureaus that maintain inaccurate client files.

- In the United States, once every 12 months, each person is entitled to one free credit report from each of the three nationwide consumer credit reporting companies: Equifax, Experian and TransUnion. Under fear of penalty, credit reporting agencies should be required to collect, maintain, and report data that is accurate, relevant, and up-to-date.

• The Government could offer a free publication called Understanding Your Credit Report and Credit Score. This publication would provide sample credit report and credit score documents with explanations of the notations and codes that are used. It would also contain general information on how to build or improve credit history, and how to check for signs that identity theft has occurred. The publication could be made available online.

4 The Right to Affordable Housing for Working Families

Recommendation—Cities and other municipalities should require that at least 30% of all new and rehabilitated market-rate construction be made available for purchase and rental by households comprising the locality's civil service workforce.

• Workforce housing includes single-family homes, townhouses, condominiums, starter homes, and apartments that are affordable to an area's workers such as: teachers, firefighters, municipal employees and the other workers who provide essential services in communities – policing, healthcare, manufacturing, and retail workers.

• A program that once held great promise in this regard – HOPE VI is broken and should be re-thought and re-built. With a vague and changing mandate, HOPE VI strayed from its initial intent of rehabilitating 6% of the nation's public housing stock; instead, it has funded the demolition of housing and displaced many thousands of poor families to meet the demands of private developers. A one-for-one replacement strategy must be employed.

• New York City provides an innovative example of one such local approach to the issue. Under their current program, known as "421-a", developers of new and rehabilitated buildings in most neighborhoods are eligible for a 10- to 15-year exemption from the increase in real estate taxes resulting from the work. Developers do not receive a tax break unless 30 percent of all the units are affordable to families earning no more that 50 percent of the median income for the area, or about $35,000 for a family of four.

5 The Right to be Free from Predatory Lending

Recommendation—Elimination of incentives for lenders to make predatory loans; a fair, competitive market that responsibly provides credit to consumers; access to justice for families caught in abusive loans; and the preservation of essential federal and state consumer safeguards.

• During recent years, responsible mortgage lenders and consumer advocates have recognized the urgent need to curb abusive lending practices that harm homebuyers and homeowners. The National Urban League supports the passage of legislation that works to better protect the consumer such as the Mortgage Reform and Anti-Predatory Lending Act of 2007 (H.R. 3915), recently passed by the U.S. House of Representatives.

6 The Right to Fairness in Lending

Recommendation—Lenders must gauge ability to repay and offer borrowers the most affordable and well-suited products for which they qualify. Lenders should demonstrate commitment to the building of personal assets. All participants in the making, collecting, holding and buying of debt have a duty to deal fairly with the borrower. Our society should pay particular attention to communities that have traditionally been underserved or at a disadvantage when obtaining credit, including communities of color and the elderly, to ensure they have full access to the most appropriate loan products that can help them build and maintain wealth. Those who are shown to have taken advantage of vulnerable populations by offering inappropriate products or charging unjustified rates fees should be held fully accountable for their actions.

• NUL believes there must be strict limits to prepayment penalties. Prepayment penalties must not apply after the expiration of teaser rates in ARM prime and subprime loans. NUL believes at least a 90 day time period is needed so that borrowers have sufficient time to shop for and receive another loan if necessary. For fixed-rate subprime loans, prepayment penalties must not extend beyond two years. Responsible lenders have voluntarily applied limits to prepayment penalties similar to NUL's recommendations. Limiting prepayment penalties prevents borrowers being trapped in abusive and predatory loans.

• NUL asserts that steering borrowers qualified for prime loans into subprime loans is an unfair and deceptive practice. Numerous studies have documented that middle- and upper-income minorities are significantly more like-ly than middle- and upper-income whites to receive subprime loans. Consequently, borrowers lose substantial amounts of wealth when they are steered into high-cost loans. NUL further urges prohibition of incentive com-pensation, such as yield spread premiums, that is based on the terms of a loan.

• NUL believes that escrows must be required for all loans, prime and sub-prime, fixed and adjustable rate. Currently, since escrows are not required, deceitful lending flourishes when unscrupulous brokers and lenders blind borrowers to the true cost of their loans by not discussing payments for insur-ance and taxes.

• NUL agrees with the Comptroller of the Currency that stated income or low doc loans are prone to abuse when predatory lenders and brokers inflate borrowers' incomes to qualify them for unsustainable loans. Stated income or low doc loans must be prohibited on subprime and/or ARM loans. Clear pro-tections and procedures must be established for reduced documentation loans including the requirement that pay stubs, tax forms, and other accept-able verification of income must be received by the lender.

• NUL maintains that lenders must be held liable for deceptive and fraudu-lent practices committed by brokers with whom they do business. Since up to 70% of the loans originated start with brokers, lenders must be motivated to strictly monitor broker behavior. Likewise, lenders and brokers must face serious financial penalties if they intimidate or pressure appraisers to meet certain home values, as fraudulent appraisals have contributed significantly to the rise of delinquencies and defaults. NUL further believes that individual mortgage brokers and loan officers must be licensed and registered, and required to act "in the best interest" of the consumer under guidelines com-parable to those that financial advisors are subject to.

7 The Right to Fair Treatment in Case of Default

Recommendation—Across the country, people have lost jobs, become tem-porarily disabled, incurred unexpected medical expenses or have had to make a choice between paying the mortgage or repairing the car that gets them to the job that pays that mortgage. Laws regarding mortgage default and foreclosure differ from state to state and mortgage lenders and servic-ing companies vary in the way they approach delinquent borrowers. NUL is generally pleased that many lenders, as well as the big mortgage gatekeepers such as Freddie Mac, FHA and the VA, have amended their approach to managing delinquencies, having finally realized that it is more cost effective to help a borrower to stay in his home than to pursue foreclosure and then confront the need to deal with owning, managing, and selling the resulting real estate. Consequently, there are myriad scenarios that can play out as a mortgage delinquency progresses; however, in the case of default NUL believes that three key provisions must be afforded to homebuyers:

• Opportunity for restructuring of a loan if the loan is determined to be onerous including the possibility of conversion to a fixed rate loan.

• Fair and unbiased counseling.

• Access to the holder of the loan for development of reasonable workout plans where the objective is preservation to the greatest extent possible and foreclosure is a least resort after all other measures are exhausted.

8 The Right to Aggressive Enforcement of Fair Housing Laws

Recommendation—Create a HUD Task Force to Vigorously Investigate and Prosecute Violations of Fair Housing Laws, and authorize Congressional Oversight Hearings to Ensure Accountability

• In a multiyear study using homebuyer "tests" funded by HUD and completed in 2005, the National Fair Housing Alliance found that potential homebuyers were steered to white or minority neighborhoods 87% of the time

• In collaboration with non-profit organizations, the Task Force would investigate and process mortgage lending complaints, including such actions as inappropriate steering to sub-prime loans, stricter qualification standards for minority borrowers and higher rates and/or conditions for minority homebuyers.

Election Reform: Protecting Our Vote from the Enemy Who Never Sleeps

by Melanie L. Campbell

The right to vote is arguably the most important right of citizenship in a democracy. Since the passage of the 15th Amendment to the U.S. Constitution in 1870, most Americans have enjoyed the legal freedom to elect candidates to serve in political offices, at city, state and federal levels.

However, exercising this civil right has traditionally been a persistent struggle for black Americans. Historically, African-American citizens have combated violence and intimidation in order to exercise their U.S. Constitutional right to vote. In addition, they have been subjected to unjust poll taxes and literacy tests in order to qualify for their voting rights.

Given the competitiveness and the diversity in ethnicity, religion and gender of the 2008 U.S. presidential candidates, black voter turnout will likely be the highest that we have seen in decades. Yet as we prepare for the 2008 presidential election, voter suppression, faulty election systems, substandard election administration and eroding voter confidence, still, unfortunately, remain primary obstacles in impeding black voter participation.

Americans of every race and ethnicity continue to face the most insidious test of their commitment to voting — a retreat into cynicism. However, we must counter cynicism by reaching into and mobilizing our communities and being vigilant in teaching and demonstrating that the power of voting brings meaningful social and economic change for our citizens. In honor of our African-American ancestors who fought and died for our right to vote, it is our duty as beneficiaries of those sacrifices to be steadfast and unwavering in fighting an enemy that still endures and attempts to hinder this U.S. Constitutional right.

Who is the Enemy?

The adversaries of minority voters are the politicians, elitists and advocates who collectively spend countless hours creating policies and schemes to marginalize and disenfranchise low-income voters, in order to maintain their political and economic advantage over the masses. Such unscrupulous practices range from enacting unjust state voter ID laws to forwarding anonymous mailings listing false information regarding election days to black households. In addition, some unethical officials have informed minority voters that those with outstanding traffic tickets will be subject to arrest if they appear at the polls. Furthermore, laws disenfranchising persons with past felony convictions, which vary from state to state, fall most harshly on the shoulders of black voters who are disproportionately convicted for felony offenses.[1]

The Help America Vote Act of 2002, along with strong enforcement of the Voting Rights Act of 1965, extended for an additional 25 years in August of 2006, are the most effective tools we have in eliminating voter disenfranchisement on a federal, state and local level. Election reform is a continuum that requires constant review, as reform policies are implemented. It also requires advocating against public policies and election administration systems that suppress voter participation, diminish voter confidence and deny the American people their right to vote without fear of reprisal.

Voter Disenfranchisement Rears Its Ugly Head in 2004 and 2006

Widespread allegations of voter disenfranchisement and suppression tainted the 2000 presidential election and the 2004 and 2006 elections encountered similar turmoil. In the last two elections, thousands of voters were not certain their votes were counted or if the election results reflected their intentions.

The African-American Human Rights Foundation brought international monitors in to observe the 2004 election and found that voter intimidation tactics or "dirty tricks" were a problem in several states:

"Controversies over the role of 'challengers' took on a highly partisan cast, especially in Ohio, but also in Michigan, South Carolina, Florida, and Mississippi as evidence gathered that, rather than ensuring the integrity of the process, challengers might intimidate voters and impede their access to the ballot. Additionally, illegal, dirty tricks were evident in many locations: calls saying your polling station was changed, when it had not been changed, and giving the wrong place for the people to vote; calls or flyers saying that voting was extended until Nov 3; flyers/mailings saying that it is a felony if people go to vote without bringing numerous types of personal identification (which most people would not have) or telling people that outstanding parking tickets, back alimony and other matters must be cleared before going to vote." [2]

In many places throughout the country, voters had to wait several hours to vote, due to misdirection of voters, poorly trained staff and an overall increase in voter registration that was not complimented by the mandated proportional increase in voting machines. It was reported that some precincts lost voting machines while gaining registered voters. [3]

In some states, voters reported widespread problems with voting machines, including suspicious and confusing functioning from direct-recording electronic voting equipment. In fact, it was reported that some polling locations were shut down entirely. [4]

Historically, state election administration has been severely under-funded and treated as a low priority for all levels of government. As a result, many eligible voters are deprived of their right to vote or to have their vote counted. Compounding this are draconian voter eligibility and registration laws - such as unfair residency requirements for students – that further encumber eligible voters ability to cast their ballots.

Among the most insidious and harmful of these measures are felon disenfranchisement laws that prohibit ex-felons from voting. According to the Sentencing Project Study on Felony Disenfranchisement, 13% of black men – nearly one and half million – are disenfranchised, a rate seven times the national average. [Move Endnote 6 here] The study forecasts that "if the current rate of incarceration continues, three in 10 of the next generation of black men can expect to be disenfranchised at some point in their lifetime." [7]

The Brennan Institute and the Leadership Conference on Civil Rights reported that, in 2006, "fliers distributed to voters with Latino surnames in Orange County, Calif., incorrectly intimated that it is illegal for naturalized citizens to vote. In Virginia, Colorado and New Mexico, voters received automated calls communicating incorrect information about where and when to vote and the requirements for voting."[8]

On Election Day, November 7, 2006, the National Coalition on Black Civic Participation, (NCBCP)—in partnership with the National Urban League and others—led a Unity '06 National "War Room Operation" to monitor and track real-time voter disenfranchisement and irregularities in 15 U.S. states. Also, NCBCP officials launched the Unity '06 Campaign national voter assistance hotline to document voter complaints and received nearly 20,000 calls in November 2006. These calls reflect an increase in complaints about voting machine malfunctions, up from 3 percent in 2004 to 20 percent in the 2006 mid-term election cycle.[9] Callers registered other complaints, including voter registration problems—such as new voter identification rules, which resulted in voters being turned away at the polls— as well as difficulty in locating the correct polling place and inadequate absentee voting procedures. The NCBCP believes that such types of complaints signal a need for continued diligence in monitoring and changing the system and reflect the fact that election reform is still an uncompleted task.

Voting System Preferences, Voter Confidence and Provisional Ballots

Controversies in Florida during the 2000 election and in Ohio and other states during the 2004 election have made election administration the primary concern of many voters. Many saw strange parallels between the actions of states in the 21st century and those of states' rights advocates from the late 19th and early 20th century who used federalism as a smoke screen for racial oppression. Because evidence has shown that voting apparatuses can have a discriminatory impact, the NCBCP was particularly interested in how confident voters were in 2006.

In November 2006, NCBCP conducted an exit poll on voters' experiences in the mid-term election.[10] On the question of voting-system confidence, the exit poll yielded a result that favored "paper balloting" and "touch screen" over punch cards that disenfranchised voters in Florida in 2000.[11]

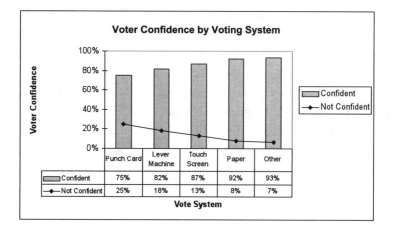

The differences in voter confidence for touch screen and paper balloting reflect heightened concern over ballot security. Our poll reconfirms voters' concern, if not wholesale suspicion, of voting without paper verification. In addition, we suspect that voter skepticism and suspicion—coupled with the failure of states to adequately systematize real ballot security—pushed voters to choose, and election administrators to suggest, provisional ballots. Although many in the civil rights community support the HAVA clauses that states provide provisional ballots in cases where voter eligibility is in question, we caution an overuse of such practices since provisional ballots are less likely to be counted that regular ballots.

State Voter ID Laws—New Corrupt Strategies to Disenfranchise Voters

Today there are still over 54 million eligible unregistered voters, including over 30 percent of African Americans and over 40 percent of Latino Americans who are unregistered.[12] Yet there are those who consistently advocate for policies that discourage eligible citizens from becoming active participants in our representative democracy and claim that voter identification laws prevent voter fraud, increase security and enhance voter confidence.

In 2006, several states passed laws with the potential to disenfranchise thousands of voters. Such enactments of new laws reflect the need for democracy reform now more than ever. For example, the state of Georgia passed a new law requiring all voters to show a "state-approved photo ID" before entering polls. Furthermore, Ohio and Florida each passed a state law making it more difficult for civic groups to register voters. Fortunately, the civil rights community legally challenged these state laws and the courts over-turned the statutes.

The NAACP Legal Defense Fund (LDF) believes that it is misguided public policy to require photo identification, and that it has an adverse impact on the country's most vulnerable citizens—minority voters, rural voters, the elderly, the disabled and the young.

The Indiana State Legislature adopted one of the most restrictive photo ID laws in the country in 2006. LDF's director-counsel and president, Theodore Shaw, said of it:

> *"Indiana's photo identification requirement threatens to fence out black voters. Lessons learned from Hurricane Katrina's unveiling of black poverty underscore this point. Many in these communities lack the necessary documentation to secure the required photo ID and must therefore pay various fees to obtain copies of these documents. This is disturbingly reminiscent of a poll tax and discourages those who are poor from taking part in our democracy."*[13]

On January 9, 2008, the U. S. Supreme Court began reviewing the Indiana photo ID law, which is alleged to be one of the most restrictive state voter ID laws implemented in recent times. The law is expected to be ruled upon in time to affect the general election in November 2008.

Conclusion

Democracy is about people, voice and opportunity; elections are about shaping the future.

In order to restore citizens' confidence that their votes count and will be counted, our nation must continue meeting the challenge of correcting the problems in our electoral system. Consequently, educating voters and protecting their rights at the polls must be an ongoing process.

As we engage in the 2008 U.S. presidential election campaign, it is important to challenge the presidential and congressional candidates to strengthen voting rights enforcement and election administration. The measures we should encourage include 1) mandating the U. S. Justice Department to fulfill its responsibility to monitor and enforce the Voting Rights Act protection provisions and the National Voter Registration Act requirements; 2) requiring public assistance agencies offer voter registration to their clients; 3) full funding of the Election Assistance Commission, so that it will be successful in achieving its mission to Help America Vote; and 4) ceasing unjust state purges of voter registration lists and photo ID requirements.

We must remember that election reform is not an end unto itself—it is a process that requires unending review, upgrading, challenge and improvement. Moreover, we the people also have the power to hold our elected officials and administrators accountable to our interests through our collective voices and votes. If our representative democracy is to be stronger and better for future generations, then it is the responsibility of current generations to continue to stand up against the enemy who never sleeps.

"Every practice that discourages people from voting is a blow to democracy."—Dr. Keith Jennings

NOTES

[1] Simson, Elizabeth, *Justice Denied: How Felony Disenfranchisement Laws Undermine American Democracy.* Americans for Democratic Action Fund (2002).

[2] Jennings, Keith, Ph.D., *Count Every Vote 2004 and The Application of International Election Observation Standards to the 2004 Election in the United States*, Atlanta, GA., African American Human Rights Foundation, p. 16 (2004).

[3] See, Miller, Mark Crispin, "None Dare Call it Stolen: Ohio, the Election and America's Servile Press," Harper's Magazine, August 2005.

[4] Election Protection 365, http://www.electionprotection2004.org/archives/cat_pennsylvania.html, People for the American Way.

[5] See, Shaw, Theodore M., "The State of Civil Rights," *The State of Black America 2007: Portrait of the Black Male*, pp. 173–182 (2007).

[6] *Felony Disenfranchisement Laws in the United States* (April 2007), U.S. Sentencing Project (http://www.sentencingproject.org/Admin/Documents/publications/fd_bs_fdlawsinus.pdf.

[7] Ibid.

[8] Welser, Wendy R., and Goldman, Jonah, 2007. "An Agenda For Election Reform." Washington, D.C., Brennan Center for Justice at New York University Law School and Lawyers' Committee For Civil Rights Under Law.

[9] National Coalition on Black Civic Participation, *2006 Year-In-Review: Lest We Forget.* pg. 25–27.

[10] Meadow, Tyson King, Ph.D., 2006, *Analysis of Exit Polls from 2006 & Black Youth Vote Surveys*, National Coalition on Black Civic Participation.

[11] Ibid.

[12] Welser, Wendy R., and Goldman, Jonah, 2007. "An Agenda For Election Reform." Washington, D.C., Brennan Center for Justice at New York University Law School and Lawyers' Committee For Civil Rights Under Law.

[13] http://www.naacpldf.org/content.aspx?article=1220

The State of Civil Rights 2008

by Kimberley Alton, J.D.

I n 2008, the civil rights community will rally its forces to confront a wide range of issues that are of key importance to the African-American community. Some of the most pressing issues this year include efforts to resolve the ongoing housing crisis in the Gulf Coast post-Hurricane Katrina as well as initiatives to provide legal assistance to those impacted by unfair mortgage lending practices. In addition, top priorities include plans to defeat anti-affirmative action ballot initiatives in several states while also lobbying Congress to restore civil rights laws that have been misinterpreted by recent U.S. Supreme Court decisions.

With the ongoing humanitarian crisis on the Gulf Coast well into its third year, the sheer loss of affordable housing caused by Hurricane Katrina has created an entirely new homeless population in the Gulf Coast. Currently, the State of Mississippi has 13,022 households in FEMA housing programs, of which 11,641 (or 89%) are still occupying travel trailers. These figures cumulatively represent an alarming estimate of 35,159 displaced individuals as of January 2008 in Mississippi alone.[1] Despite the affected states receiving billions of dollars from the federal government to rebuild, too many individuals remain unable to return home and pick back up with their lives. Instead, they remain stuck in cramped and toxic trailers utterly vulnerable to the next hurricane.

A major barrier for these families is the lack of available affordable housing. As a result, civil rights advocates will continue to push federal, state and local governments to correct the missteps of their post-Katrina housing-assistance programs.

The lack of affordable housing is not isolated to the Gulf Coast. A 2005 study found that for every 100 households earning 50% or less of the median area income, there were just 76.7 housing units that were affordable (costing less than 30% of household income) and available (not rented by higher income households).[2] This is down from 81.4 housing units from just two years prior in 2003. With just over 16 million households in this country earning 50% or less of the median area income, this translates into a total shortage of housing stock of about 3.7 million housing units.[3]

In light of these stark statistics, civil rights advocates will mark this year's 40th anniversary of the Fair Housing Act as a renewed opportunity to highlight and combat racial discrimination in the housing market. Signed into law in April 1968, the landmark Fair Housing Act includes broad prohibitions on discriminatory activity in the sale and rental of housing. Yet, the law has had a disappointing impact in deterring continued housing discrimination. Racial discrimination in the real estate market, rental market, and in financing continues at high rates. According to the National Law Center on Homelessness and Poverty, every year, more than 1.7 million fair housing violations are committed solely against African Americans.[4] An annual report by the U.S. Department of Housing and Urban Development indicates that of the 10,328 housing-related complaints handled by the agency in 2006, race and disability made up the largest percentiles.[5] In an earlier HUD study, the agency found that among Blacks, Asians, and Pacific Islanders, one in every five customers encountered discrimination by rental agents.[6] The harmful effects of these discriminatory housing practices have led to hyper segregated communities and schools across the country.

In too many cities, the quality of K-12 educational opportunities is directly linked to the racial makeup and economic level of the community. Last year's Supreme Court decision in the Seattle/Louisville cases hampered local school boards' efforts to achieve racial integration.[7] Nevertheless, civil rights lawyers continue to defend school integration plans and work with local administrators to develop strategies that promote diversity in a manner that complies with the Court's opinion.

As the U.S. Supreme Court prepares to deliver opinions in several important civil rights cases this year, advocates will closely monitor the activities of the Court. Special focus will be given to employment discrimination cases as well as a voter ID case pending before the Court. The outcome of these cases will have huge implications in determining an individual's success in pursuing employment discrimination claims in court and in their ability to exercise their right to vote.

With the 2008 election cycle in full swing, the civil rights community is particularly interested in how the Supreme Court will rule in the voter identification case, Indiana Democratic Party v. Rokita.[8] In January 2008, the Supreme Court heard oral arguments in two consolidated challenges to an Indiana law that requires in-person voters to show government-issued photo identification. The challengers claim that the law violates the fundamental right to vote contained within the Equal Protection Clause of the U.S. Constitution. The State of Indiana contends that the law was passed to prevent voter fraud.

Over the past several years, state legislatures in Indiana, Georgia, and Arizona have passed laws that impose restrictive identification requirements as a condition to casting a ballot at the polls. For voters who cannot meet these strict and unnecessary requirements, the ID law equates to a 21st century poll tax by requiring voters to purchase acceptable forms of identification. By creating a price tag to vote, these laws will disproportionately disenfranchise minority voters, the elderly, the disabled and students. Advocates remain hopeful that the Supreme Court will recognize the importance of the fundamental right to vote and not permit this modern day poll tax.

In response to recent Supreme Court decisions which undermine the intent and effectives of our nation's civil rights laws, civil rights groups will continue to lobby Congress in support of the Civil Rights Act of 2008 and the Fair Pay Restoration Act. These pieces of legislation will ensure that Congress keeps the promises it made to the American people when it passed civil rights laws prohibiting unfair treatment.

In light of the new leadership now in place at the U.S. Department of Justice, civil rights advocates remain hopeful that the agency will improve its poor track record in the area of civil rights enforcement. Civil rights supporters commend the Justice Department's January 2008 indictment of Jeremiah Munsen on federal hate crime and conspiracy charges for his role in threatening and intimidating marchers who participated in a civil rights rally in Jena, Louisiana, by displaying two hangman's nooses from the back of a pickup truck.

Much has been written about the groundbreaking and historical significance of the 2008 presidential primary contest between Hillary Clinton and Barack Obama. Their success provides unquestionable proof of the progress this country has made over the decades. Their success also provides an opportunity for some to claim that discrimination no longer exists and that we now live in a color-blind society. Opponents of race-conscience affirmative action programs will emphasize this theme in 2008 as they roll-out their anti-affirmative action ballot initiatives in Arizona, Colorado, Missouri, Oklahoma, and Nebraska. A success in all five of these states would establish a U.S. population base of over 25 percent living in states with affirmative action bans.[9] In response, the civil rights community is mobilizing its resources from across the country to defeat these harmful measures.

The civil rights priorities for 2008 can be achieved through the collective efforts of those who support equal opportunity for all. Civil rights supporters will tirelessly push our agenda within each branch of government and at all levels this year.

Thanks to John C. Brittain, Sarah Crawford, Jon Greenbaum, Joe Rich, and David Tipson for their contributions.

NOTES

[1] FEMA, Mississippi 1604, GCRO, IA Global Report No. 23.0, Report Date: 01/16/08: http://www.fema.gov/pdf/harzard/hurricane/2005katrina/ms_iag.pdf: Note: The aggregate number reported uses FEMA's standardized formula of: [# of households x 2.7 (average MS household size) = total aggregate population].

[2] Submission on Racial Segregation and the Right to Housing, Prepared by Allard K. Lowenstein International Human Rights Clinic at Yale Law School on Behalf of Poverty & Race Research Action Council, Before the Inter-American Commission on Human Rights, Situation of the Right to Adequate Housing in the Americas Hearing – 122nd Period of Sessions at 37 (2005) (describing the U.S.'s history of discriminatory housing policies), www.prrac.org/pdf/IACHRLetter2005.pdf.

[3] *Id.* at 56.

[4] National Law Center on Homelessness & Poverty, *Housing Rights for All: Promoting and Defending Housing Rights in the United States*, at 58 (2005) (citing National Fair Housing Alliance, *2004 Fair Housing Trends Report*, at 2 (2004). Note that this figure does not include discrimination in lending, insurance, racial and sexual harassment, planning and zoning.

[5] The Office of Fair Housing & Equal Opportunity, *FY 2006: Annual Report on Fair Housing*, at 3-8 (2007), http://www.hud.gov/offices/fheo/fy2006rpt.pdf.

[6] Margery Austin Turner et al., *All Other Things Being Equal: A Paired Testing Study of Mortgage Lending Institutions*, Urban Institute (2002).

[7] *Parents Involved in Community Schools v. Seattle School District*, 127 S.Ct. 2738 (2007).

[8] *Indiana Democratic Party v. Rokita*, Supreme Court Docket No. 07-25: 472 F.3d 949 (7th Cir. 2007).

[9] Peter Schmidt, *5 More States May Curb Use of Race in Hiring and Admissions*, The Chronicle on Higher Education, Oct.12, 2007.

The Impact of Health Disparities in African-American Women

by Doris Browne, M.D., M.P.H.

Introduction

Over the past two decades the overall health of the nation has improved significantly. However, research shows that wide disparities in health and health-care continue to persist throughout the United States. Particularly striking are disparities in the occurrence of illness and death experienced by African Americans[1] caused by higher rates of cardiovascular disease (CVD), cancer, stroke, diabetes, AIDS, and a shorter life expectancy. Possible explanations for these disparities are the complex interaction of biological factors, environment, ethnicity, insurance, and certain health behaviors or lifestyle choices. Equally important are the effects of socioeconomic factors (SES), education and income in creating health disparities. For AA women, poverty, race and ethnicity play a significant role in lower health quality and health outcomes.

The leading causes of death for all women in the U.S. are heart disease, cancer, AIDS, stroke, and diabetes.[2] The number of new cases (incidence) and death rates for these diseases among AA women continues to rise despite declining rates for whites. AA women have the highest cancer death rates for breast, colorectal, and pancreatic cancers.[3] Overcoming persistent health disparities and promoting healthy behaviors for AAs is a formidable health challenge.

Heart Disease, Hypertension, and Stroke

Data from 2001 indicates that coronary heart disease (CHD) is the leading cause of death (498,863) for women in the U.S. followed by lung cancer (65,632) and breast cancer (41,394).[4] Over the past decade the number of deaths from cardiovascular (CVD) has declined. However, the rate of decline is smaller for women and for African Americans. For example, 38 % of women die within the first year after diagnosis compared to 25 % of men.

Coronary heart disease (CHD), which is a sub-set of cardiovascular disease, occurs when plaque builds up in the arteries. The death rate for African American women is 377 per 100,000 compared to 274 per 100,000 in white women. One in five women has some type of heart disease; the death rate is 20% higher for African Americans than whites. The incidence rate of stroke is disproportionately higher in African Americans, and the death rate is nearly 28% higher than in whites.[5]

Major risk factors for developing heart disease are: unhealthy cholesterol level; high blood pressure (greater than 130/85 for an extended time period); smoking- which leads to damaged blood vessels and blocked oxygen delivery to the body's tissue; insulin resistance—inability of the body to utilize insulin appropriately; diabetes; obesity; metabolic syndrome—a group of factors related to excess weight and obesity that leads to heart disease, stroke and diabetes; no physical activity; increasing age; and family history of early heart disease (before age 55 for men and 65 for women). Having a family history of early heart disease and aging are uncontrollable risk factors, which if present, do not necessarily mean that developing heart disease is imminent, but that the risk is elevated. It is important, particularly as we get older, to make healthy lifestyle changes that minimize other risk factors.

Nearly 1 in 3 adult Americans has high blood pressure is defined as blood pressure at or above 140/90. A normal blood pressure is 120/80 mmHg or lower. Once high blood pressure develops it usually lasts a lifetime. Nevertheless, it is treatable and in many cases can be controlled with diet, exercise and medications. When the blood pressure is elevated and left untreated it can cause an enlarged heart, leading to heart attack, heart failure, kidney failure, and stroke. Often, blood pressure problems are undetected and untreated until there is heart, brain, or kidney trouble; hence, hypertension has been called the 'silent killer'. High blood pressure accounts for 18% of the overall death rate. However, it accounts for 41% of deaths in AA women and 50% in AA men.[6]

Cancer

Cancers are the second leading cause of death in women of all ages, especially in AA women. The disparity for AA women related to cancer is evidenced by higher overall numbers of new cases and death rates for certain cancers when compared to other racial and ethnic groups. Five-year survival rates for all cancers after diagnosis is lowest for AA women (57 % versus 67 % in whites).[7] Many of the differences in incidence and death rates among racial and ethnic groups may be attributable to factors associated with social status rather than ethnicity. SES, in particular, appears to play a major role in the differences in incidence, death rate, risk factors, and screening prevalence among racial and ethnic minorities.[8]

Lung cancer

Lung cancer is the third most common cancer in the U.S. and the leading cause of cancer death in women. In 2007, there were an estimated 98,620 new lung cancer cases and 70,880 lung cancer deaths in AA women. The lung cancer death rate among African Americans is 17 % higher then in whites and is the highest among all racial and ethnic groups in the United States.[9] Both small cell and non-small cell subtypes of lung cancer present at a higher stage and with a poor performance[10] status, which leads to a poorer outcome in AAs. Over the past few years, new cases of lung cancer in men have declined, while rates for women have increased. Currently more women die from lung cancer than from breast cancer. The greatest known risk factor for lung cancer is smoking. The level of education an individual has plays a role in determining the chances of becoming a smoker. Thus, a higher education level yields a lower percentage chance of smoking. SES also impacts the number of cigarettes smoked and duration of smoking. AAs are more likely to be diagnosed with a more advanced stage of lung cancer and have a poorer prognosis. Scientific studies have demonstrated that a substantial number of African Americans with early stage lung cancer fail to receive potentially curative treatments of any type—surgery, radiation or chemotherapy, compared to whites. Numerous studies, including an Institute of Medicine Report, [11] confirm that minorities have higher cancer rates and receive unequal treatment.

Breast cancer

Breast Cancer is the second leading cause of cancer death among women in U.S. and throughout the world.[12] Despite many years of extensive research, the incidence and death rates for breast cancer remain alarmingly high.

Breast cancer development appears to be significantly impacted by hormones. Risk factors for breast cancer are gender, early menarche (periods), late menopause, age at first birth, number of pregnancies, family history, age, and excess weight. Approximately one-third of breast cancer cases diagnosed in the U.S. are estrogen receptor negative (ERN). ERN tumors include distinct subtypes. One subtype, basal-like, has been associated with race and age. It has a poor outcome, more aggressive growth rate, larger tumor size, increased number of involved lymph nodes, shorter disease free interval and overall survival. Basal-like breast cancer is diagnosed in 39% of premenopausal (young) and 21% of postmenopausal (older) African American women.[13] No biologically targeted agent exists to treat this type of breast cancer, but it may respond to chemotherapy. In women with the breast cancer gene, known as BRCA-1 gene mutation, over 80% have ERN breast cancer or have features that are consistent with basal-like tumors.[14] Overall less than 2% AA women have the BRCA1 mutation, but about 17% of those under age 35 have the mutation.[15]

Diabetes

Diabetes is the fourth leading cause of death in women in the United States. Roughly 35 million people, approximately 7% of the U.S. population has diabetes. Approximately 1/3 are unaware that they have the disease or are undiagnosed because the affected person either has no symptoms, does not inform the health care provider about symptoms, or mistakes the symptoms for something else (such as aging). There are 15 million AA adult women with diabetes. The incidence of diabetes in African Americans is almost twice that of their white counterparts; one in four AA women 55 and over has diabetes.[16] Certain racial and ethnic communities, including African Americans, other minorities, older people and economically disadvantaged individuals suffer disproportionately from diabetes when compared to whites.[17]

Unfortunately, in addition to a higher number of new cases, 23% of African Americans also experience higher incidence of diabetic complications such as: end-stage renal disease (ESRD) and a higher death rate.[18] The risk of death from diabetes is nearly twice that of those without the disease. Devastating complications, such as stroke, heart attack, amputation, kidney disease, blindness, birth defects, and death can result from poorly controlled diabetes. Heart disease and stroke kill two-thirds of people with diabetes. Controlling blood sugar (blood glucose), blood pressure and cholesterol is very important for preventing these and other complications.

Diabetes is the leading cause of blindness in adults. It is also the leading cause of kidney failure. More than 45,000 diabetics in the U.S. are on treatment for ESRD and more than 160,000 people with ESRD are on chronic dialysis or have a kidney transplant as a result of diabetes. Nearly two-thirds of diabetics have some form of mild to severe nerve damage contributing to loss of sensation or pain in the extremities, slower food digestion, carpal tunnel syndrome, or other nerve damage. About one-third of diabetics over age 40 lose sensation in their feet resulting in lower limb amputations. The risk for gum disease (gingivitis) is twice that of non-diabetics. One third of diabetics are more prone to severe gum disease, which leads to deep pockets around the teeth.[19] If diabetes is not tightly controlled it can lead to a biochemical imbalance, which may result in coma or other life threatening conditions.

In addition, poorly controlled diabetes can lead to complications during pregnancy such as birth defects, spontaneous abortions and excessively large babies.[20] Successfully managing diabetes requires changes in eating habits, possibly taking daily medications, increasing physical activity, smoking cessation and coping with the consequences of living with a chronic disease.

It is important for a diabetic to know the ABCs of Diabetes–A1C, Blood pressure, and Cholesterol:

• A1C (also called hemoglobin A1C) measures average blood sugar over the past 3 months. An ideal A1C level is less than 7.0.

• Controlling Blood pressure (BP) is very important for diabetics. High BP can lead to heart attack, stroke, eye and kidney disease. An ideal BP goal is less than 130/80.

• Cholesterol is fat that clogs the arteries blocking blood flow. There are several types of cholesterol – LDL, "bad" cholesterol; HDL, "good" cholesterol; and VLDL cholesterol. A high level of LDL can cause circulation problems and increases the risk of a heart attack or stroke. An LDL level below 100 is an ideal goal for diabetics. The LDL goal for people with multiple risk factors (diabetes, high blood pressure, and tobacco use) is less than 70.

HIV and AIDS

HIV—human immunodeficiency virus (HIV) is a viral infection that kills or damages cells of the body's immune system leading to AIDS (acquired immunodeficiency syndrome), which is the most advanced state of the infection. HIV most often spreads through unprotected sex with an infected person; sharing drug needles or through contact with the blood of an infected person. The signs and symptoms of HIV and AIDS may be non-specific. The first signs of HIV infection may be swollen glands and flu-like symptoms, which may come and go over several weeks after exposure to the viral infection. Severe symptoms may not appear until months or years later. Women can convey it to their babies during pregnancy or childbirth; 65% of the perinatally infected infants are AAs.[21]

The HIV/AIDS epidemic in the U.S. is a health crisis for AAs. AAs are disproportionately affected by HIV/AIDS. In the U.S. since the beginning of the epidemic nearly 385,000 cases and 212,000 deaths from AIDS were AAs. 49% of the estimated new cases of HIV/AIDS are AA. 61% of those under age 25 with the diagnosis of HIV/AIDS are AAs. AA women are diagnosed with AIDS at a rate nearly 24 times higher than white women. AA women are more likely to be infected by heterosexual means (74%)—sexual contact with men who are HIV positive; compared to other racial and ethnic groups.[22]

Injection drug use is the second leading cause of HIV infection in AA women.[23] Having other sexually transmitted diseases (e.g., gonorrhea, syphilis, etc) increases the risk 3 to 5 fold of contracting HIV infection.[24] AIDS is incurable, but there are many treatment regimens that can control HIV/AIDS, infections and cancers associated with the advanced stages of AIDS. Today, people can live with HIV and AIDS for many years if a treatment regimen is followed closely. Ideally, HIV and AIDS prevention strategies, which include: education/awareness, HIV testing and counseling are crucial to controlling this disease. A screening blood test can tell if the HIV infection is present and should be performed regularly in women who are sexually active, especially those with multiple partners, and intravenous drug users.

Women are the caregivers for the family and generally take little time to care for their own health needs. Education, awareness and screening are essential to preventing and controlling chronic diseases in women. AA women tend to use preventive screening tools at a similar level as women of other racial and ethnic groups. However, once an abnormality is detected they face a worse prognosis. Multiple influences such as access to care, SES, insurance status, belief systems, physician–patient relationship issues, education, tobacco use, environmental factors, physical inactivity, and other factors play an important role in health outcomes. Research on genetics, biological, and environmental factors as well as health policies that address access, equal treatment and SES factors that impact AA women are needed. AA women also need to be proactive in altering their lifestyle choices in order to improve their health. Most of the risk factors (obesity, physical inactivity, and smoking) for heart disease, breast cancer diabetes, hypertension, and stroke are modifiable and related to lifestyle choices. The journey towards improving the health status of African American women and quality health care for all has just begun. Take charge of your health status;

NOTES

[1] African American(s) will be abbreviated to AA(s) throughout the paper.

[2] Heron, M.P., Smith, B.L. Deaths: Leading Causes for 2003. National Vital Statistics Report. Vol. 55, No. 10. Hyattsville, MD. National Center for Health Statistics. 2007.

[3] Smigal, C., Jemal, A., Ward, E., Cokkinides, V., Smith, R., Howe, H.L. and Thun, M.J. (2006). Trends in Breast Cancer by Race and Ethnicity: Update 2006. *A Cancer Journal for Clinicians*, 56 (3):168-183.

[4] American Heart Association. Heart Disease and Stroke Statistics–2004 Update. Dallas, Tex.: American Heart Association; 2003. Smigal C, Jemal A, Ward E, Cokkinides V, Smith R, Howe HL and Thun MJ. (2006). Trends in Breast Cancer by Race and Ethnicity: Update 2006. *A Cancer Journal for Clinicians*, 56 (3):168-183.

[5] National Center for Health Statistics. Health, United States, 2004 with Chartbook on Trends in the Health of Americans. Hyattsville, MD 2004.

[6] Huff, D., Leigh, W. (2006). Women of Color Data Book: Adolescents to Seniors. Bethesda, MD: Office of Research on Women's Health, Office of the Director, National Institute of Health.

[7] Smigal, C., Jemal, A., Ward, E., Cokkinides, V., Smith, R., Howe, H.L. and Thun, M.J. (2006). Trends in Breast Cancer by Race and Ethnicity: Update 2006. *A Cancer Journal for Clinicians*, 56 (3):168-183.

[8] American Cancer Society. Cancer Facts and Figures, 2006

[9] Smigal, C., Jemal, A., Ward, E., Cokkinides, V., Smith, R., Howe, H.L. and Thun, M.J. (2006). Trends in Breast Cancer by Race and Ethnicity: Update 2006. *A Cancer Journal for Clinicians*, 56 (3):168-183.

[10] Performance status is a classification used in cancer care for the functional level of an individual; it a person is unable to take care of activities of daily living and is bedridden the classification would be poor and the prognostic outcome is not good

[11] Smedley BD, Stith AY, Nelson AR. (2002). Institute of Medicine Report: Unequal Treatment Confronting Racial and Ethnic Disparities in Health Care. Washington, DC: National Academy of Science Press 2002.

[12] Jemal, A., Siegel, R., Ward, E., Murray, T., Xy, J., Thun, M.J. (2007). Cancer Statistics, 2007. A Cancer Journal for Clinicians, 57(1): 43-66.

[13] Carey, L.A., Perou, C.M., Livasy, C.A., Dressler, L.G., et al. (2006). Race, Breast Cancer Subtypes, and Survival in the Carolina Breast Cancer Study. *Journal of the American Medical Association*, 295(21):2492-2502.

[14] Carey, L.A., Perou, C.M., Livasy, C.A., Dressler, L.G., et al. (2006). Race, Breast Cancer Subtypes, and Survival in the Carolina Breast Cancer Study. *Journal of the American Medical Association*, 295(21):2492-2502.

[15] John, E.M., Miron, A., Gong, G. et al. (2007). Prevalence of Pathogenic BRCA1 Mutation Carriers in 5 US Racial/Ethnic Groups. *Journal of the American Medical Association*, 298 (24):2869-2876.

16 National Institute of Diabetes and Digestive and Kidney Diseases. National Diabetes Statistics fact sheet: general information and national estimates on diabetes in the United States, 2005. Bethesda, MD: U.S. Department of Health and Human Services, National Institute of Health, 2005.

[17] Department of Health and Human Services, *Minority Health Disparities at a Glance Fact Sheet*, http://www.omhrc.gov/templates/content.aspx?ID=2139.

[18] American Heart Association. Heart Disease and Stroke Statistics – 2004 Update. Dallas, Tex.: American Heart Association; 2003.

[19] National Institute of Diabetes and Digestive and Kidney Diseases. National Diabetes Statistics fact sheet: general information and national estimates on diabetes in the United States, 2005. Bethesda, MD: U.S. Department of Health and Human Services, National Institute of Health, 2005.

[20] National Institute of Diabetes and Digestive and Kidney Diseases. National Diabetes Statistics fact sheet: general information and national estimates on diabetes in the United States, 2005. Bethesda, MD: U.S. Department of Health and Human Services, National Institute of Health, 2005.

[21] Center for Disease Control and Prevention. (2007) HIV/AIDS among African Americans. Atlanta, GA: U.S. Department of Health and Human Services, Center for Disease Control and Prevention 2007.

[22] Center for Disease Control and Prevention. (2007) HIV/AIDS among African Americans. Atlanta, GA: U.S. Department of Health and Human Services, Center for Disease Control and Prevention 2007.

[23] CDC. *HIV/AIDS Surveillance Report, 2005*, Vol. 17. Rev ed. Atlanta: US Department of Health and Human Services, CDC: 2007:1–46. Accessed June 28, 2007.

[24] Fleming DT, Wasserheit JN. From epidemiological synergy to public health policy and practice: the contribution of other sexually transmitted diseases to sexual transmission of HIV infection. *Sexually Transmitted Infections* 1999;75:3–17.

By the Numbers: Uninsured African-American Women

by Eboni D. Morris

Health insurance, one of the most critical issues in the 2008 presidential election, is a fundamental component of quality access to healthcare in the United States. Eighteen percent of all women in the United States are uninsured. Sixteen percent—or 2 million—of these women are African-American.[1] These women face daunting health outcomes and lower quality of care then those who have health insurance. Those who are uninsured lack access to care, and when they enter the health care system they may receive lower standards of care. Uninsured women, especially those who are members of a racial or ethnic group, are at the greatest risk within our healthcare system, due to the barriers they face in accessing and receiving health care. Financial barriers, transportation issues, and lack of childcare all play a role in accessing and receiving care.

Women are also more vulnerable than men to losing their insurance because they more likely than men to be covered as dependents. Becoming

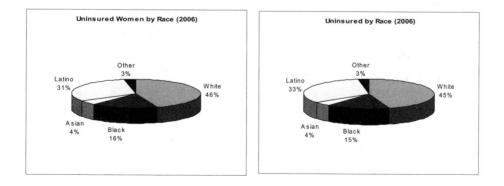

173

divorced, widowed, having a spouse lose their job, the spouse's employer dropping family coverage, or the spouse's employer increasing premiums all can cause married women to become uninsured.[2]

Uninsured African-American Women[3]

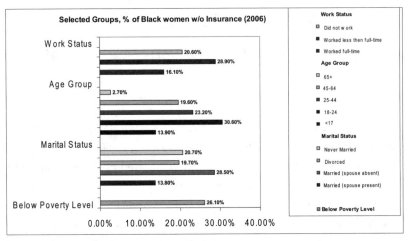

- Women who are younger and have low incomes are at risk for being uninsured, especially women of color.
- About 1/3 of African-American uninsured women are between the ages of 18–24.
- Most uninsured African-American women are married, approximately 40%.
- Most uninsured adults in the United States are in the job market.[4] This is also true for African-American women. About 45% of uninsured African-American women are employed: 28% less then full time and 16% working full time.
- About 1/3 of uninsured African-American women are living below the poverty level.

Implications for overall health and health outcomes[5]

Health insurance is imperative to the overall health of African-American women due to the various chronic health conditions that adversely affect this particular group and the resulting need to have access to quality health care. The Institute of Medicine found that the general health status of the uninsured decreases over time compared to insured adults with continuous coverage. Uninsured adults are less likely to receive care to manage chronic diseases, thus have worse clinical health outcomes.[6]

• African-American women are more likely to report a disability or condition the limits their activity versus white and Latina women.

• Hypertension and Arthritis affect about half of African-American women 45 and older. With high cholesterol and diabetes being fairly common.

• Approximately one in three African-American women has delayed care due to costs as compared to white women.

Implications for financial stability

The uninsured typically have to pay for medical expense out-of-pocket. Persons or families that are uninsured also are likely to have lower incomes and little to no assets, therefore unable to use savings to cover medical expenses. Medical expense can potentially pull financial resources away from essential household expenses such as rent, food, and utilities. A survey by the Commonwealth Fund found that many of the uninsured rack up "medical debt" due to increase medical bills. Some resort to using credit cards and loans to cover these expenses. This debt can adversely affect one's credit score. On average, African Americans are more likely to have lower credit ratings and receive unfavorable rates and terms on loans and credit cards.[7]

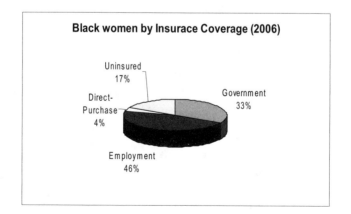

Black women by Insurace Coverage (2006)

Uninsured 17%

Direct-Purchase 4%

Government 33%

Employment 46%

Possible solutions

• Tax credits—permit individuals and employers to use pre tax dollars to pay for insurance premiums through a credit or tax deduction.

• Institute a single payer system- where health care providers would remain private but the government would administer the payments The government receives funding for payments through taxing employers who do not offer coverage.

• Expanding public programs—Medicaid/SCHIP through federal state and local tax revenue.

• Requiring employers to cover all workers—pay or play systems which require employers to provide insurance to their workers or contribute or finance coverage through a tax which covers all of their workers usually through an insurance pool.

• Insurance pools—letting individuals and employer buy into an existing pool.

• Individual Insurance Mandates- requiring everyone to have some type of basic health insurance coverage.

• Vouchers—the government can provide financial assistance to buy health insurance i.e. through a benefit transfer card similar to Food Stamps.viii

There needs to be a combination of public and private efforts to expand coverage, especially for African-American women who are more likely to be uninsured. Improved rates of health insurance coverage would most likely reduce morbidity and mortality among African-American women

NOTES

[1] Current Population Survey (CPS) 2007

[2] 2004 Kaiser Women's Health Survey. Women and Health Care: A National Profile. Kaiser Family Foundation

[3] Current Population Survey (CPS) 2007

[4] Alliance for Health Reform. Health Care Coverage in America: Understanding the Issues and Proposed Solutions March 2007.

[5] 2004 Kaiser Women's Health Survey. Women and Health Care: A National Profile. Kaiser Family Foundation.

6 National Academy of Sciences. Care Without Coverage: Too Little Too Late. Committee on the Consequences of Uninsurance 2002.

7 Alliance for Health Reform. Health Care Coverage in America: Understanding the Issues and Proposed Solutions March 2007.

8 American Medical Association. Expanding health insurance coverage and choice: The AMA proposed reform 2008.

Black Love Under Siege

by Susan Taylor

> There are things sadder
> than you and I. some people
> do not touch.
>
> —*Sonia Sanchez*

Maria W. Stewart, born in Connecticut in 1803, believed as fervently as today's activist black women do that sisters must organize and act on our own behalf and on behalf of our struggling communities. Hers is the story of a powerful and progressive black woman. Orphaned at age five, she served as a domestic servant until she was 15. In 1826 she married, and three years later when her husband, James Stewart, died, she was cheated out of her inheritance by an unscrupulous lawyer and left indigent. But less than six years later she would rise up and speak out, demanding social and economic equality for black women. In 1831, Maria Stewart became the first American-born woman of any race to give a lecture in this nation. In her speeches, she challenged Black women to see that racism and sexism, forms of oppression not radically different from each other, were the fundamental causes of their subjugation.

Though she herself had little formal education, Stewart bluntly stated, "It is of no use for us to wait any longer for a generation of well-educated men to arise." Weary and even frustrated, Stewart's searing words reflected those of a black woman who felt strongly that free African Americans were lacking in commitment. We weren't unified and we didn't have a plan and because that was true, by extension, it was also true that we were ultimately responsible for the continuance of slavery and black suffering, Stewart believed. And like many women today, when Stewart raised her critiques, she looked at brothers and wondered, where are you? What are you doing to move us ahead? And if you're doing nothing, or not enough, should we, black women, look to you, wait for you, love you? That question punctures many of our lives now, but what is the answer?

Any sincere attempt to answer that complex and wrenching question must begin with an honest examination of the history of the black family. From a tribal system of ancient laws that ordered family life and held the clan together over the millennia, enslaved Africans were thrown into a system that ripped away all that was dear and familiar to them. Yet throughout the Americas, enslaved black people developed and cherished solid and stable families. The greatest punishment rendered against a slave wasn't the whip or the lash. It was separation from his family. Beyond individual freedom, a common mission of runaways was finding their loved ones. And even though there were no legally recognized marital bonds between enslaved women and men, still they formed deep spiritual bonds, a legacy passed down through generations that made them feel responsible for one another. Not permitted to be married by a preacher, they created jumping the broom, their own ritual to seal the sacred union.

Amazingly, black women and men emerged from slavery with their families—and their love for one another—relatively intact. There are moving stories about the desperate search for family members they'd been separated from—husbands and wives looking for one another, mothers and fathers for their children. And things might have stayed this way had the concept of freedom meant more for us than enforced servitude. It did not, and the aftermath of slavery did as much to unwrap us from one another as did that mean, peculiar institution.

After 1865, since we had neither money nor land, black people were still dependent on former slaveholders and privileged whites for sustenance. And as we suffered and struggled under the heavy tarp of Jim Crow and the share-cropping system, we had more than feeding our families to worry about. The country proved to be a dangerous place for us. Historian Howard Zinn, in his powerful book *A People's History of the United States,* documents that in a black Memphis, Tennessee, community we were trying to make safe and loving and our own, in one month alone, May 1866, white mobs murdered 46 black men, raped five black women and burned down 90 homes, 12 schools and four churches.[1] Any time that African Americans began making any headway, rape, lynchings, beatings and burnings were introduced to break us, turn us away from ourselves, from our joy. From our love.

More recently, the dumping of drugs and weapons into black communities characterizes how racist hearts and minds have organized to limit black advancement. Life for black people in America is still a dangerous, perilous thing. It has wounded and crippled so many of our men—if not physically, then surely mentally and spiritually. Even the Bible shows that those in power attempt to ensure the continued oppression of a people through the cruel strategy of killing the boys. Today, murder is the number-one cause of death among ours.

This is the nightmare in which black love has sought to thrive; this is the context in which black love has steadily lost ground. We are a strong and determined people. Our survival proves that. It took 100 years to set black women and men apart from each other, but it has happened and the question now before us is what are we willing to do about it?

Consider that stable, two-parent families were the rule after the Civil War. In 1900—and continuing on until post World War II, 90 percent of all back children were born in wedlock.[2] Black men were employed as craftsmen and in factories and earned enough to maintain male breadwinner families, even though the majority of black women were in the workforce as well. According to Marvin Harris, former chairman of the anthropology department at Columbia University, it was only after the great wave of European immigration during World War II that black men were forced out of their jobs as mechanics, house painters, carpenters and plumbers by racist hiring practices. More and more men left the home to seek out work in other towns, other cities and states which gave rise to mother-centered black households. A century after the Emancipation Proclamation, black families showed an alarming rate of dissolution. Then, Harris states, during the 1970s, the U. S. welfare system placed its stamp of approval on the fatherless inner-city family by instituting "the no-man in the house rule." If an unemployed father moved in with his family, payment ceased. The number of families led by black single mothers, Harris notes, rose 257 percent in the 1970s. [3]

The problems faced by the black family are compounded by the structural racism inherent in public policy. The schools our children attend have fewer and fewer public dollars put into them. Throughout the nation there are public schools in underserved communities that don't have well-trained teachers, books for the children or even running water and working toilets! That is a policy matter—who gets good public education and who does not. Who has a decent, nurturing school environment and who does not. Today 58 percent of black fourth graders are functionally illiterate.[4] Couple this with the fact that some 70 percent of people who are in jails and prisons are also functionally illiterate[5] and it's clearly seen that failing schools are the pipeline to prison. Indeed, in some states the failure rates of black boys in the third grade are measured as an indicator of the number of prison cells that will be needed for the future of a for-profit prison system.

In 2007, the number of incarcerated black men reached a new high: A million black men are on lockdown. While African Americans constitute 13 percent of the population, they account for more than 50 percent of all drug-related arrests.[6] Which brings us back to the focal question: how can we love each other when we live in a world that does not love us, where even young people's recent memory does not take them back to a time of love? Intent on basic survival, love may seem like a luxury when in fact it is the very bridge that will carry us across our days of challenge and into a life worth living.

Black women are not a monolithic group. I know that. We speak in many voices. But as I've met and spoken and bonded with sisters far and wide, for all of our many thoughts, feelings and opinions on everything from prayer to politics, there is still a common thread uniting us. We want inner peace. We want happiness. We want our children safe and we want our hearts filled with goodness. We want the black community restored yesterday and every vulnerable child made whole this day. But how can we have this, how can we hope for it without the financial stability that comes from being honored in the workplace and at home? More often than not, those who are successful look back on their lives and point to deep family connections as the reason they made it. And families are not only who we are born into. Families are also who we are able to seek out and partner with as we grow and mature. As much as we need family though, as critical as the skill is to be able to build family, we cannot do it—and therefore cannot reap its benefits—if we buy into the notions of self offered up by the very system of white supremacy that does not care for us.

A quick and painful example is put before us every day in the media. "From early childhood through adulthood, many black women, pressured to be physically attractive and to live up to Eurocentric beauty standards, experience tremendous pain and shame related to their skin color, hair texture, body shape, or weight," say co-authors of *Shifting: The Double Lives of Black Women in America,* Charisse Jones and Kumea Shorter-Gooden.[7] Feelings of being unattractive haunt many black women, the writers' research showed, and this undermines our self-esteem and relationships with men. But we cannot ignore the fact that someone in some boardroom is making a very deliberate decision about who will be made a celebrity; who will represent womanhood. We don't come up with these notions on our own and there are huge industries financially bound to keeping them in place—from the private prisons to public media companies.

Still, to the degree that we have bought into the values of white supremacy and the dominant society's dictates, we have become fragmented and disconnected from our self. Many black women and men throughout the Diaspora and in our Motherland have internalized a hatred for black looks—physical attributes that are uniquely African. Bleaching creams and hair relaxers are the top-selling grooming products in West African nations today. Here in the U. S., look at the women who are included in black music videos. Who is exalted? Who is not? When we reject our men for not earning enough or being positioned enough because structural racism has marginalized them, they are wounded. When our men don't "see" us because they think light skin or blonde hair equals beauty, it is equally wounding. How do we become a salve to our wounds, rather than salt? And what are the benefits?

Over the decades, black thinkers have debated whether it is even possible for us to love, given our emotional scars from the humiliation and heinous acts of violence we have withstood over the centuries. "We have been wounded in the places where we would know love," says feminist scholar and author bell hooks.

While that is true, hooks also recalls the words of the great James Baldwin who said we are more than our pain. We must love in order to heal, but to love means we must risk opening our hearts, moving out of our comfort zones, and yes, compromise. It might seem counterintuitive to ask a people so compromised to do so themselves. But the truth is we are interconnected and if we close out spaces for others in our homes and in our hearts, we will awaken one day with no space for ourselves. When we risk loving someone else, in truth, we are risking loving ourselves.

Essentially, it comes down to this. We can either continue to lament the state of affairs in Black America or we can, as Maria Stewart encouraged us to do, choose ourselves, beginning in our homes. We cannot sit in silence when our children are being undereducated or underemployed. Black love requires us to speak out when the laws unequally target our people. We can't go silent just months after the protests about nooses hanging from trees in Jena, Louisiana or Columbia University—no. In fact, our tradition and survival demands that we organize and speak. Sadly, the Montgomery Bus Boycott, more than 50 years ago, is the only sustained organized effort on the part of Black people in recent times.

Some problems are so breathtakingly large they require our mighty and combined muscle. But we know that if Brad Pitt can bring together public and private interests to reinvigorate parts of New Orleans, so too can we. Perhaps not scores of us, but enough of us have access to power and real power to restore that city. But for those among us who do not, there is power right in our houses and neighborhoods. Begin with the children. One friend of mine, exhausted by the idea of going and joining a group, still chooses to mentor children and for her part, runs a homework helper once a week. Her payment? Her own daughter's grades have gone up, scholarship possibilities are presenting themselves, and Mom gets an unending well of love and bragging rights when all the babies do better on their spelling tests and math tests each week. The first solution, and what I want to underscore the most through my work with the organization I founded at *Essence,* the National Cares Movement, is this: turn to our children and they will turn away from the horrors that abound. They will reach for the sky.

But in turning to our children, we must also turn to ourselves, to our own energies and spirits which created them. Whether it was love or lust, in the moment we come together and make a life, there is usually something tender afoot between us. How do we call that back, pull it out of the bedroom and into the living room of our life? What do we win when we set aside cruel words—and cruel hands? African Americans are the most unwed people in the nation. We need marriages of true minds. Partnerships are our strength, the glue that holds families and communities together. All the mighty forces arrayed against us would be rendered powerless in the face of mutual black love. This is the connection we must make again. What can conscious black women and men do?

1) We can begin this second to love more fully and deeply who we are and who we are with. Turn down the volume in our interactions. Stop going gangster on one another. Let all we say have three purposes alone: to heal, to bless, to prosper. I have a friend whose sister instructs her children to, before they speak, think: is it helpful, is it necessary, is it kind? We can make the choice every day not to speak to one another as though our very lovers are our enemies. If this is true, then move on. If we are not partnered, walking through this harsh world a little more gently will surely increase our chances of meeting our soul mate. We think we want the finest person but if we live long enough we learn: we want the kindest person. And of critical importance, introduce other single seekers. So many women and men are longing for deep connections, partnerships. The many who say they want to stay single forevermore, have simply lost faith that they'll ever connect with a soul mate.

2) In our partnerships we must commit to working toward making them healthier, and must commit to staying together. Marriage is, as we know, a public as much as a private affair. Invite in a wise and trusted elder, a faith leader, a therapist if help is needed getting through a rough patch. We've been giving up too easily. We can learn forgiveness. Holding onto anger is like taking poison every day.

We mustn't buy the hype; we are not the headlines. While the statistics that are out in the universe have their truths they are not the truth of who we are. We come from a long line of can-do, make-do people, spiritual people. But living in a world of negative thought, we become unconscious of our inner eye, the Watcher at the gate that never sleeps. "If therefore thine eye be single, thy whole body is full of light." Let Divine, spirit-filled ideas crowd our consciousness. Let us cease magnifying our obstacles. Instead, magnify goodness, magnify love, magnify God. We combine with what we focus on. We are born to love together. The possibilities are without limits.

NOTES

[1] Zinn, Howard, *A People's History of the United States*, 1942.

[2] Mendel, Charles N. and Haberstein, Robert W. eds., *Ethnic Families in America*, New York: Elsier Scientific Publishing, 1976, p.225.

[3] See, Harris, Marvin, *In America Now: The Anthropology of a Changing Culture*, Simon and Schuster, 1981.

[4] Baxter, Sandra L., Ed.D., *Effort to Build Skills Among African-American Youth* National Institute for Literacy, Institute Director.

[5] "Literacy Behind Prison Walls,"Profiles of the Prison Population from the *National Adult Literacy Survey*, 1994.

[6] Beatty, Phillip, Petteruti, Amanda and Ziedenberg, Jason, *The Vortex: The Concentrated Racial Impact of Drug Imprisonment and the Characteristics of Punitive Counties*, 2007, p.2.

[7] Charisse Jones and Kumea Shorter-Gooden, *Shifting: The Double Lives of Blac Women in America*, HarperCollins, September 2003.

Weaving the Fabric: The Political Activism of Young African-American Women

by Tiffany Lindsay

It began the summer before my term as student government association president officially started, with a call at 11:00 pm to read about six black boys in Louisiana. I did not believe it; there was no way that—in 2007—six young black men could be expelled from school and arrested for events, all sparked from a peaceful response to nooses hanging from a high school tree. Our government should not have allowed this to happen, and our media would not miss the opportunity to uncover this injustice. Moreover, if all else failed, our national black leaders would not separate this from any platform they had. I e-mailed every leader, college student and media outlet I could think of; however, the responses were few. Although people were surprised, any action beyond that was non-existent.

Then came a collegiate leadership conference in August, and I was in the presence of nearly every student government president of a historically black college or university. We discussed the case and the magnitude of the injustice it posed. The majority of us agreed that it was up to us individually to take this issue back to our student bodies and communities. Our Student Government Association at Bennett planned a "Jena 6" week for November. As we told our students about Jena, and our plans for November, they wanted to do something sooner, and we weren't alone in those sentiments. Just a few days later, Michael Baisden began calling on black people everywhere to go down to Jena on September 20 for a march to demand for justice in this case. And it did not take much after that.

The words nooses, Louisiana, and young black men were enough. We as student government presidents stayed in contact with each other about events and plans we had surrounding the march. Some of us held large community rallies, and some sent funds to support their legal defense. But a large amount of us gathered our student bodies and prepared for the journey of justice to Jena, La.

The Importance of Activism

At Bennett, we did all three. Our activism is a fundamental part of our sisterhood, and we were not going to sit in Greensboro while our people across the country were preparing to stand valiantly for the Jena 6. It was not going to be easy organizing 50 students for the trip and raising $10,000 in two weeks for their scholarship and legal defense fund—but it certainly was not impossible. We separated our sisters into several groups and simultaneously began working together to reach our goal. Some sent e-mails and letters to local businesses about the situation in Jena and our goals for the trip. Others went door to door, informing the Greensboro community about the momentous event. We stood at bus stations, Wal-mart parking lots and hosted our own campus rally to increase awareness and raise funds for the Jena 6.

However, our biggest challenges during this time were not organizing and fundraising campaigns. The biggest hurdle was convincing people, even with the march in the black media, why they should support or even more so, why they should care. Nevertheless, we continued and on September 19, we embarked on a 22-hour bus ride with 50 students and collected over $9,600 for their legal aid.

The Jena Crusade and Beyond

A few weeks after the Jena 6 march, we took that spirit to West Virginia. The story of the rape and torture of Megan Williams filled the media and entered into each of our hearts and minds. How could anyone rape, beat and torture this woman for a week because of her race? To add insult to injury, the assailants were not charged with hate crimes. A rally was planned in Charleston, WV, to draw attention and demand that the proper charges be brought forth. Because of opinions about the event organizers, some key churches and religious organizations in the area, along with the NAACP, failed to endorse the event. As a result, more media attention focused on the dispute, rather than the cause for the march.

Nonetheless, we took another group of 50 students to West Virginia to let Megan Williams know that she was not alone. By our presence, we said that we as women have to support each other, even if our leaders suggest otherwise. We gave her letters of encouragement and shared our gifts of poetry and music with her. Though we were the only college present, I knew that day we stood behind her for all black women. Martin Luther King Jr. once said, "That there is an invisible book of life that faithfully records our vigilance or our neglect." The scope of our vigilance is not always in the confines of our comfort zone. We have much to keep watch of as African-American women, but we have to stand tall enough on our strengths, our pride and our ancestors for our sisters and brothers to see it.

In November, we took the vigilance from the Jena 6 and Megan William's marches and demanded justice. This time we headed to Washington D.C., to attend the march planned by Al Sharpton and other black leaders. Their goal was to demand that the Justice Department prosecute cases like Megan Williams and the Jena 6 as hate crimes. It was a powerful experience and nearly 20 of us marched with thousands of other people seven times around the Justice Department, symbolic to the walls of Jericho story in the bible. Once again, we as Bennett Belles were able to unite with other leaders and demand justice in the cases we rallied behind all year. Helen Keller once said, "Never doubt that a small group of thoughtful, committed people can change the world; indeed, it's the only thing that ever has."

The Force of African-American Women

We as black women can be that small group in our communities. We move one step closer to changing the world each time we come together with our gifts and talents in service to our people. Rarely does activism come with a surplus of people waiting to join the ranks of civic engagement, but it does come with a courageous few. Black women have no choice but to display that courage and use it to demand justice and equality in our own individual unique way. Change first occurs in self and in understanding the role and environment that God has placed us to work. Those courageous few have to understand the necessity and power of service is through activism.

We do at Bennett College, as our entire culture is about molding the girl into a woman that will change the world through service. We are a small school of nearly 600 students, but our numbers are no measurement for the power we have when we unite as one. The methodologies at Bennett are applicable to all black women in their efforts of contributing to our race. As black women, we culturally inherit positions of leadership that force us to create a vision for ourselves and those connected to us. This is the story of the sister who takes her cosmetology license and opens her own beauty salon. It is the story of our aunts who took that "knack for doin' for others peoples kids" and formed a daycare center. Such female role models are our educators, our doctors, and our first ladies, with each in their own way serving as architects of tenacity and faith for our people. It is imperative that we delve into the problems that face our community with hands-on experience and action.

We can get signatures to draw attention to a local slum lord and go to a city council to demand change. The task is irrelevant but the action imperative. We were able to raise $9,600 in two weeks, because we were honest and committed. However, the most important factor was that we made people understand the reality and urgency of their action. Once people understand the power of their individual contribution, they will never compromise it. Imagine the looks on our elders' faces if they know their one vote is the key to erasing the ills of their community for their grandchildren. We must make a black father understand that if he does not become a mentor, his son could be the next statistic. Often in our communities, people have become so accustomed to injustice and racism that they accept it. Education is our freedom, and once we have gained it, we must go back and ensure that our people reap the same benefits.

We Must Work Together

The reality is that not all of us are fortunate enough to have access to resources that make a difference, but those who do must use them for the advancement of our race. A college degree is a key component in this work, but it is not the sole factor. Some of our greatest achievements from women as a race have been by those who were just fed up. They used their families, their church networks and that spirit of urgency as vehicles of justice. Toni Morrison once said I wrote my first book, because I wanted to read it. I cherish this fortitude and ingenuity. It is a hallmark to that "do it yourself spirit" we as black women hone in on to create powerful change.

That service to our community cannot be out of pity but obligation. Though I am a young African-American woman, soon to be a college graduate, I am not removed from the struggle of my community. I am subject to the same plight as my sister, who is 22-years-old with three kids and a high school diploma. There is no difference, and the moment we give power to this form of separation, we are just as accountable as outside forces that labor to tear our people apart. We walked side by side in Jena, we stood behind Megan for support in West Virginia, and we formed a circle of unity around the Justice Department. Not once did we ever look down, nor can we ever afford to.

The following is an excerpt from my journal of my Jena experience:

"For the last few weeks we've ate, slept and lived Jena. Throughout the march, I did not have many words. I do not know when I will have the next opportunity to bask in this much blackness. I thought of movements in the past. This was our civil rights march, and we did not miss it. I marched next to black panthers, and I listened to our black elders as they reminisced of how they did the same in the 60's. I kept asking myself why we did not do this sooner and more often. But now that that we were here, the responsibility seems greater. How do we move forward from here with the same power and unity? Or as a brother's tee shirt read in large letters: "what about tomorrow?"

Tomorrow included more of the same work at Bennett. Once we as women recognize the power behind our collective strength, activism is only the beginning. Activism captures the minds and propels the actions of women at Bennett College historically and now. I am certain that the approach we use toward activism is inclusive enough for everyone to play a part, and powerful enough to change the world that we enter.

We walk in the footprints of Dr. Willa B. Player, the first African-American woman to serve as president of a four-year institution. I serve as the student government association president, the same position as Sandra Neely Smith, who was shot and killed in the Greensboro Massacre on Nov. 3, 1979, by the Klu Klux Klan while she and others were fighting for workers' rights at a local textile plant. The ideology is that each woman will take each component of the Bennett experience and weave it into her own God-given gifts to make the world better.

Who would have thought that little old Bennett College could make such a difference by demonstrating that unity is the essence of activism. Each individual action, woven together, creates the fabric that sustains the advancement of our people. Each failure to act shreds that fabric and stalls our forward movement. Although we are torn, we cannot look to anyone but ourselves to mend our race. We each have a piece to contribute and an act to sow. We are the mothers of justice, the carriers of courage. The load is not heavy and the laborers are not few. The only requirement is a heart to serve and the faith that the progression of our people is more than a dream.

Going in Circles: The Struggle to Diversify Popular Images of Black Women

by Moya Bailey

A s a junior at Spelman College and president of the Feminist Majority Leadership Alliance (FMLA) on campus, the spring of 2004 proved to be a pivotal time in my life. It was that year that rapper Nelly had planned to come to Spelman's campus for a bone marrow registration drive. The FMLA thought it would be a good idea to talk with Nelly about the lyrics to his song Tip Drill and the video's less than flattering portrayal of black women, as well as inform the campus about their content. However, upon learning that there might be some trouble with his appearance, his foundation pulled the plug on the event.

This launched substantial news coverage for a number of reasons. First, here we were, young black women responding to music that was presumably for us and about us. It's one thing for Tipper Gore and C. Delores Tucker to have their say, but young black women in college questioning these depictions came as a shock to some. As a result, we found ourselves both venerated and vilified for our desire to directly address Nelly about his lyrics and video. While predecessors in the black feminist movement and black conservatives sent us words of encouragement and praise, many of our peers and other popular artists gave us flack. Needless to say it was an interesting position for us to be in, raising critical questions about popular depictions of black female sexuality.

Let me say up front, we were in no way promoting censorship. Clearly, Nelly and other artists have the constitutional right to say whatever they want, just as we have the right to object to it. Nor were we interested in policing depictions of black sexuality. What we were interested in was why black sexuality so often reflects black women as sex objects without agency waiting to fulfill men's fantasies; why popular images of sex are generally equated with violence and roughness and why physical appearance is valued over all other aspects of a woman's identity.

Representations of black women in U.S. media remain largely unchanged since their inception. What has changed somewhat is who produces the images and who profits from them. In too many of today's songs and music videos, old tropes about black sexuality as animalistic and bestial are revived, more often than not reinforcing stereotypes that date back to the late 19th century. Current day "gold diggers", "hoes", "trap/dough boys" and "thugs" are simply reincarnations of the "jezebel", "sapphire" and "strong black buck" of before. As such, many rappers (unwittingly or not) collude with the racism and sexism that has existed in this country for centuries by repackaging images that have been instrumental in justifying institutional oppression of women and people of color for decades. It is no longer as easy as saying "white people oppress black people" or "men oppress women." Rather, white privilege and patriarchy have informed what we believe about each other as black men and women. In other words, Nelly's lyrics, "Now mama girl you gotta friend that don't mind joinin' in Ima tip drill, I need a tip drill" or White Chocolate's decision to have a credit card swiped through her backside are framed within a context that offers them rewards as individuals for creating imagery that negatively affects the representation of the whole.

While the immediate response has been to criticize the artist, the situation is more complex than asking Nelly to stop making the kind of music he makes or to ask women to stop participating in the videos. After all, we live in a capitalist society that is quick to say "sex sells." This in no way, however, lets the artists off the hook, but raises questions about who is in a position to challenge the status quo and when. Nelly, though clearly in a position to choose what to write about or weigh in on the theme of a video, is still subject to an exploitative industry that cares more about selling millions of CDs than who is affected in the process of achieving this end. Quite simply, it seems that there is no financial incentive for rappers or so-called video vixens to change their negative behavior either. In the end, while individual black (and white) people profit from the degrading images that come to represent the whole of Black America, individuals get rich but communities remain marginalized.

However, some entertainers are trying to use the media to shift negative notions and show that "positive" images can sell too. Yet, even in camps that are supposedly creating positive images for the black community, the representation of black women still harkens back to traditional images. For example, what we hear most often from middle class Black America is a desire to return to the good old days of respectability. If women put their clothes back on; if men return to being the head of the household; if black people go to church, all our problems will be solved.

Tyler Perry's and Will Smith's projects, Daddy's Little Girls, Why Did I Get Married?, and The Pursuit of Happyness respectively, reflect their self-proclaimed agency to create the pictures they want and rewrite popular misunderstandings of black masculinity. However, in the process of creating these alternative "positive" representations of black male characters, stereotypes about black women are re-inscribed. Additionally, positive black masculinity in these films is equated with the black male character's ability to achieve the model nuclear family, be the primary breadwinner and have a middle class lifestyle. This goal is reached through the often violent reassertion of hierarchal gender roles. Black women are physically put back in their place or pushed out of the way by the black men in the narratives. Through these acts of masculine reassertion, violence against black women is made normal, comic, and necessary for the attainment of a "positive" black masculinity, further alienating black women from human rights claims in the real world. Furthermore, as black men align themselves with traditional western ideas of masculinity that position black women in a subordinate or dysfunctional role, the twisted notions behind white racism and sexism receive validation from the resulting construction of "bad black women" and "good black men".

The complexity and diversity of blackness and femininity remain illegible when the same recycled images are repeatedly thrust forward. My hope is that black folks make more of an effort to see the complexity that exists within our own communities and that we learn to embrace the multiple ways in which we inhabit the world both as men and women. I wish the media were able to reflect this diversity instead of continually reinforcing a monolithic blackness that constrains us all. Until then, performance artists like Sarah

Jones and Staceyann Chin remain peripheral to invocations of black poetry; Kimya Dawson and Hanifah Walidah don't have videos on BET and documentaries like AfroPunk, Paris is Burning, and No! remain unseen by large segments of our communities.

Having more images to choose from is helpful but is not a solution in itself. Beyond opening up space for different voices, we have to continue to challenge the images that assail our humanity as women and as black people. This means refusing to financially support the artists and entertainers who popularize degrading images of black women and continuing to hold them accountable for their actions. We must remain vigilant in our objections even when we are small in number. After all, who knew that a small group of determined students at a historically black college for women would force the hand of an internationally recognized rap star? This may be a long and difficult process, but in the meantime, we have to equip young folks with the tools to critically evaluate what they are seeing. If the images won't change fast enough, we must change how we think about the images. Black women...we are more powerful than we think and if we raise our voices together we can create the changes we want to see in how we are represented in the media.

Black Women's Hands Can Rock The World: Global Involvement and Understanding*

By Julianne Malveaux Ph.D

W hile globalization has been a reality since Christopher Columbus "discovered" America, or since people were snatched from their African homes and became our nation's foundational workforce and involuntary immigrants, the world's global economic intertwining is more pronounced now than it has ever been. The United States deploys military forces in 130 countries,[1] and much of our economic growth has been fueled by our ability to export goods and services to other countries. As the world's largest global power (our waning influence notwithstanding), our nation has the opportunity to and the possibility of influencing the realities of people all over the world. Our failure to fully engage in Darfur may well have, for example, continued a carnage that has cost thousands of lives. Our trade policies can improve or devastate economies in developing countries, even as we ourselves may be influenced by the changing role China plays in the world economy and the trade policies of that country (including the diversification of portfolio to include more euros and fewer dollars). In an increasingly complex global landscape, what role must African-American women play, and what linkages must we develop around the globe, especially with women of African descent? We are inextricably linked, and African-American women, as some of the most privileged women of African descent in the world, have an obligation to develop global understanding and maintain global involvement.

Global Awareness

Organizations like the TransAfrica Forum and Africa Action[2] have dedicated themselves to raising awareness, involvement, and understanding of issues facing the African continent and the Diaspora, with aggressive awareness campaigns. Indeed, TransAfrica is rooted in the Free South Africa movement, leading the fight to end apartheid in South Africa. It is among the organizations that continue the fight to empower African descendents around the world, making connections between Afro-descendents in Haiti, Venezuela, Cuba, and other countries, including those on the African continent. The challenge for organizations like TransAfrica is to make a case to a broad base of African-American people that their involvement in diasporan issue, by exerting influence on political leaders, making contributions to critical issues and organizations, and raising awareness through activism. Far too many African-American people feel that our policy plate overflows with domestic issues of social and economic justice. Yet there are compelling reasons why African-American women should attempt to "rock the world" for sisters around the globe.

Poverty. Half of the world lives on less than two dollars a day. More than 26,500 children die each day because of poverty.[3] According to President George W. Bush, "A world where some live in comfort and plenty, while half the human race lies on less than $2 a day is neither just nor stable."[4] Our awareness of distribution issues in the United States must extend to an awareness of distribution issues around the world, especially on the African continent, where GDP per capita is less than $750 in a majority of countries. An outgrowth of this poverty, especially on the African continent, is malnutrition, malaria and diseases associated with malnutrition. Additionally, the HIV/AIDS crisis that has devastated populations in parts of Africa is partly a result of the crippling poverty that people in some countries experience. As in the United States and other parts of the world, women and children are those most likely to experience poverty.

Debt. Irresponsible lending policies, and predatory repayment arrangements, cripple developing countries around the world. Some are forced to repay debt at the expense of investing in education or health systems, effectively crippling their country's development in the long run. Indeed, according to the Dakar Declaration, a n initiative that called for the total elimination of African and Third World debt, described debt and structural adjustment plans are the major reason for the erosion of health, education, nutrition, food security, environmental and social cultural values in developing countries. In addition to social and economic destabilization, excessive debt, which is partly a result of unreasonable repayment terms, causes a brain drain in developing countries and forces countries into unfair terms of trade. Indeed, the passage of the African Growth and Opportunity Act (AGOA) in 2000, and its subsequent modifications, inspired a slogan, "trade not aid". But trade will not eliminate debt or close gaps between developed and developing countries. The slogan really ought to be, "Trade, aid, and debt forgiveness". To the extent that uneven debt erodes social development, women and children are most likely affected by the economic injustice associated with excessive debt.

Environmental Devastation. Nobel Prize winner Wangari Maathai, who founded the Green Belt Movement in Kenya, pointed to the key role that African women play in caring for families and noted, in her Nobel Peace Prize acceptance speech, that women are "the first to become aware of environmental damage as resources become scarce and incapable of sustaining their families."[5] Responding to scarcities in firewood and clean drinking water, Maathai's Green Belt Movement has been responsible for planting more than 30 million trees in Kenya, improving both the environment and the employment situation for many women. Additionally, tree-planting activities raised questions and issues about democracy and peace because, says Maratha, "governance of the environment was impossible without democratic space." As the United States is challenged to address our disproportionate resource use, global warming and the abuse of our own environment, we should be motivated, encouraged, and indeed, galvanized by the work Wangari Maathai has done and use it as a template for our environmental activism.

The Condition of Education. Liberian President Ellen Johnson Sirleaf was elected in 2005 after more than two decades of political instability in that country. She faces high expectations, and has been the beneficiary of significant international support, yet she inherited an infrastructure shattered by war. One of the most pressing needs is for education, because when a woman is educated, so is a family. The Liberian Education Trust is one of the organizations that focus on restoring the educational infrastructure, and providing education to Liberian women.[6] The uphill battle that President Sirleaf has had to fight illustrates the carnage resulting from political instability on the

African continent, and is a cause for concern. In other countries, less war-rav-
aged than Liberia, parents often find education unaffordable because of the
high fees imposed by schools that are not fully supported by cash-poor governments. The opportunities for African-American women's involvement in
developing educational opportunities on the African continent are numerous
and have the potential to be life altering. Indeed, as we work to provide more
educational opportunities to African-American women in the United States,
we can use the same rationale to work for increased educational opportunities for women of African descent both on the African continent and in the
Diaspora. The International Foundation for Education and Self Help (IFESH),
founded by Dr. Leon Sullivan and now led by his daughter, Dr. Julie Sullivan
has provided aid, for 25 years, to sub Saharan Africa, focusing some of its
efforts on the educational enterprise.[7]

Political Instability. The Darfur region of western Sudan has been in the
news for five years, and, while many have condemned the carnage in that
country, these five years have been years of international inaction. To be
sure there have been protests here, pickets there, fundraising and awareness activities, but ever since the Janjaweed, a militia group, has killed hun-
dreds of thousands of civilians and terrorized as many as 2.5 million who
have been burned out of their homes. While an entire society has been
destabilized, the rape of women and the murder of children are among the
glaring atrocities in this conflict that seems at least partly land-based.
Hostilities in Darfur threaten to destabilize Chad and other parts of the
region, as countries neighboring the Sudan are harboring refuges, which
cause strain on their economic structure. Although the United Nations was
conducting peace talks and committed to sending troops in February 2008,
some rebel groups indicate unreadiness for peace talks. The conflict in
Darfur makes a strong case for black women's activism, and many have
been involved in some of the humanitarian efforts to bring relief to that part
of the Sudan. The carnage in Darfur is only one example of the effects of
political instability on the African continent. A disputed presidential election in Kenya in December 2007 has led to riots, looting, and violence.
Former UN Secretary Kofi Anan was negotiating a peace and political
power sharing agreement between rival political factions, but questions
have been raised about the stability of such a brokered peace and some of

the challenges from Darfur—with violence causing forced population shifts and neighboring countries absorbing refuges—are likely.

This list of compelling concerns is not meant to be exhaustive. Instead, it is intended to motivate understanding, interest, and involvement. African-American women have been involved in the global arena in small ways—such as building wells, adopting villages, and supporting humanitarian causes. We have also been involved in large and official ways, with women like career Foreign Service officer Robin Renee Sanders serving as ambassador to Nigeria, and women like Constance Berry Newman serving (2004-2005) as Assistant Secretary of State for Africa and Assistant Administrator for the US Agency for International Development. The pinnacle of our global involvement has been the State Department leadership of Dr. Condoleezza Rice. In promoting Bush administration policies during a time of global conflict, Dr. Rice's leadership has been controversial, especially among African Americans. Still, there is no denying her historic achievement as the first African-American woman to lead the State Department. African-American women also work in the nongovernmental sector on global issues, including women like Dr. Helene Gayle, who heads CARE, the international anti-poverty organization, and Gay McDougall, who led Global Rights, an international human rights advocacy group, from 1994 to 2007. These women's work should inspire us all to embrace global issues and, yes, to rock the world.

*"Black Women's Hands Can Rock the World" was the program theme for the National Association of Negro Business and Professional Women's Clubs, Inc. from 1995-1999.

NOTES

[1] www.globalsecurity.org/military/ops/global-deployments.htm

[2] TransAfrica and Africa Action are among the DC based activist organizations that raise awareness around African and diasporic issues. Their websites are www.transafricaforum.org and www.africaaction.org.

[3] Anup Shah, Poverty Facts and Stats, Global Issues, November 24, 2006. www.globalissues.org.

[4] New York Times Quote of the Day, July 18, 2001

[5] Wangari Maathai, Nobel Peace Prize Acceptance Speech, December 10, 2004

[6] Founded in 2006, the Liberian Education Trust is a project of the Phelps Stokes Fund. In full disclosure, I served as a member of its Board of Advisors. More information can be found at www.liberianeducationtrust.org

[7] Rev. Leon Sullivan, author of the "Sullivan Principles" of corporate engagement with African founded, was a leader in African-American engagement with the African continent. He also founded the African/African-American summit, which encourages economic ties between Africans and African Americans. Information on IFESH is available at www.ifesh.org

Women's Voices, Women's Power

by Stephanie J. Jones, J.D.

Children, I come back today
To tell you a story of the long dark way
That I had to climb, that I had to know
*In order that the race might live and grow.**

Since eternity's birth, our mothers' voices have soothed, scolded, taught, warned, guided and prodded us to do a little bit better than we thought we could and to travel just a little bit further than we imagined we'd ever go.

Our sisters' voices have sustained and encouraged us, shielding us from the bitter winds of the world like a warm, familiar, favorite cloak.

And our daughters' voices—so new and still untested, individual as snowflakes yet uncannily reminiscent of our own—remind us why we do it at all.

This edition of the *State of Black America: In the Black Woman's Voice* channels and conveys this multidimensional, intergenerational, indestructible power of the black woman's voice. Originally conceived as a companion piece to last year's *State of Black America 2007: Portrait of the Black Male,* this year's book—like the women who inspired and created it—developed its own unique personality and, ironically, found its own collective voice, separate from, yet complimentary to, its Male counterpart.

While the burdens that black women bear may not seem as dire as those facing African-American men—captured in *Portrait of the Black Male*—we nevertheless deal consistently with unique and serious challenges of our own. These challenges are all-too-often swept aside or outright ignored—perhaps because women often handle them quietly, under the radar, behind the "indomitable black woman" façade/stereotype/trap, subordinating our concerns to the alarming problems facing our black men. But just as we have learned, in the case of emergency, to don our own oxygen mask first before we assist anyone else while traveling by air, we must empower ourselves before we can empower those around us on our life journey.

But God put a song and a prayer in my mouth.
God put a dream like steel in my soul.
Now, through my children, I'm reaching the goal.

The National Urban League hopes that by presenting issues facing black women—and all African Americans—through the lens and voices of black women, we offer a helpful collage of perspectives, assessments and opinions that reflect the diversity, intelligence and depth of black women in all walks of American life. But we don't only present these issues, we offer real solutions through our *Opportunity Compact*. We are enormously grateful for the remarkable women who have contributed to this effort, from our noble movement mother Dr. Dorothy I. Height, who still guides our steps on the path that she paved, to our dynamic and gifted guest editor, Dr. Julianne Malveaux, whose love and leadership helps light the way, to Tiffany Lindsay and Moya Bailey, committed carriers of courage just starting their journey, to each of the other women who have poured their hearts, minds and voices into this book. Thanks to all of them, and the other women and men who participated in this project, *The State of Black America: In the Black Woman's Voice* is a painstakingly researched yet uniquely inspirational reference tool for anyone seeking a deeper understanding of the issues, challenges, successes and beauty of the African-American woman and the communities she graces. .

Make of my past a road to the light
Out of the darkness, the ignorance, the night . . .
But march ever forward, breaking down bars.
Look ever upward at the sun and the stars.

February 2008

*From "The Negro Mother" by Langston Hughes

In Memoriam

Effi Barry

Effi Barry was a former First Lady of the District of Columbia and a former wife of Marion Barry, past mayor of the District and a current D.C. city councilman.

She was born Effi Slaughter in Toledo, OH, in 1944 and was raised by a single mother in a middle-class area of the city. She later attended Hampton Institute (later renamed Hampton University) in Virginia, where she received a bachelor's degree in home economics. Upon graduating from Hampton, she relocated to New York City and worked as a flight attendant and a high school teacher. She earned a master's degree in public health from City College of New York and also married her high school sweetheart Stanley Cowell, a professional jazz musician. However, their marriage ended in divorce, and during the mid-1970s, she moved to Washington, D.C.

Shortly after relocating to the Nation's Capital in 1976, she began working for the city as a restaurant inspector; soon thereafter, she met Marion Barry, a prominent District politician. The two were married in 1978, and during the same year, Barry also was elected mayor of Washington. As only the second elected mayor of the District, Barry held the office for three consecutive terms.

During her early days as First Lady of the District, she was initially ostracized by some within D.C.'s black establishment because of her inexperience in civil rights activism and her reserved and, what some perceived, "bourgeois" demeanor. However, she would later earn widespread respect for her tireless work in AIDS/HIV awareness campaigns in the District. Her husband Marion also maintained that she was instrumental in securing funding for AIDS awareness programs for the District's impoverished residents.

Public reverence for her further increased during the early 1990s, while her husband Marion, still mayor of the District, was standing trial on federal charges of perjury and drug possession. She impressed many with the stoicism and loyalty she displayed throughout his trial, despite repeated nationwide airings of a videotape depicting his use of illicit drugs and philandering.

Yet the marriage ended in divorce in 1993, and she returned to Hampton University, her alma mater, where she taught health classes for the next 11 years. She returned to Washington in 2004, and although still estranged from her husband Marion, she publicly supported him in his successful campaign for a seat on the District's city council.

However, in 2006 Effi Barry was diagnosed with acute myeloid leukemia. Despite being afflicted with the potentially fatal disease, she courageously used the plight of her condition to call attention to the illness—a rare form of leukemia—and encourage more African Americans to join the registry for bone-marrow transplants. Unfortunately, she succumbed to the disease on September 5, 2007, at the age of 63.

Jane Bolin

Jane Bolin was a female legal pioneer who became the first African-American woman to be appointed a judge in the U.S. judicial system. In addition, she was the first black women to graduate from Yale Law School and the first African-American woman to join the New York City Bar Association.

Jane Matilda Bolin was born in Poughkeepsie, N.Y. on April 11, 1908. Her father, Gaius Bolin, was also a lawyer and the first black student to graduate from Willams College in Williamstown, Mass. She often remarked that he was her greatest inspiration in pursing a legal career.

She attended Wellesley College where she encountered numerous instances of bigotry and discrimination. As only one of the two black students in her class, she was often rebuffed by white classmates and only allowed to share rooming accommodations with the other black student of the college.

Despite being an excellent student and achieving the status of Wellesley Scholar, an honor given to the top 20 students in the senior class, her guidance counselor tried to dissuade her from applying to law school, saying that a career in law was an unrealistic endeavor for a black woman. Nevertheless, Bolin applied to Yale Law School and was accepted in 1928. At the time, she was the institution's only black student.

After her graduation in 1931, she returned to Poughkeepsie and worked as a law clerk for her father. Soon thereafter, she started a legal practice in New York with another attorney, Ralph Mizelle, who would later become her first husband. Six years later, she accepted a position in the New York City corporation counsel's office as assistant corporation counsel and was assigned to the Domestic Relations Court. She made history on July 22, 1939, when New York City Mayor, Fiorello LaGuardia, appointed her as a judge of the court.

As a judge, Bolin used her authority to eliminate discriminatory practices in New York City's child welfare system. She ended the assignment of probation officers to families based on race and abolished segregation in child placement facilities. She was also instrumental in desegregating New York City treatment centers for male juvenile delinquents. Subsequent New York City mayors renewed her appointments three times, and she served on the bench of the Domestic Relations Court for 40 years. However, she left the court in 1979 when she reached the age of 70, the state's mandatory age for retirement.

Upon her retirement from New York's City judicial system, she became a volunteer reading instructor in the New York City public school system and also served on the Regents Review Committee of the New York Board of Regents. She passed way on January 8, 2007, at the age of 98.

Daniel A. Collins

Dr. Daniel A. Collins was the first African-American dentistry professor of the University of California at San Francisco and founder of the Bay Area Urban League. He was also the first African American to serve on the California State Board of Education.

He was a graduate of Paine College in Augusta, Ga., and in 1941, he earned his D.D.S. at Meharry Medical College in Nashville, TN. In addition to having a successful dental practice for 33 years, he was also an instructor and assistant professor at the University of California at San Francisco School of Dentistry, where he earned his master's degree. He also served on the board of directors of the San Francisco Dental Society and as a trustee of the American Fund for Dental Education.

In 1946, Dr. Collins founded the San Francisco Chapter of the Urban League, later to be re-named the Bay Area Urban League. In 1965, he became a board member of the National Urban League, where he served for 12 years and later served as vice chairman from 1973 to 1975. During his tenure at the San Francisco affiliate and the national office of the Urban League, he was instrumental in numerous fundraising activities. In recognition for his contributions and tireless work, the National Urban League awarded him the Whitney M. Young Medallion in 1989.

Collins and his wife were also the co-founders of Marin Aid to Retarded Children, now called Lifehouse, a counseling facility for developmentally challenged individuals and also played an integral role in the passage of the Lanterman Developmental Disabilities Services Act of 1969.

Dr. Daniel A. Collins died on September 13, 2007, at the age of 91.

Oliver Hill

Oliver Hill was a prominent civil rights attorney who played an integral role in ending segregation and making discrimination illegal. He was founder of the Virginia chapter of the NAACP, and his legal team won numerous civil rights cases with respect to voting rights, employment rights and jury selection in the state. In 1949, he became the first African American since reconstruction to serve on the city council of Richmond, Va.

Oliver White Hill was born in Richmond, Va., on May 1, 1907. His family later moved to Washington, D.C., and Hill attended Howard University Law School. He graduated in 1933, second in his class behind future Supreme Court Justice Thurgood Marshall. Marshall and Hill became part of the NAACP Legal Defense and Education Fund and worked together on numerous civil rights cases throughout their legal careers. They remained close friends until Marshall's death in 1993.

In 1940, Hill won his first civil rights case, Alston v. School Board of Norfolk, Va., which ordered equal pay for black and white teachers. From the early 1940s through the early 1960s, he headed the Virginia legal team of the NAACP. During the era of segregation, it was said that Hill and his legal team filed more civil rights cases in the state of Virginia than were filed in any other state in the South.

In 1951, Hill argued a civil rights case on the behalf of black students' complaints of deplorable conditions in a Farmville, Va. school. The case would later become one of the five cases the NAACP Legal Defense and Education Fund used in the 1954 landmark Brown v Board of Education Supreme Court case, which ruled that segregation in schools was unconstitutional.

Hill received numerous honors and awards, in recognition of his outstanding accomplishments. In 1959, National Bar Association National Bar Association honored him with the "Lawyer of the Year Award," and he also received the American Bar Association Justice "Thurgood Marshall Award" in 1993. And in 1999, President William Clinton awarded Hill the Presidential Medal of Freedom, the nation's most prestigious honor.

In 2005, a newly constructed building in Virginia's Capitol Square was named after him, making him the first African American in the state to be bestowed with such an honor. Also during that year, Hill received the Spingarn Award for distinguished achievement from the NAACP. Oliver White Hill died on August 5, 2007, at the age of 100.

Yolanda King

Yolanda King, the eldest child of the Rev. Dr. Martin Luther King, Jr., was a human rights activist, motivational speaker, and an accomplished actress and playwright. She devoted her life to the pursuit of his ideals for social equality through both her work in civil rights activism and her theatrical talents.

Yolanda, or more affectionately known by family members and friends as "Yoki," was born on November 17, 1955, in Montgomery, Ala., and was ingrained into the civil rights movement from birth. Less than two weeks after she was born, Rosa Parks made her defiant refusal to give her seat to a white bus passenger, an incident that spawned the historic Montgomery bus boycott. About two months later, Yolanda and her mother miraculously escaped injury after racists had firebombed their family house in Montgomery.

She was only 12 years-old when her father was assassinated in 1968 and learned of the tragic event by watching a news bulletin on television. On year after the assassination, Yolanda and her younger siblings assisted their mother, Coretta, in continuing Dr. King's civil rights work through the finding of the Martin Luther King Jr. Center for Nonviolent Social Change. As an adult, she would become an organizational board director and the founding director of the King Center's cultural affairs program.

In addition to her interest in human rights activism, which she showed at an early age, Yolanda also displayed a strong interest in theatrical drama. She wrote her first play at the age of eight and began taking acting lessons a year later. During her years in college, she performed in numerous stage plays. In addition to earning a bachelor's of arts degree from Smith College in Northampton, Mass., she earned a master's degree in theatre from New York University.

During her career as a film actress, she portrayed prominent figures from the civil rights movement. In her first film role in 1978, Yolanda played Rosa Parks in a made-for-TV movie entitled King, a biographical account of her father. Three years later, she co-starred in the film Death of a Prophet, portraying Malcolm X's widow Betty Shabazz.

Interestingly, Yolanda's work as actress also linked her with two other daughters of slain civil rights leaders. In the mid 1980s, she co-founded Nucleus, a performing arts company, with Attallah Shabazz, the eldest daughter of Malcolm X. Also, she portrayed Reena Evers, daughter of Megar Evers, in the 1996 movie Ghosts of Mississippi.

She died on May 15, 2007, at the home of a family friend in Santa Monica, Calif. Family members speculated that a heart ailment may have been the cause of her death. She was 51 years-old.

Calvin Lockhart

Calvin Lockhart had an illustrious acting career in which he played a variety of roles on stage and film across the world. During his career, the handsome Bahamian actor was cast in over two dozen movies and made numerous appearances on television shows in both the United States and Europe. However, he is probably best known for his villainous roles in "blaxploitation" movies of the 1970s.

He was born Bert Cooper in 1934 in Nassau, Bahamas and was the youngest of eight children. He moved to New York City at the age of eighteen to study civil engineering at the Cooper Union School of Engineering, but he dropped out after one year, as his passions shifted to acting. In 1960, he was cast in the Ketti Frings play, Cool World, which was followed by a role in a short-lived Broadway play, Taste of Honey, playing opposite of Angela Lansbruy in a story about an interracial relationship. It was also in and around this time that he changed his name to Calvin Lockhart.

However, during the early 1960s, acting opportunities were still very limited for blacks in the United States, on both stage and film. By the mid-sixties, Lockhart relocated across seas to London, where he found work in the theatre and also appeared in several British television shows. It was also there where he made his film debut in a starring role in the 1968 movie Joanna, which received critical acclaim and was nominated for a 1969 Golden Globe Award for best foreign picture.

Lockhart returned back to the United States in 1969 and found prominent roles in films, with the sudden emergence of African-American movies in Hollywood during the early 1970s. Although this revolutionary period of black filmmaking is known today in retrospect, and somewhat deprecatingly, as "blaxploitation," the film era did, however, mark a turning point in which African Americans were portrayed in a more intelligent and assertive manner than the passive and submissive images Hollywood had traditionally depicted. During the seventies, Lockhart starred in several box-office hits of the genre, including Cotton Comes To Harlem, Uptown Saturday Night and Let's Do It Again.

However, by the seventies as the blaxpliotation era began to wane, so too did Lockhart's work as a Hollywood actor. During the 1980s, his roles in movies and on television were minor and sporadic, occasionally making guest appearances on the eighties' TV series Dynasty and playing a cameo role in the 1987 movie Coming to America, starring Eddie Murphy.

During the mid-1990s, Lockhart returned to his homeland, Nassua, Bahmas, where he worked as a director for the Freeport Players Guild and married for the fourth time. But on March 29, 2007, he passed away at the age of 72 from complications of a stroke.

In an effort to honor and preserve his legacy, his family has planned to establish a scholarship fund bearing his name to assist young Bahamians interested in studying acting and/or filmmaking.

Mahlon Puryear

Mahlon Puryear was a senior staff member with the National Urban League who for decades played a significant role in organizing activities, particularly with respect to the League's efforts to enhance job opportunities for African Americans.

Mahlon Puryear was born January 27, 1915, in Winston Salem, NC. Puryear was only 14 years old when he graduated from Columbian Heights High School in 1930. He received his bachelor's degree from Hampton Institute (later re-named Hampton University) in 1942 and earned a master's degree from Columbia University Teachers College in 1948.

He joined the National Urban League in 1940 the associate director of the League's Southern Regional Office and held 25 different titles during his tenure. Puryear relocated to the League's New York offices in 1962, and in 1972, he was Director of the Economic Development Department, overseeing a budget of more than $30 million. In addition, Puryear opened new Urban League affiliates in Charlotte, NC, and Orange County, Cali. during the early eighties.

Puryear also had an integral role in establishing the league's Labor Education Advancement Program (LEAP), which for years placed thousands of workers in trade occupations. During the 1970s, Puryear also oversaw the Urban Leagues' New Skills Bank, which found jobs for highly skilled workers at an estimated rate of 60,000 jobs per year. In addition, Puryear was highly instrumental in orchestrating career placement seminars at Historical Black Colleges and Universities (HBCU), in an effort to find employment for recent African-American college graduates.

From 1997 to 2004, he served as both president and historian for the National Urban League's Quarter Century Club, and he was a recipient of both the Whitney M. Young Medallion and the Ann Tanneyhill Award, two of the Urban League's most prestigious honors.

He died on September 26, 2007. He was 92 years old.

Max Roach

Max Roach was an innovative jazz drummer and a significant pioneer in the development of bebop, a predominant musical form of modern jazz. Many musical experts contend that he redefined the manner in which jazz drums were played and was a major catalyst in making jazz drumming more sophisticated.

Maxwell Roach was born in Newland, N.C., on January 10, 1924. His family relocated to Brooklyn, N.Y when Roach was four, and at the age of 12, he took up playing the drums.

By the time he was 16, he was studying music composition at the Manhattan School of Music and sitting in on drums with Duke Ellington's orchestra. By the mid 1940s, and still in his teens, Roach was playing drums with Jazz legends Charlie Parker, Miles Davis and Dizzy Gillespie in Harlem night clubs.

During the 1940s, Roach, along with Kenny Clarke, another groundbreaking jazz drummer, created a revolutionary concept of musical time by playing the beat-by-beat pulse of standard 4/4 time on the "ride" cymbal, instead of on the bass drum. In doing so, Roach and Clarke developed an unprecedented drumming style that enabled drum soloists to play more freely. The innovative style became the standard method of modern jazz drumming, which persists to this day. As opposed to constantly playing of the traditional 4/4 time, Roach also revolutionized jazz drumming by experimenting with waltz time and other unorthodox meters.

During the 1950s, he formed a quintet with trumpet legend Clifford Brown, where the young jazz musicians developed a well-received musical derivative of jazz bebop, known as "hard bop." Although the quintet was extremely popular in the jazz clubs of New York City in the 1950s, Brown's untimely death in a car accident in 1956 led to its demise.

In 1960, Roach collaborated with lyricist Oscar Brown and vocalist Abbey Lincoln, whom Roach would later marry, to record *We Insist!— Max Roach's Freedom Now Suite,* a jazz album entailing musical themes about the freedom struggle for blacks in Africa and the United States. Though not a commercial success, the album was a timely statement that coincided with the burgeoning civil right movement of the 1960s.

In 1972, Roach taught Jazz at the University of Massachusetts and toured the country as music lecturer. In later years, he formed a jazz group M'Boom Re: Percussion,' a 10-piece drum ensemble, and worked with avant-garde musicians Cecil Taylor, Anthony Braxton and Archie Shepp. He also performed outside of the Jazz genre by playing drums with symphony orchestras and Japanese musicians. In early the 1980s, he even tried his hand at hip hop music, performing at a concert with rapper Fab Five Freddy and the New York Break Dancers.

He died at his home in New York City on April 16, 2007, at the age of 83.

Eddie Robinson

The legendary Eddie Robinson was the first college football coach in the history of the NCAA to win more than 400 games, and at the time of his retirement in 1997, was the all-time winningest coach in college football. During his coaching career at Grambling State University, he won 408 games and compiled an astounding winning percentage of .707 during his illustrious tenure.

Edward Robinson was born on February 13, 1919, in Jackson, La.. He attended Leland College in Baker, La., where he starred as a quarterback on the football team and received a bachelor's degree in English in 1941. Soon after graduating from Leland, he accepted a job to coach football at the Louisiana. Negro Normal and Industrial Institute, which was later renamed Grambling State University in 1946.

Despite having no paid coaching staff and only meager facilities and equipment for his players when he first became head coach, Robinson transformed the football team into a perennial winner. In just his second season coaching at the college in 1943, his football team amassed an unde-feated record of 9-0 and subsequently had six consecutive non-losing sea-sons. He had 45 winning seasons during his 57-year coaching career at Grambling and won nine national championships and 17 Southwestern Athletic Conference titles.

Robinson also sent over 200 players into professional football, including NFL hall of famers Willie Brown, Charlie Joiner, Willie Davis and the first black college player in the NFL, Tank Younger. In addition, two players he coached—James Harris and Doug Williams—became groundbreaking black quarterbacks in the NFL. In 1971, forty-three players in NFL training camps were from Grambling University, a record that still stands to this day.

In view of this tremendous success, some misperceived Grambling as a "football factory," or a training farm for professional football prospects. But throughout his coaching career, Robinson, a one-time educator himself, placed a higher priority on academics than athletics. In addition to his numer-ous accomplishments as a football coach, he took great pride in the fact that over 80 percent of his players graduated from the university.

In 1997, the year he retired, he was inducted in the College Football Hall of Fame. In honor and recognition of his legendary achievements, the Football Writers' Association of America annually gives the "Eddie Robinson Coach of the Year" award to the best football coach in Division I-A college football. Coach Robinson died on April 3, 2007, at the age of 88.

William Simms

William Simms worked with the Urban League for 25 years, most of which was served as a director of development. By initiating the League's first national fundraising campaign, he played a pivotal role in substantially increasing funding for the organization during his tenure.

He was born on January 23, 1914. Upon serving in the U.S. Army in World War II, he became the director of public relations for the American Council on Race Relations in Chicago. Soon thereafter in the late 1940s, he became one of the first African-Americans to work in sales for the Pepsi Company, in a marketing campaign aimed at promoting the soft drink to the African-American community.

In 1949, Simms accepted a position to work for the New York City Urban League as a public affairs officer, and six years later, he became the assistant director of the Urban League Fund at the national office. Using his extensive background in public relations and marketing, Simms helped raise millions of dollars for the National Urban League through national fundraisers. In recognition of his accomplishments, he was awarded the Whitney M. Young Medallion in 1992.

After his retirement from the Urban League, Simms became a fundraising consultant for Tuskegee Institute's Centennial Program and through the sponsorship of the Lily Foundation, he also served as a mentor to young professionals embarking on careers in fundraising. He was also a co-founder of the Association of Fundraising Professionals, an organization that sets the professional standards for best practices in fundraising.

William Simms passed away on December 17, 2007, at the age of 94.

Darryl Stingley

Darryl Stingley was an NFL wide receiver for the New England Patriots during the 1970s who tragically suffered a permanent paralyzing injury during an NFL exhibition game in 1978. The incident, one of the darkest moments in the history of the NFL, spurred controversy about excessive violence in the sport, and many also believe that it was a forerunner for the implementation of rule changes enacted to make the game much safer.

Darryl Stingley was born on September 18, 1951, in Chicago, IL. Reared in impoverished conditions on Chicago's West Side, Stingley demonstrated exceptional athletic ability as a youth. He was a standout running back at John Marshall High School, and in his senior year, a local Chicago newspaper named him "Schoolboy Athlete of the Year." He accepted a football scholarship to Purdue University, where he had a stellar career as wide receiver and broke several school records in receiving. In 1973, he was a first-round draft choice of the New England Patriots and played his entire five-year career with the team. During his brief NFL tenure, he was considered to be one of the league's premier receivers.

However, fate took a cruel turn for the worse for the 26-year-old professional athlete during an exhibition game with the Oakland Raiders on August 12, 1978. During the game, Stingley leaped into the air in a futile attempt to catch a pass. Although the pass was overthrown, making it impossible for Stingley to make a reception, Raider safety Jack Tatum delivered a vicious helmet-to-helmet hit on the receiver. The devastating blow fractured two of the young receiver's vertebrae, permanently paralyzing his body from the neck down.

Yet despite having to live as a quadriplegic, Stingley went on to lead a highly productive life and never harbored bitterness about his condition. A few years after the accident and his subsequent stint in physical rehabilitation, he co-authored a memoir entitled, Happy to Be Alive, in which he explained how he learned to overcome both the physical and mental challenges of living with quadriplegia. He also became a prominent speaker on the issue of wanton violence in the NFL and called on league officials to take measures to curb unnecessary roughness in the sport. And in 1991, he founded the Darryl Stingley Foundation, an organization geared to providing guidance to disadvantaged youth on the west side of Chicago.

He died suddenly at his home in Chicago on April 5, 2007, at the age of 55. A later autopsy revealed that his death was the result of medical complications stemming from quadriplegia and pneumonia.

During his life, he had come to symbolize, to some, the dangerous risk involved in the play of an intensely brutal and violent sport. But to many, he will probably be best remembered for the immense strength of character and courage he displayed in the wake of extreme adversity.

Ike Turner

Ike Turner was best known as part of the legendary singing duo, Ike & Tina Turner. Despite a less-than flattering portrayal of him in the film, *What's Love Gotta Do With It?*," a biographical account of his former wife, Tina, that depicted disturbing instances of spousal abuse, he was widely respected for his talents as a musician and is regarded as one of R&B/rock music's most significant pioneers. Some music authorities, in fact, assert that his band's recording of the song "Rocket 88" in 1951, credited to Turner's sax player, Jackie Brenston, may have been the first rock-n-roll song ever recorded.

Born on November 5, 1931, Turner learned piano and guitar as a youngster and eventually became a highly demanded studio session musician, backing up blues greats, such as B.B. King, Elmore James, Howlin' Wolf, and Otis Rush. In his late teens, he formed a band called the Kings of Rhythm that became popular at clubs in cities and towns along the Mississippi River.

In 1956, while playing at a club date in St. Louis, Turner met a young teenage girl named Anna Mae Bullock, whom he made the lead singer of his band. He changed her name to Tina and renamed his band the "Ike & Tina Turner Revue." Throughout the early1960s, the husband-wife singing duo played in clubs, concert halls and on the "chitlin' circuit." The duo and their high-energy band eventually attained international fame in the early 1970s, scoring hits with covers of rock songs, such as the Beatles' "Come Together," Sly Stone's "I Want to Take You Higher" and "Proud Mary."

The couple divorced in 1975, and Ike and Tina moved into opposite directions, both personally and professionally. During the 1980s, as Tina was achieving astounding worldwide success as a solo artist, both Ike's personal life and musical career, in contrast, went into a downward spiral. Turner continued to struggle with drugs and served a prison term for drug possession. During his incarceration, Ike and Tina Turner were inducted into the Rock and Roll Hall of Fame, with Tina accepting the award on her former husband's behalf.

After his release from jail in 1991, Turner resumed his music career by performing at concerts and recording songs with other artists. During the final years of his life, he returned to his blues-music roots, where, fittingly enough, he would receive his greatest success and recognition as a solo artist. In 2007, his album "Risin' with the Blues" won a Grammy Award for best traditional blues album.

Ike Turner died at the age of 76 in San Diego, CA, on December 12, 2007 from a cocaine overdose.

About the Authors

Kimberley Alton, J.D.

Kimberly Alton is the public policy counsel at the Lawyers' Committee for Civil Rights Under Law where she monitors numerous civil rights issues at the federal and state level. She served in the Clinton Administration as a special assistant to the staff director at the U.S. Commission on Civil Rights. She was previously deputy chief of staff to U.S.. Representative Eddie Bernice Johnson.

Moya Bailey

Moya Bailey is a third year Fellow in Women's Studies at Emory University, where her research is focused on health care disparities in marginalized groups. She received her undergraduate degree in Women's Studies with a concentration in Health from Spelman College and also served as President of the Feminist Majority Leadership Alliance.

Doris Browne, M.D., M.P.H.

Dr. Doris Browne is president and CEO of Browne and Associates, Inc., a health consultancy company. She manages diversified health programs, including women's health, breast and prostate cancers, and HIV/AIDS, with an emphasis on health promotion and disease prevention.

Melanie L. Campbell

Melanie Campbell is the CEO and executive director of the National Coalition on Black Civic Participation. Ms. Campbell is a highly regarded authority on voting rights and coalition building and spearheaded such coalition projects as the Unity Civic Engagement & Voter Empowerment Campaign and the award-winning Black Youth Voted development program.

Johnnetta B. Cole, Ph.D.

Dr. Johnnetta Cole is president emerita of both Bennett College for Women and Spelman College, the only two exclusively black female colleges in the United States. She is also a prominent speaker, lecturing on issues pertaining to justice, diversity, and the health and safety of women. She currently chairs the Johnnetta B. Cole Global Diversity & Inclusion Institute at Bennett College for Women.

Maudine R. Cooper

Maudine Cooper is president and CEO of the Greater Washington Urban League, an affiliate of the National Urban League. She was formerly chief of staff of the executive office of the mayor in the District of Columbia and headed the District's Minority Business Opportunity Commission. She previously served as director of the National Urban League's Washington Operations (now known as the National Urban League Policy Institute).

Renee R. Hanson

Renee Hanson is a resident scholar at the National Urban League Policy Institute, where she focuses on sociological issues, such as education, children and poverty. She received her Master of Arts degree in Sociology from American University.

Andrea Harris

Andrea Harris is the president and co-founder of the North Carolina Institute for Minority Economic Development. As president, she directs the Institute staff in the development of project and programs that remain consistent with the organization's mission and purpose. Ms. Harris is a graduate of Bennett College, and sits on numerous boards and commissions.

Alexis Herman

Alexis Herman was the first African American to serve as U.S. Secretary of Labor and also served as director of the Labor Department's Women's Bureau, the youngest person ever to hold the position. She is currently a board member of numerous organizations, including the National Urban League, Coca-Cola, MGM and Toyota.

Stephanie J. Jones, J.D.

Stephanie Jones is the executive director of the National Urban League's Policy Institute and is also editor-in-chief of the organization's two flagship publications—the Opportunity Journal magazine and the State of Black America report. She previously served as chief counsel to former North Carolina Sen. John Edwards and in the Clinton Administration as secretary's regional representative in the U.S. Department of Education.

Julianne Malveaux, Ph.D.

Dr. Julianne Malveaux is president of the Bennett College for Women in Greensboro, North Carolina. She is also a syndicated columnist and an accomplished editor, and her edited works include Voices of Vision: African-American Women on the Issues and Slipping Through the Cracks: The Status of Black Women.

Lisa Mensah

Lisa Mensah is the executive director of the Aspen Institute's Initiative on Financial Security and is a leading authority on economic improvement measures for the impoverished and working class. She is a former deputy director of economic development for the Ford Foundation, where she oversaw issues pertaining to microfinance and economic development for women.

Lucy Reuben, Ph.D.

Dr. Lucy Reuben is a noted lecturer, author and consultant on issues of financial management, including black economic development. She was a former provost at North Carolina Central University and a past dean of the South Carolina State University School of Business.

Susan L. Taylor

Susan Taylor is the founder and director of Essence Cares national mentoring movement. She is the editorial director of Essence magazine and author of the magazine's popular monthly column, "In the Spirit." In addition, she is the author of several books, including In the Spirit: The Inspirational Writings of Susan L. Taylor, and is the first African-American woman to receive the "Henry Johnson Fisher Award" from the Magazine Publishers of America.

Valerie R. Wilson, Ph.D.

Dr. Valerie Rawlston Wilson is Senior Resident Scholar at the National Urban League Policy Institute where she is responsible for directing the Policy Institute's research agenda. Her research focuses on labor economics, economics of higher education, poverty and discrimination. She serves on the National Urban League President's Council of Economic Advisers.

Index of Authors and Articles 1987–2008

In 1987, the National Urban League began publishing *The State of Black America* in a smaller, typeset format. By so doing, it became easier to catalog and archive the various essays by author and article name.

The 2008 edition of *The State of Black America* is the fourteenth to contain an index of the authors and articles that have appeared since 1987. The articles have been divided by topic and are listed in the alphabetical order of their authors' names.

Reprints of the articles catalogued herein are available through the National Urban League, 120 Wall Street, New York, New York 10005; 212/558-5316.

Affirmative Action

Arnwine, Barbara R., "The Battle Over Affirmative Action: Legal Challenges and Outlook," **2007**, pp. 159-172.

Special Section. "Affirmative Action/National Urban League Columns and Amici Brief on the Michigan Case," **2003**, pp. 225–268.

Afterword

Daniels, Lee A., "Praising the Mutilated World," **2002**, pp. 181–188.

Jones, Stephanie J., "Women's Voices, Women's Power," **2008**, pp. 203–204.

AIDS

Rockeymoore, Maya, "AIDS in Black America and the World," **2002**, pp. 123–146.

An Appreciation

National Urban League, "Ossie Davis: Still Caught in the Dream," **2005**, pp. 137-138.

Jones, Stephanie J., "Rosa Parks: An Ordinary Woman, An Extraordinary Life," **2006**, pp. 245-246.

Black Males

Bell, William C., "How are the Children? Foster Care and African-American Boys," **2007**, pp. 151-157.

Carnethon, Mercedes R., "Black Male Life Expectancy in the United States: A Multi-level Exploration of Causes," **2007**, pp. 137-150.

Dyson, Eric Michael, "Sexual Fault Lines: Robbing the Love Between Us," **2007**, pp. 229-237.

Hanson, Renee, Mark McArdle, and Valerie Rawlston Wilson, "Invisible Men: The Urgent Problems of Low-Income African-American Males," **2007**, pp. 209-216.

Holzer, Harry J., "Reconnecting Young Black Men: What Policies Would Help," **2007**, pp. 75-87.

Johns, David J., "Re-imagining Black Masculine Identity: An Investigation of the 'Problem' Surrounding the Construction of Black Masculinity in America," **2007**, pp. 59-73.

Lanier, James R., "The Empowerment Movement and the Black Male," **2004**, pp. 143–148.

———, "The National Urban League's Commission on the Black Male: Renewal, Revival and Resurrection Feasibility and Strategic Planning Study," **2005**, pp. 107–109.

Morial, Marc H., "Empowering Black Males to Reach Their Full Potential," **2007**, pp. 13-15.

Reed, James, and Aaron Thomas, The National Urban League: The National Urban League: Empowering Black Males to Reach Their Full Potential, **2007**, pp. 217-218.

Rodgers III, William, M., "Why Should African Americans Care About Macroeconomic Policy," **2007**, pp. 89-103.

Wilson, Valerie Rawlston, "On Equal Ground: Causes and Solutions for Lower College Completion Rates Among Black Males," **2007**, pp. 123-135.

Business

Emerson, Melinda F., "Five Things You Must Have to Run a Successful Business," **2004**, pp. 153–156.

Glasgow, Douglas G., "The Black Underclass in Perspective," **1987**, pp. 129–144.

Henderson, Lenneal J., "Empowerment through Enterprise: African-American Business Development," **1993**, pp. 91–108.

Price, Hugh B., "Beacons in a New Millennium: Reflections on 21st-Century Leaders and Leadership," **2000**, pp. 13–39.

Tidwell, Billy J., "Black Wealth: Facts and Fiction," **1988**, pp. 193–210.

Turner, Mark D., "Escaping the 'Ghetto' of Subcontracting," **2006**, pp. 117–131.

Walker, Juliet E.K., "The Future of Black Business in America: Can It Get Out of the Box?," **2000**, pp. 199–226.

Children and Youth

Bell, William C., "How are the Children? Foster Care and African-American Boys," **2007,** pp. 151-157.

Comer, James P., "Leave No Child Behind: Preparing Today's Youth for Tomorrow's World," **2005**, pp. 75–84.

Cox, Kenya L. Covington, "The Childcare Imbalance: Impact on Working Opportunities for Poor Mothers," **2003**, pp.197–224d.

Edelman, Marian Wright, "The State of Our Children," **2006**, pp. 133–141.

———, "Losing Our Children in America's *Cradle to Prison Pipeline*," **2007**, pp. 219-227.

Fulbright-Anderson, Karen, "Developing Our Youth: What Works," **1996**, pp. 127–143.

Hare, Bruce R., "Black Youth at Risk," **1988**, pp. 81–93.

Howard, Jeff P., "The Third Movement: Developing Black Children for the 21st Century," **1993**, pp. 11–34.

Knaus, Christopher B., "Still Segregated, Still Unequal: Analyzing the Impact of No Child Left Behind on African-American Students," **2007**, pp. 105-121.

McMurray, Georgia L. "Those of Broader Vision: An African-American Perspective on Teenage Pregnancy and Parenting," **1990,** pp. 195–211.

Moore, Evelyn K., "The Call: Universal Child Care," **1996**, pp. 219–244.

Scott, Kimberly A., "A Case Study: African-American Girls and Their Families," **2003**, pp. 181–195.

Williams, Terry M., and William Kornblum, "A Portrait of Youth: Coming of Age in Harlem Public Housing," **1991**, pp. 187–207.

Civic Engagement

Alton, Kimberley, "The State of Civil Rights 2008," **2008**, pp. 157–161.

Campbell, Melanie L., "Election Reform: Protecting Our Vote from the Enemy That Never Sleeps," **2008**, pp. 149–156.

Lindsay, Tiffany, "Weaving the Fabric: The Political Activism of Young African-American Women," **2008**, pp. 187–192.

Civil Rights

Alton, Kimberley, "The State of Civil Rights **2008**," 2008, pp. 157–161.

Archer, Dennis W., "Security Must Never Trump Liberty," **2004**, pp. 139–142.

Burnham, David, "The Fog of War," **2005**, pp. 123-127.

Campbell, Melanie L., "Election Reform: Protecting Our Vote from the Enemy That Never Sleeps," **2008,** pp. 149–156.

Jones, Nathaniel R., "The State of Civil Rights," **2006**, pp. 165–170.

Ogletree, Jr., Charles J., "Brown at 50: Considering the Continuing Legal Struggle for Racial Justice," **2004**, pp. 81–96.

Shaw, Theodore M., "The State of Civil Rights," **2007,** pp. 173-183.

Criminal Justice

Curry, George E., "Racial Disparities Drive Prison Boom," **2006**, pp. 171–187.

Drucker, Ernest M., "The Impact of Mass Incarceration on Public Health in Black Communities," **2003**, pp. 151–168.

Edelman, Marian Wright, "Losing Our Children in America's *Cradle to Prison Pipeline*," **2007**, pp. 219-227.

Lanier, James R., "The Harmful Impact of the Criminal Justice System and War on Drugs on the African-American Family," **2003**, pp. 169–179.

Diversity

Bell, Derrick, "The Elusive Quest for Racial Justice: The Chronicle of the Constitutional Contradiction," **1991**, pp. 9–23.

Cobbs, Price M., "Critical Perspectives on the Psychology of Race," **1988**, pp. 61–70.

———, "Valuing Diversity: The Myth and the Challenge," **1989**, pp. 151–159.

Darity, William Jr., "History, Discrimination and Racial Inequality," **1999**, pp. 153–166.

Jones, Stephanie J., "Sunday Morning Apartheid: A Diversity Study of the Sunday Morning Talk Shows," **2006**, pp. 189-228.

Watson, Bernard C., "The Demographic Revolution: Diversity in 21st-Century America," **1992**, pp. 31–59.

Wiley, Maya, "Hurricane Katrina Exposed the Face of Diversity," **2006**, pp. 143–153.

Drug Trade

Lanier, James R., "The Harmful Impact of the Criminal Justice System and War on Drugs on the African-American Family," **2003**, pp. 169–179.

Economics

Alexis, Marcus and Geraldine R. Henderson, "The Economic Base of African-American Communities: A Study of Consumption Patterns," **1994**, pp. 51–82.

Bradford, William, "Black Family Wealth in the United States," **2000**, pp. 103-145.

———, "Money Matters: Lending Discrimination in African-American Communities," **1993**, pp. 109–134.

Burbridge, Lynn C., "Toward Economic Self-Sufficiency: Independence Without Poverty," **1993**, pp. 71–90.

Edwards, Harry, "Playoffs and Payoffs: The African-American Athlete as an Institutional Resource," **1994**, pp. 85–111.

Hamilton, Darrick, "The Racial Composition of American Jobs," **2006**, pp. 77-115.

Harris, Andrea, "The Subprime Wipeout: Unsustainable Loans Erase Gains Made by African-American Women," **2008**, pp. 125–133.

Henderson, Lenneal J., "Blacks, Budgets, and Taxes: Assessing the Impact of Budget Deficit Reduction and Tax Reform on Blacks," **1987**, pp. 75–95.

———, "Budget and Tax Strategy: Implications for Blacks," **1990**, pp. 53–71.

———, "Public Investment for Public Good: Needs, Benefits, and Financing Options," **1992**, pp. 213–229.

Herman, Alexis, "African-American Women and Work: Still a Tale of Two Cities," **2008,** pp. 109–113

Holzer, Harry J., "Reconnecting Young Black Men: What Policies Would Help," **2007**, pp. 75-87.

Jeffries, John M., and Richard L. Schaffer, "Changes in the Labor Economy and Labor Market State of Black Americans," **1996**, pp. 12-77.

Malveaux, Julianne, "Shouldering the Third Burden: The Status of African-American Women," **2008**, pp. 75–81.

Malveaux, Julianne M., "The Parity Imperative: Civil Rights, Economic Justice, and the New American Dilemma," **1992**, pp. 281–303.

Mensah, Lisa, "Putting Homeownership Back Within Our Reach," **2008**, pp. 135–142.

Morial, Marc H. and Marvin Owens, "The National Urban League Economic Empowerment Initiative," **2005**, pp. 111-113.

Myers, Jr., Samuel L., "African-American Economic Well-Being During the Boom and Bust," **2004**, pp. 53–80.

National Urban League, The National Urban League's Homebuyer's Bill of Rights, **2008**, pp. 143–147.

National Urban League Research Staff, "African Americans in Profile: Selected Demographic, Social and Economic Data," **1992**, pp. 309–325.

———, "The Economic Status of African Americans During the Reagan-Bush Era: Withered Opportunities, Limited Outcomes, and Uncertain Outlook," **1993**, pp. 135–200.

———, "The Economic Status of African Americans: Limited Ownership and Persistent Inequality," **1992**, pp. 61–117.

———, "The Economic Status of African Americans: 'Permanent' Poverty and Inequality," **1991**, pp. 25–75.

———, "Economic Status of Black Americans During the 1980s: A Decade of Limited Progress," **1990**, pp. 25–52.

———, "Economic Status of Black Americans," **1989**, pp. 9–39.

———, "Economic Status of Black 1987," **1988**, pp. 129–152.

———, "Economic Status of Blacks 1986," **1987**, pp. 49–73.

Reuben, Lucy J., "Make Room for the New 'She'EOs: An Analysis of Businesses Owned by Black Females," **2008**, pp. 115–124.

Rodgers III, William, M., "Why Should African Americans Care About Macroeconomic Policy," **2007**, pp. 89-103.

Shapiro, Thomas M., "The Racial Wealth Gap," **2005**, pp. 41–48.

Taylor, Robert D., "Wealth Creation: The Next Leadership Challenge," **2005**, pp. 119–122.

Tidwell, Billy J., "Economic Costs of American Racism," **1991**, pp. 219–232.

Turner, Mark D., "Escaping the 'Ghetto' of Subcontracting," **2006**, pp. 117-131.

Watkins, Celeste, "The Socio-Economic Divide Among Black Americans Under 35," **2001**, pp. 67-85.

Webb, Michael B., "Programs for Progress and Empowerment: The Urban League's National Education Initiative," **1993**, pp. 203-216.

Education

Allen, Walter R., "The Struggle Continues: Race, Equity and Affirmative Action in U.S. Higher Education," **2001**, pp. 87-100.

Bailey, Deirdre, "School Choice: The Option of Success," **2001**, pp. 101-114.

Bradford, William D., "Dollars for Deeds: Prospects and Prescriptions for African-American Financial Institutions," **1994**, pp. 31–50.

Cole, Johnnetta Betsch, "The Triumphs and Challenges of Historically Black Colleges and Universities," **2008**, pp. 99–107.

Comer, James P., Norris Haynes, and Muriel Hamilton-Leel, "School Power: A Model for Improving Black Student Achievement," **1990**, pp. 225–238.

——, "Leave No Child Behind: Preparing Today's Youth for Tomorrow's World," **2005**, pp.75–84.

Dilworth, Mary E. "Historically Black Colleges and Universities: Taking Care of Home," **1994**, pp. 127–151.

Edelman, Marian Wright, "Black Children In America," **1989,** pp. 63–76.

Freeman, Dr. Kimberly Edelin, "African-American Men and Women in Higher Education: 'Filling the Glass' in the New Millennium," **2000**, pp. 61–90.

Gordon, Edmund W., "The State of Education in Black America," **2004**, pp. 97–113.

Guinier, Prof. Lani, "Confirmative Action in a Multiracial Democracy," **2000**, pp. 333–364.

Hanson, Renee R., "A Pathway to School Readiness: The Impact of Family on Early Childhood Education," **2008,** pp. 89–98.

Journal of Blacks in Higher Education (reprint), "The 'Acting White' Myth," **2005**, pp.115–117.

Knaus, Christopher B., "Still Segregated, Still Unequal: Analyzing the Impact of No Child Left Behind on African American Students," **2007**, pp. 105-121.

McBay, Shirley M. "The Condition of African American Education: Changes and Challenges," **1992**, pp. 141–156.

McKenzie, Floretta Dukes with Patricia Evans, "Education Strategies for the 90s," **1991**, pp. 95–109.

Robinson, Sharon P., "Taking Charge: An Approach to Making the Educational Problems of Blacks Comprehensible and Manageable," **1987**, pp. 31–47.

Rose, Dr. Stephanie Bell, "African-American High Achievers: Developing Talented Leaders," **2000**, pp. 41–60.

Ross, Ronald O., "Gaps, Traps and Lies: African-American Students and Test Scores," **2004**, pp. 157–161.

Sudarkasa, Niara, "Black Enrollment in Higher Education: The Unfulfilled Promise of Equality," **1988**, pp. 7–22.

Watson, Bernard C., with Fasaha M. Traylor, "Tomorrow's Teachers: Who Will They Be, What Will They Know?" **1988**, pp. 23–37.

Willie, Charles V., "The Future of School Desegregation," **1987,** pp. 37–47.

Wilson, Reginald, "Black Higher Education: Crisis and Promise," **1989**, pp. 121–135.

Wilson, Valerie Rawlston, "On Equal Ground: Causes and Solutions for Lower College Completion Rates Among Black Males," **2007**, pp. 123-135.

Wirschem, David, "Community Mobilization for Education in Rochester, New York: A Case Study," **1991**, pp. 243-248.

Emerging Ideas

Huggins, Sheryl, "The Rules of the Game," **2001**, pp. 65-66.

Employment

Anderson, Bernard E., "African Americans in the Labor Force,: **2002**, pp. 51-67.

Darity, William M., Jr., and Samuel L.Myers, Jr., "Racial Earnings Inequality into the 21st Century," **1992**, pp. 119–139.

Hamilton, Darrick, "The Racial Composition of American Jobs," **2006**, pp. 77–115.

Hammond, Theresa A., "African Americans in White-Collar Professions," **2002**, pp. 109–121.

Herman, Alexis, "African-American Women and Work: Still a Tale of Two Cities," **2008,** pp. 109–113.

Reuben, Lucy J., "Make Room for the New 'She'EOs: An Analysis of Businesses Owned by Black Females," **2008**, pp. 115–124.

Thomas, R. Roosevelt, Jr., "Managing Employee Diversity: An Assessment," **1991**, pp. 145–154.

Tidwell, Billy, J., "Parity Progress and Prospects: Racial Inequalities in Economic Well-being," **2000**, pp. 287–316.

———, "African Americans and the 21st- Century Labor Market: Improving the Fit," **1993**, pp. 35–57.

———, "The Unemployment Experience of African Americans: Some Important Correlates and Consequences," **1990**, pp. 213–223.

———, "A Profile of the Black Unemployed," **1987**, pp. 223–237.

Equality

Raines, Franklin D., "What Equality Would Look Like: Reflections on the Past, Present and Future, **2002**, pp. 13-27.

Equality Index

Global Insight, Inc., The National Urban League Equality Index, **2004**, pp. 15-34.

———, The National Urban League Equality Index, **2005**, pp. 15-40.

Parker, Sophia and Ana Orozco of Global Insight, Inc., The National Urban League 2008 Equality Index, **2008**, pp. 26–41.

Thompson, Rondel and Sophia Parker of Global Insight, Inc.,The National Urban League Equality Index, **2006**, pp. 13-60.

———, The National Urban League Equality Index, **2007** pp. 17-58.

Wilson, Valerie Rawlston, The National Urban League 2008 Equality Index: Analysis, **2008**, pp.15–24.

Families

Battle, Juan, Cathy J. Cohen, Angelique Harris, and Beth E. Richie, "We Are Family: Embracing Our Lesbian, Gay, Bisexual, and Transgender (LGBT) Family Members," **2003**, pp. 93-106.

Billingsley, Andrew, "Black Families in a Changing Society," **1987**, pp. 97–111.

———, "Understanding African-American Family Diversity," **1990**, pp. 85–108.

Cox, Kenya L. Covington, "The Childcare Imbalance: Impact on Working Opportunities for Poor Mothers," **2003**, pp. 197-224d.

Drucker, Ernest M., "The Impact of Mass Incarceration on Public Health in Black Communities," **2003**, pp. 151-168.

Dyson, Eric Michael, "Sexual Fault Lines: Robbing the Love Between Us," **2007**, pp. 229-237.

Hanson, Renee R., "A Pathway to School Readiness: The Impact of Family on Early Childhood Education," **2008**, pp. 89–98

Hill, Robert B., "Critical Issues for Black Families by the Year 2000," **1989**, pp. 41–61.

———, "The Strengths of Black Families' Revisited," **2003**, pp. 107-149.

Ivory, Steven, "Universal Fatherhood: Black Men Sharing the Load," **2007**, pp. 243-247.

Rawlston, Valerie A., "The Impact of Social Security on Child Poverty," **2000**, pp. 317–331.

Scott, Kimberly A., "A Case Study: African-American Girls and Their Families," **2003**, pp. 181-195.

Shapiro, Thomas M., "The Racial Wealth Gap," **2005**, pp. 41-48

Stafford, Walter, Angela Dews, Melissa Mendez, and Diana Salas, "Race, Gender and Welfare Reform: The Need for Targeted Support," **2003**, pp. 41-92.

Stockard (Jr.), Russell L. and M. Belinda Tucker, "Young African-American Men and Women: Separate Paths?," **2001**, pp. 143-159.

Teele, James E., "E. Franklin Frazier: The Man and His Intellectual Legacy," **2003**, pp. 29-40

Thompson, Dr. Linda S. and Georgene Butler, "The Role of the Black Family in Promoting Healthy Child Development," **2000**, pp. 227–241.

West, Carolyn M., "Feminism is a Black Thing"?: Feminist Contribution to Black Family Life, **2003**, pp. 13-27.

Willie, Charles V. "The Black Family: Striving Toward Freedom," **1988**, pp. 71–80.

Foreword

Height, Dorothy I., "Awakenings," **2008**, pp. 9–10

Obama, Barack, Foreword, **2007**, pp. 9-12.

From the President's Desk

Morial, Marc H., "The State of Black America: The Complexity of Black Progress," **2004**, pp. 11–14.

————, "The State of Black America: Prescriptions for Change," **2005**, pp. 11–14.

————, "The National Urban League Opportunity Compact," **2006**, pp. 9–1.

————, "Empowering Black Males to Reach Their Full Potential," **2007**, pp. 13-15.

————, From the President's Desk, **2008**, pp. 11–14.

Health

Browne, Doris, "The Impact of Health Disparities in African-American Women," **2008**, pp. 163–171.

Cooper, Maudine R., "The 'Invisibility Blues' of Black Women in America," **2008**, pp. 83–87.

Carnethon, Mercedes R., "Black Male Life Expectancy in the United States: A Multi-level Exploration of Causes," **2007**, pp. 137-150.

Christmas, June Jackson, "The Health of African Americans: Progress Toward Healthy People 2000," **1996**, pp. 95–126.

Leffall, LaSalle D., Jr., "Health Status of Black Americans," **1990**, pp. 121–142.

McAlpine, Robert, "Toward Development of a National Drug Control Strategy," **1991**, pp. 233–241.

Morris, Eboni D., "By the Numbers: Uninsured African-American Women," **2008**, pp. 173–177.

Nobles, Wade W., and Lawford L. Goddard, "Drugs in the African-American Community: A Clear and Present Danger," and **1989**, pp. 161–181.

Primm, Annelle and Marisela B. Gomez, "The Impact of Mental Health on Chronic Disease," **2005**, pp. 63–73.

Primm, Beny J., "AIDS: A Special Report," **1987**, pp. 159–166.

————, "Drug Use: Special Implications for Black America," **1987**, pp. 145–158.

Smedley, Brian D., "Race, Poverty, and Healthcare Disparities," **2006**, pp. 155–164.

Williams, David R., "Health and the Quality of Life Among African Americans," **2004**, pp. 115-138.

Housing

Calmore, John O., "To Make Wrong Right: The Necessary and Proper Aspirations of Fair Housing," **1989**, pp. 77–109.

Clay, Phillip, "Housing Opportunity: A Dream Deferred," **1990**, pp. 73–84.

Cooper, Maudine R., "The 'Invisibility Blues' of Black Women in America," **2008**, pp. 83–87.

Freeman, Lance, "Black Homeownership: A Dream No Longer Deferred?," **2006**, pp. 63–75.

Harris, Andrea, "The Subprime Wipeout: Unsustainable Loans Erase Gains Made by African-American Women," **2008**, pp. 125–133.

James, Angela , "Black Homeownership: Housing and Black Americans Under 35," **2001**, pp. 115-129.

Leigh, Wilhelmina A., "U.S. Housing Policy in 1996: The Outlook for Black Americans," **1996**, pp. 188–218.

Mensah, Lisa, "Putting Homeownership Back Within Our Reach," **2008**, pp. 135–142.

National Urban League, The National Urban League's Homebuyer's Bill of Rights, **2008**, pp. 143–147.

In Memoriam

National Urban League, "William A. Bootle, Ray Charles, Margo T. Clarke, Ossie Davis, Herman C. Ewing, James Forman, Joanne Grant, Ann Kheel, Memphis Norman, Max Schmeling," **2005**, pp. 139–152.

————, "Renaldo Benson, Shirley Chisholm, Johnnie Cochran, Jr., Shirley Horn, John H. Johnson, Vivian Malone Jones, Brock Peters, Richard Pryor, Bobby Short, C. Delores Tucker, August Wilson, Luther Vandross, and NUL members Clarence Lyle Barney, Jr., Manuel Augustus Romero;" **2006**, pp. 279–287.

————, "Ossie Davis: Still Caught in the Dream," **2005**, pp. 137–138.

————, "Ed Bradley, James Brown, Bebe Moore Campbell, Katherine Dunham, Mike Evans, Coretta Scott King, Gerald Levert, Gordon Parks, June Pointer, Lou Rawls, and Helen E. Harden," **2007**, pp. 249-257.

————, "Effi Barry, Jane Bolin, Daniel A. Collins (NUL Member), Oliver Hill, Yolanda King, Calvin Lockhart, Mahlon Puryear (NUL Member), Max Roach, Eddie Robinson, William Simms (NUL Member), Darryl Stingley, and Ike Turner," **2008**, pp. 205–217.

Jones, Stephanie J., "Rosa Parks: An Ordinary Woman, An Extraordinary Life," **2006**, pp. 245–246.

Military Affairs

Butler, John Sibley, "African Americans and the American Military," **2002**, pp. 93-107.

Music

Boles, Mark A., "Breaking the 'Hip Hop' Hold: Looking Beyond the Media Hype," **2007**, pp. 239-241.

Brown, David W., "Their Characteristic Music: Thoughts on Rap Music and Hip-Hop Culture," **2001**, pp. 189–201.

Bynoe, Yvonne, "The Roots of Rap Music and Hip-Hop Culture: One Perspective," **2001**, pp. 175–187.

Op-Ed/Commentary

Archer, Dennis W., "Security Must Never Trump Liberty," **2004**, pp. 139–142.

Bailey, Moya, "Going in Circles: The Struggle to Diversify Popular Images of Black Women," **2008**, pp. 193–196.

Boles, Mark A., "Breaking the 'Hip Hop' Hold: Looking Beyond the Media Hype," **2007**, pp. 239-241.

Burnham, David, "The Fog of War," **2005**, pp. 123–127.

Covington, Kenya L., "The Transformation of the Welfare Caseload," **2004**, pp. 149–152.

Dyson, Eric Michael, "Sexual Fault Lines: Robbing the Love Between Us," **2007**, pp. 229-237.

Edelman, Marian Wright, "Losing Our Children in America's *Cradle to Prison Pipeline*," **2007**, pp. 219-227.

Emerson, Melinda F., "Five Things You Must Have to Run a Successful Business," **2004**, pp. 153–156.

Ivory, Steven, "Universal Fatherhood: Black Men Sharing the Load," **2007**, pp. 243-247.

Journal of Blacks in Higher Education (reprint), "The 'Acting White' Myth," **2005**, pp. 115–117.

Lanier, James R., "The Empowerment Movement and the Black Male," **2004**, pp. 143–148.

Lindsay, Tiffany, "Weaving the Fabric: The Political Activism of Young African-American Women," **2008**, pp. 187–192.

Malveaux, Julianne, "Black Women's Hands Can Rock the World: Global Involvement and Understanding," **2008**, pp. 197–202.

Ross, Ronald O., "Gaps, Traps and Lies: African-American Students and Test Scores," **2004**, pp. 157–161.

Taylor, Susan L., "Black Love Under Siege," **2008**, pp. 179–186.

Taylor, Robert D., "Wealth Creation: The Next Leadership Challenge," **2005**, pp. 119–122.

West, Cornel, "Democracy Matters," **2005**, pp. 129–132.

Overview

Morial, Marc H., "Black America's Family Matters," **2003**, pp.9-12.

Price, Hugh B., "Still Worth Fighting For: America After 9/11," **2002**, pp. 9-11.

Politics

Alton, Kimberley, "The State of Civil Rights 2008," **2008**, pp. 157–161.

Campbell, Melanie L., "Election Reform: Protecting Our Vote from the Enemy Who Never Sleeps," **2008**, pp. 149–156.

Coleman, Henry A., "Interagency and Intergovernmental Coordination: New Demands for Domestic Policy Initiatives," **1992**, pp. 249–263.

Hamilton, Charles V., "On Parity and Political Empowerment," **1989**, pp. 111–120.

———, "Promoting Priorities: African-American Political Influence in the 1990s," **1993**, pp. 59–69.

Henderson, Lenneal J., "Budgets, Taxes, and Politics: Options for the African-American Community," **1991**, pp. 77–93.

Holden, Matthew, Jr., "The Rewards of Daring and the Ambiguity of Power: Perspectives on the Wilder Election of 1989," **1990**, pp. 109–120.

Kilson, Martin L., "African Americans and American Politics 2002: The Maturation Phase," **2002**, pp. 147–180.

———, "Thinking About the Black Elite's Role: Yesterday and Today," **2005**, pp. 85-106.

Lee, Silas, "Who's Going to Take the Weight? African Americans and Civic Engagement in the 21st Century," **2007,** pp. 185-192.

Lindsay, Tiffany, "Weaving the Fabric: The Political Activism of Young African-American Women," **2008**, pp. 187–192.

McHenry, Donald F., "A Changing World Order: Implications for Black America," **1991,** pp. 155–163.

Persons, Georgia A., "Blacks in State and Local Government: Progress and Constraints," **1987**, pp. 167–192.

Pinderhughes, Dianne M., "Power and Progress: African-American Politics in the New Era of Diversity," **1992**, pp. 265–280.

———, "The Renewal of the Voting Rights Act," **2005**, pp. 49–61.

———, "Civil Rights and the Future of the American Presidency," **1988**, pp. 39–60.

Price, Hugh B., "Black America's Challenge: The Re-construction of Black Civil Society," **2001**, pp. 13-18.

Tidwell, Billy J., "Serving the National Interest: A Marshall Plan for America," **1992**, pp. 11–30.

West, Cornel, "Democracy Matters," **2005**, pp. 129–132.

Williams, Eddie N., "The Evolution of Black Political Power", **2000**, pp. 91–102.

Poverty

Cooper, Maudine R., "The 'Invisibility Blues' of Black Women in America," **2008,** pp. 83–87.

Edelman, Marian Wright, "The State of Our Children," **2006**, pp. 133–141.

Prescriptions for Change

National Urban League, "Prescriptions for Change," **2005**, pp. 133-135.

Relationships

Taylor, Susan L., "Black Love Under Siege," **2008**, pp. 179–186.

Religion

Lincoln, C. Eric, "Knowing the Black Church: What It Is and Why," **1989**, pp. 137–149.

Richardson, W. Franklyn, "Mission to Mandate: Self-Development through the Black Church," **1994**, pp. 113–126.

Smith, Dr. Drew, "The Evolving Political Priorities of African-American Churches: An Empirical View," **2000**, pp. 171–197.

Taylor, Mark V.C., "Young Adults and Religion," **2001**, pp. 161–174.

Reports from the National Urban League

Hanson, Renee, Mark McArdle, and Valerie Rawlston Wilson, "Invisible Men: The Urgent Problems of Low-Income African-American Males," **2007**, pp. 209-216.

Lanier, James, "The National Urban League's Commission on the Black Male: Renewal, Revival and Resurrection Feasibility and Strategic Planning Study," **2005**, pp. 107–109.

Jones, Stephanie J., "Sunday Morning Apartheid: A Diversity Study of the Sunday Morning Talk Shows" **2006**, pp. 189–228.

National Urban League Policy Institute, The Opportunity Compact: A Blueprint for Economic Equality, **2008**, pp. 43–74.

Reports

Joint Center for Political and Economic Studies, A Way Out: Creating Partners for Our Nation's Prosperity by Expanding Life Paths for Young Men of Color - *Final Report of the Dellums Commission*, **2007**, pp. 193-207.

Reed, James and Aaron Thomas, The National Urban League: Empowering Black Males to Meet Their Full Potential, **2007**, pp. 217-218.

Sexual Identity

Bailey, Moya, "Going in Circles: The Struggle to Diversify Popular Images of Black Women," **2008**, pp. 193–196.

Battle, Juan, Cathy J. Cohen, Angelique Harris, and Beth E. Richie, "We Are Family: Embracing Our Lesbian, Gay, Bisexual, and Transgender (LGBT) Family Members," **2003**, pp. 93-106.

Taylor, Susan L., "Black Love Under Siege," **2008**, pp. 179–186.

Sociology

Cooper, Maudine R., "The 'Invisibility Blues' of Black Women in America," 2008, pp. 83–87.

Taylor, Susan L., "Black Love Under Siege," **2008**, pp. 179–186.

Teele, James E., "E. Franklin Frazier: The Man and His Intellectual Legacy," **2003**, pp. 29-40.

Special Section: Black Women's Health

Browne, Doris, "The Impact of Health Disparities in African-American Women," **2008,** pp. 163–171.

Morris, Eboni D., "By the Numbers: Uninsured African-American Women," **2008**, pp. 173–177.

Special Section: Katrina and Beyond

Brazile, Donna L., "New Orleans: Next Steps on the Road to Recovery," **2006**, pp. 233–237.

Morial, Marc H., "New Orleans Revisited," **2006**, pp. 229–232.

National Urban League, "The National Urban League Katrina Bill of Rights," **2006**, pp. 239–243.

Surveys

The National Urban League Survey, **2004**, pp. 35-51.

Stafford, Walter S., "The National Urban League Survey: Black America's Under-35 Generation," **2001**, pp. 19-63.

Stafford, Walter S., "The New York Urban League Survey: Black New York—On Edge, But Optimistic," **2001**, pp. 203-219.

Technology

Dreyfuss, Joel, "Black Americans and the Internet: The Technological Imperative," **2001**, pp. 131-141.

Wilson Ernest J., III, "Technological Convergence, Media Ownership and Content Diversity," **2000**, pp. 147–170.

Urban Affairs

Allen, Antonine, and Leland Ware, "The Socio-Economic Divide: Hypersegregation, Fragmentation and Disparities Within the African-American Community," **2002**, pp. 69–92.

Bates, Timothy, "The Paradox of Urban Poverty," **1996**, pp. 144–163.

Bell, Carl C., with Esther J. Jenkins,"Preventing Black Homicide," **1990**,pp. 143–155.

Bryant Solomon, Barbara, "Social Welfare Reform," **1987**, pp. 113–127.

Brown, Lee P., "Crime in the Black Community," **1988**, pp. 95–113.

Bullard, Robert D. "Urban Infrastructure: Social, Environmental, and Health Risks to African Americans," **1992**, pp.183–196.

Chambers, Julius L., "The Law and Black Americans: Retreat from Civil Rights," **1987**, pp. 15–30.

———, "Black Americans and the Courts: Has the Clock Been Turned Back Permanently?" **1990**, pp. 9–24.

Cooper, Maudine R., "The 'Invisibility Blues' of Black Women in America," **2008**, pp. 83–87.

Edelin, Ramona H., "Toward an African-American Agenda: An Inward Look," **1990**, pp. 173–183.

Fair, T. Willard, "Coordinated Community Empowerment: Experiences of the Urban League of Greater Miami," **1993**, pp. 217–233.

Gray, Sandra T., "Public-Private Partnerships: Prospects for America...Promise for African Americans," **1992**, pp. 231–247.

Harris, David, " 'Driving While Black' and Other African-American Crimes: The Continuing Relevance of Race to American Criminal Justice," **2000**, pp. 259–285.

Henderson, Lenneal J., "African Americans in the Urban Milieu: Conditions, Trends, and Development Needs," **1994**, pp. 11–29.

Hill, Robert B., "Urban Redevelopment: Developing Effective Targeting Strategies," **1992**, pp. 197–211.

Jones, Dionne J., with Greg Harrison of the National Urban League Research Department, "Fast Facts: Comparative Views of African-American Status and Progress," **1994**, pp. 213–236.

Jones, Shirley J., "Silent Suffering: The Plight of Rural Black America," **1994**, pp.171–188.

Massey, Walter E. "Science, Technology, and Human Resources: Preparing for the 21st Century," **1992**, pp. 157–169.

Mendez, Jr. Garry A., "Crime Is Not a Part of Our Black Heritage: A Theoretical Essay," **1988**, pp. 211–216.

Miller, Warren F., Jr., "Developing Untapped Talent: A National Call for African-American Technologists," **1991**, pp. 111–127.

Murray, Sylvester, "Clear and Present Danger: The Decay of America's Physical Infrastructure," **1992**, pp. 171–182.

Pemberton, Gayle, "It's the Thing That Counts, Or Reflections on the Legacy of W.E.B. Du Bois," **1991**, pp. 129–143.

Pinderhughes, Dianne M., "The Case of African-Americans in the Persian Gulf: The Intersection of American Foreign and Military Policy with Domestic Employment Policy in the United States," **1991**, pp. 165–186.

Robinson, Gene S. "Television Advertising and Its Impact on Black America," **1990**, pp. 157–171.

Sawyers, Dr. Andrew and Dr. Lenneal Henderson, "Race, Space and Justice: Cities and Growth in the 21st Century," **2000**, pp. 243–258.

Schneider, Alvin J., "Blacks in the Military: The Victory and the Challenge," **1988**, pp. 115–128.

Smedley, Brian, "Race, Poverty, and Healthcare Disparities," **2006**, pp. 155–164.

Stafford, Walter, Angela Dews, Melissa Mendez, and Diana Salas, "Race, Gender and Welfare Reform: The Need for Targeted Support," **2003**, pp. 41–92.

Stewart, James B., "Developing Black and Latino Survival Strategies: The Future of Urban Areas," **1996**, pp. 164–187.

Stone, Christopher E., "Crime and Justice in Black America," **1996**, pp. 78–94.

Tidwell, Billy J., with Monica B. Kuumba, Dionne J. Jones, and Betty C. Watson, "Fast Facts: African Americans in the 1990s," **1993**, pp. 243–265.

Wallace-Benjamin, Joan, "Organizing African-American Self-Development: The Role of Community-Based Organizations," **1994**, pp. 189–205.

Walters, Ronald, "Serving the People: African-American Leadership and the Challenge of Empowerment," **1994**, pp. 153–170.

Ware, Leland, and Antoine Allen, "The Socio-Economic Divide: Hypersegregation, Fragmentation and Disparities Within the African-American Community," **2002**, pp. 69–92.

Wiley, Maya, "Hurricane Katrina Exposed the Face of Poverty," **2006**, pp. 143–153.

Welfare

Bergeron, Suzanne, and William E. Spriggs, "Welfare Reform and Black America," **2002**, pp. 29–50.

Cooper, Maudine R., "The 'Invisibility Blues' of Black Women in America," **2008,** pp. 83–87.

Covington, Kenya L., "The Transformation of the Welfare Caseload," **2004**, pp. 149–152.

Spriggs, William E., and Suzanne Bergeron, "Welfare Reform and Black America," **2002**, pp. 29–50.

Stafford, Walter, Angela Dews, Melissa Mendez, and Diana Salas, "Race, Gender and Welfare Reform: The Need for Targeted Support," **2003**, pp. 41-92.

Women's Issues

Bailey, Moya, "Going in Circles: The Struggle to Diversify Popular Images of Black Women," **2008**, pp. 193–196.

Browne, Doris, "The Impact of Health Disparities in African-American Women," **2008,** pp. 163–171.

Cooper, Maudine R., "The 'Invisibility Blues' of Black Women in America," **2008**, pp. 83–87.

Harris, Andrea, "The Subprime Wipeout: Unsustainable Loans Erase Gains Made by African-American Women," **2008**, pp. 125–133.

Herman, Alexis, "African-American Women and Work: Still a Tale of Two Cities," **2008**, pp. 109–113.

Lindsay, Tiffany, "Weaving the Fabric: The Political Activism of Young African-American Women," **2008**, pp.187–192.

Malveaux, Julianne, "Black Women's Hands Can Rock the World: Global Involvement and Understanding," **2008,** pp. 197–202.

———, "Shouldering the Third Burden: The Status of African-American Women," **2008**, pp. 75–81.

Morris, Eboni D., "By the Numbers: Uninsured African-American Women," **2008**, pp. 173–177.

Mensah, Lisa, "Putting Homeownership Back Within Our Reach," **2008**, pp. 135–142.

Reuben, Lucy J., "Make Room for the New 'She'EOs: An Analysis of Businesses Owned by Black Females," **2008**, pp. 115–124.

Stafford, Walter, Angela Dews, Melissa Mendez, and Diana Salas, "Race, Gender and Welfare Reform: The Need for Targeted Support," **2003**, pp. 41–92.

Taylor, Susan L., "Black Love Under Siege," **2008**, pp.179–186.

West, Carolyn M., "Feminism is a Black Thing"?: Feminist Contribution to Black Family Life, **2003**, pp. 13–27.

World Affairs

Malveaux, Julianne, "Black Women's Hands Can Rock the World: Global Involvement and Understanding," **2008**, pp. 197–202.

History of the National Urban League

The National Urban League grew out of that spontaneous grassrootsmovement for freedom and opportunity that came to becalled the Black Migrations. When the U.S. Supreme Court declared its approval of segregation in the 1896 Plessy v. Ferguson decision, the brutal system of economic, social and political oppression the White South quickly adopted rapidly transformed what had been a trickle of African Americans northward into a flood.

Those newcomers to the North soon discovered that while they had escaped the South, they had by no means escaped racial discrimination. Excluded from all but menial jobs in the larger society, victimized by poor housing and education, and inexperienced in the ways of urban living, many lived in terrible social and economic conditions.

Still, in the North and West blacks could vote; and in that and other differences between living in the South and not living in the South lay opportunity—and that African Americans clearly understood.

But to capitalize on that opportunity, to successfully adapt to urban life and to reduce the pervasive discrimination they faced, they would need help. That was the reason the Committee on Urban Conditions Among Negroes was established on September 29, 1910 in New York City. Central to the organization's founding were two extraordinary people: Mrs. Ruth Standish Baldwin and Dr. George Edmund Haynes, who would become the Committee's first executive secretary. Mrs. Baldwin, the widow of a railroad magnate and a member of one of America's oldest families, had a remarkable social conscience and was a stalwart champion of the poor and disadvantaged. Dr. Haynes, a graduate of Fisk University, Yale University, and Columbia University (he was the first African American to receive a doctorate from the latter), felt a compelling need to use his training as a social worker to serve his people.

A year later, the Committee merged with the Committee for the Improvement of Industrial Conditions Among Negroes in New York (founded in 1906), and the National League for the Protection of Colored Women (founded in 1905) to form the National League on Urban Conditions Among Negroes. In 1920, the name was later shortened to the National Urban League.

The interracial character of the League's board was set from its first days. Professor Edwin R. A. Seligman of Columbia University, one of the leaders in progressive social service activities in New York City, served as chairman from 1911 to 1913. Mrs. Baldwin took the post until 1915.

The fledgling organization counseled black migrants from the South, helped train black social workers, and worked in various other ways to bring educational and employment opportunities to blacks. Its research into the problems blacks faced in employment opportunities, recreation, housing, health and sanitation, and education spurred the League's quick growth. By the end of World War I the organization had 81 staff members working in 30 cities.

In 1918, Dr. Haynes was succeeded by Eugene Kinckle Jones who would direct the agency until his retirement in 1941. Under his direction, the League significantly expanded its multifaceted campaign to crack the barriers to black employment, spurred first by the boom years of the 1920s, and then, by the desperate years of the Great Depression. Efforts at reasoned persuasion were buttressed by boycotts against firms that refused to employ blacks, pressures on schools to expand vocational opportunities for young people, constant prodding of Washington officials to include blacks in New Deal recovery programs and a drive to get blacks into previously segregated labor unions.

As World War II loomed, Lester Granger, a seasoned League veteran and crusading newspaper columnist, was appointed Jones' successor. Outspoken in his commitment to advancing opportunity for African Americans, Granger pushed tirelessly to integrate recalcitrant trade unions, and led the League's effort to support A. Philip Randolph's March on Washington Movement to fight discrimination in defense work and in the armed services. Under Granger, the League, through its own Industrial Relations Laboratory, had notable success in cracking the color bar in numerous defense plants. The nation's demand for civilian labor during the war also helped the organization press with greater urgency its programs to train black youths for meaningful blue-collar employment. After the war those efforts expanded to persuading Fortune 500 companies to hold career conferences on the campuses of Negro Colleges and place blacks in upperechelon jobs.

Of equal importance to the League's own future sources of support, Granger avidly supported the organization of its volunteer auxiliary, the National Urban League Guild, which, under the leadership of Mollie Moon, became an important national force in its own right.

The explosion of the civil rights movement provoked a change for the League, one personified by its new leader, Whitney M. Young, Jr., who became executive director in 1961. A social worker like his predecessors, he substantially expanded the League's fundraising ability—and, most critically, made the League a full partner in the civil rights movement. Indeed, although the League's tax-exempt status barred it from protest activities, it hosted at its New York headquarters the planning meetings of A. Philip Randolph, Martin Luther King, Jr., and other civil rights and labor leaders for the 1963 March on Washington. Young was also a forceful advocate for greater government and private-sector involvement in efforts to eradicate poverty. His call for a domestic Marshall Plan, a ten-point program designed to close the huge social and economic gap between black and white Americans, significantly influenced the discussion of the Johnson Administration's War on Poverty legislation.

Young's tragic death in 1971 in a drowning incident off the coast of Lagos, Nigeria brought another change in leadership. Vernon E. Jordan, Jr., formerly Executive Director of the United Negro College Fund, took over as the League's fifth Executive Director in 1972 (the title of the office was changed to President in 1977).

For the next decade, until his resignation in December 1981, Jordan skillfully guided the League to new heights of achievement. He oversaw a major expansion of its social-service efforts, as the League became a significant conduit for the federal government to establish programs and deliver services to aid urban communities, and brokered fresh initiatives in such League programs as housing, health, education and minority business development. Jordan also instituted a citizenship education program that helped increase the black vote and brought new programs to such areas as energy, the environment, and non-traditional jobs for women of color—and he developed *The State of Black America report.*

In 1982, John E. Jacob, a former chief executive officer of the Washington, under Jordan, took the reins of leadership, solidifying the League's internal structure and expanding its outreach even further.

Jacob established the Permanent Development Fund in order to increase the organization's financial stamina. In honor of Whitney Young, he established several programs to aid the development of those who work for and with the League: The Whitney M. Young, Jr. Training Center, to provide training and leadership development opportunities for both staff and volunteers; the Whitney M. Young, Jr. Race Relations Program, which recognizes affiliates doing exemplary work in race relations; and the Whitney M. Young, Jr. Commemoration Ceremony, which honors and pays tribute to long-term staff and volunteers who have made extraordinary contributions to the Urban League Movement. Jacob established the League's NULITES youthdevelopment program and spurred the League to put new emphasis on programs to reduce teenage pregnancy, help single female heads of households, combat crime in black communities, and increase voter registration.

Hugh B. Price, appointed to the League's top office in July 1994, took its reins at a critical moment for the League, for Black America, and for the nation as a whole. The fierce market-driven dynamic known as "globalization," swept the world, fundamentally altering economic relations among and within countries, including the United States. Price, a lawyer by training, with extensive experience in community development and other public policy issues, intensified the organization's work in three broad areas: in education and youth development, in individual and community-wide economic empowerment, and in the forceful advocacy of affirmative action and the promotion of inclusion as a critical foundation for securing America's future as a multiethnic democracy.

In the spring of 2003, Price stepped down after a productive nine-year tenure, and Marc H. Morial, the former two-term Mayor of New Orleans, Louisiana, was appointed president and chief executive officer. Since taking the helm, Morial has helped thrust the League into the forefront of major public policy issues, research and effective community-based solutions.

From Hurricane Katrina and the extension of the Voting Rights Act to creating jobs and housing through effective economic strategies, he is considered one of the nation's foremost experts on a wide range of issues related to cities and their residents. He has also been recognized by the *Non-Profit Times* as one of America's top 50 non-profit executives and has been named by *Ebony Magazine* as one of the 100 "Most Influential Blacks in America."

Upon his appointment to the League, Morial established an ambitious five-point empowerment agenda encompassing Education & Youth, Economic Empowerment, Health & Quality of Life, Civic Engagement and Civil Rights & Racial Justice that informs the League's programs, research and advocacy efforts. He created the new quantitative "Equality Index" to effectively measure the disparities in urban communities across these five areas. The Index is now a permanent part of the League's annual and muchheralded *The State of Black America* report.

In 2004, Mr. Morial launched the League's first Annual Legislative Policy Conference (LPC) in Washington, D.C. Armed with a common agenda of jobs, education and civil rights, the Urban League leadership (staff, board and volunteers) from across the country served as frontline advocates in discussions with congressional lawmakers.

During the 2007 National Urban League Annual Conference, Morial unveiled the National Urban League's Opportunity Compact.

The *Opportunity Compact* is our blueprint for economic equality. It is a comprehensive set of principles and policy recommendations designed to empower all Americans to be full participants in the economic and social mainstream of this nation. There are four cornerstones of the Opportunity Compact that reflect the values represented by the American dream: The Opportunity to Thrive (Children), The Opportunity to Earn (Jobs), The Opportunity to Own (Housing) and The Opportunity to Prosper (Entrepreneurship).

BOARD OF TRUSTEES
2007–2008

OFFICERS

Chair
John D. Hofmeister

Senior Vice Chair
Robert D. Taylor

Vice Chair
Alma Arrington Brown

Vice Chair
Martha "Bunny" Mitchell

Secretary
Alexis M. Herman

Treasurer
Willard "Woody" W. Brittain

President and Chief Executive Officer
Marc H. Morial

TRUSTEES

Lanesha T. Anderson
Ajay Banga
Mark Adin Boles
Robert J. Brown
David L. Cohen
Cassye D. Cook
Michael J. Critelli
Michelle Crockett
Roderick D. Gillum
"Suzy" Annette Hoffman Hardy
Effenus Henderson
Harold R. Henderson
Theresa Hopkins-Staten, Esq.
Thomas D. Hyde
Harry E. Johnson, Sr
Gregory W. Jones
John F. Killian
Michael K. Lee, Esq.
Dale LeFebvre
John W. Mack
Robert A. Malone
Jonathan D. McBride
Brenda W. McDuffie
Liam E. McGee
Anne Nobles
William F. Pickard, Ph.D.

Stephen S. Rasmussen
Russell Simmons
Rodney E. Slater
Michael Sourie
Gina Stikes
Andrew C. Taylor
Nicole C. Whittington, Esq.
Dale LeFebvre
John W. Mack
Robert A. Malone
Jonathan D. McBride
Brenda W. McDuffie
Liam E. McGee
Anne Nobles
William F. Pickard, Ph.D.
Stephen S. Rasmussen
Russell Simmons
Rodney E. Slater
Michael Sourie
Gina Stikes
Andrew C. Taylor
Nicole C. Whittington, Esq.
Jim Winestock
B. Michael Young
Andrea Zopp

NUL COUNSEL

Charles J. Hamilton, Jr., Esq

HONORARY TRUSTEES

Reginald K. Brack, Jr.
M. Anthony Burns
Coy Eklund
David T. Kearns
Theodore W. Kheel
Robert C. Larson
Kenneth D. Lewis
Jonathan S. Linen

NATIONAL URBAN LEAGUE

Chair
John D. Hofmeister

President and Chief Executive Officer
Marc H. Morial

Executive Vice President & Chief Operating Officer
Deborah S. Coleman

Senior Vice President
Development
Dennis G. Serrette

Senior Vice President
Programs
Donald E. Bowen

Executive Director
Policy Institute
Stephanie J. Jones

Senior Vice President
Affiliate Service
Annelle Lewis

Senior Vice President
Marketing & Communications
Cheryl F. McCants

NATIONAL URBAN LEAGUE POLICY INSTITUTE

Executive Director
Stephanie J. Jones

Vice President & Chief of Staff
Lisa Bland Malone

Senior Resident Scholar
Valerie Rawlston Wilson

Senior Legislative Director
Suzanne M. Bergeron

Resident Scholar
Renee R. Hanson

Research Analyst
Mark McArdle

Publications Director
Larry Williamson

Publications Manager
Rose Jefferson-Frazier

Office Manager
Gail Thomas

Assistant
Clarissa McKithen

Receptionist
Richard E. Lawrence

ROSTER OF NATIONAL URBAN LEAGUE AFFILIATES

AKRON, OHIO
Akron Community Service Center
And Urban League

ALEXANDRIA, VIRGINIA
Northern Virginia Urban League

ANCHORAGE, ALASKA
Urban League of Anchorage-Alaska

ALTON, ILLINOIS
Madison County Urban League

ANDERSON, INDIANA
Urban League of Madison County, Inc.

ATLANTA, GEORGIA
Atlanta Urban League

AURORA, ILLINOIS
Quad County Urban League

AUSTIN, TEXAS
Austin Area Urban League

BALTIMORE, MARYLAND
Greater Baltimore Urban League

BATTLE CREEK, MICHIGAN
Southwestern Michigan Urban League

BINGHAMTON, NEW YORK
Broome County Urban League

BIRMINGHAM, ALABAMA
Birmingham Urban League

BOSTON, MASSACHUSETTS
Urban League of Eastern Massachusetts

BUFFALO, NEW YORK
Buffalo Urban League

CANTON, OHIO
Greater Stark County Urban League, Inc.

CHAMPAIGN, ILLINOIS
Urban League of Champaign County

CHARLESTON, SOUTH CAROLINA
Charleston Trident Urban League

CHARLOTTE, NORTH CAROLINA
Urban League of Central Carolinas, Inc.

CHATTANOOGA, TENNESSEE
Urban League Greater Chattanooga, Inc.

CHICAGO, ILLINOIS
Chicago Urban League

CINCINNATI, OHIO
Urban League of Greater Cincinnati

CLEVELAND, OHIO
Urban League of Greater Cleveland

COLORADO SPRINGS, COLORADO
Urban League of Pikes Peak Region

COLUMBIA, SOUTH CAROLINA
Columbia Urban League

COLUMBUS, GEORGIA
Urban League of Greater Columbus, Inc.

COLUMBUS, OHIO
Columbus Urban League

DALLAS, TEXAS
Urban League of Greater Dallas and
North Central Texas

DAYTON, OHIO
Dayton Urban League

ENGLEWOOD, NEW JERSEY
Urban League for Bergen County

GARY, INDIANA
Urban League of Northwest Indiana, Inc.

GRAND RAPIDS, MICHIGAN
Grand Rapids Urban League

GREENVILLE, SOUTH CAROLINA
The Urban League of the Upstate

HARTFORD, CONNECTICUT
Urban League of Greater Hartford

HOUSTON, TEXAS
Houston Area Urban League

INDIANAPOLIS, INDIANA
Indianapolis Urban League

JACKSON, MISSISSIPPI
Urban League of Greater Jackson

JACKSONVILLE, FLORIDA
Jacksonville Urban League

JERSEY CITY, NEW JERSEY
Urban League of Hudson County

KANSAS CITY, MISSOURI
Urban League of Kansas City

KNOXVILLE, TENNESSEE
Knoxville Area Urban League
LANCASTER, PENNSYLVANIA
Urban League of Lancaster County

LAS VEGAS, NEVADA
Las Vegas- Clark County Urban League

LEXINGTON, KENTUCKY
Urban League of Lexington-Fayette County

LONG ISLAND, NEW YORK
Urban League of Long Island

LOS ANGELES, CALIFORNIA
Los Angeles Urban League

LOUISVILLE, KENTUCKY
Louisville Urban League

MADISON, WISCONSIN
Urban League of Greater Madison

MEMPHIS, TENNESSEE
Memphis Urban League

MIAMI, FLORIDA
Urban League of Greater Miami

MILWAUKEE, WISCONSIN
Milwaukee Urban League

MINNEAPOLIS, MINNESOTA
Minneapolis Urban League

MORRISTOWN, NEW JERSEY
Morris County Urban League

MUSKEGON, MICHIGAN
Urban League of Greater Muskegon

NASHVILLE, TENNESSEE
Urban League of Middle Tennessee

NEW ORLEANS, LOUISIANA
Urban League of Greater New Orleans

NEW YORK, NEW YORK
New York Urban League

NEWARK, NEW JERSEY
Urban League of Essex County

NORFOLK, VIRGINIA
Urban League of Hampton Roads

OKLAHOMA CITY, OKLAHOMA
Urban League of Oklahoma City

OMAHA, NEBRASKA
Urban League of Nebraska

ORLANDO, FLORIDA
Metropolitan Orlando Urban League

PEORIA, ILLINOIS
Tri-County Urban League

PHILADELPHIA, PENNSYLVANIA
Urban League of Philadelphia

PHOENIX, ARIZONA
Phoenix Urban League

PITTSBURGH, PENNSYLVANIA
Urban League of Pittsburgh

PORTLAND, OREGON
Urban League of Portland

PROVIDENCE, RHODE ISLAND
Urban League of Rhode Island

RACINE, WISCONSIN
Urban League of Racine & Kenosha,Inc.

RALEIGH, NORTH CAROLINA
Triangle Urban League

RICHMOND, VIRGINIA
Urban League of Greater Richmond, Inc.

ROCHESTER, NEW YORK
Urban League of Rochester

SACRAMENTO, CALIFORNIA
Sacramento Urban League

SAINT LOUIS, MISSOURI
Urban League Metropolitan St. Louis

SAINT PAUL, MINNESOTA
St. Paul Urban League

SAINT PETERSBURG, FLORIDA
Pinellas County Urban League

SAN DIEGO, CALIFORNIA
Urban League of San Diego County

SEATTLE, WASHINGTON
Urban League of Metropolitan Seattle

SOUTH BEND, INDIANA
Urban League of South Bend
and St. Joseph County

SPRINGFIELD, ILLINOIS
Springfield Urban League, Inc.

SPRINGFIELD, MASSACHUSETTS
Urban League of Springfield

STAMFORD, CONNECTICUT
Urban League of Greater Fairfield County
Connecticut, Inc.

TACOMA, WASHINGTON
Tacoma Urban League

TALLAHASSEE, FLORDIA
Tallahassee Urban League

TOLEDO, OHIO
Greater Toledo Urban League

TUCSON, ARIZONA
Tucson Urban League

TULSA, OKLAHOMA
Metropolitan Tulsa Urban League

WARREN, OHIO
Greater Warren-Youngstown Urban League

WASHINGTON, D.C.
Greater Washington Urban League

WEST PALM BEACH, FLORIDA
Urban League of Palm Beach County, Inc.

WHITE PLAINS, NEW YORK
Urban League of Westchester County

WICHITA, KANSAS
Urban League of Kansas, Inc.

WILMINGTON, DELAWARE
Metropolitan Wilmington Urban League

WINSTON-SALEM, NORTH CAROLINA
Winston-Salem Urban League